THE STRANGERS
WHO CAME HOME

BY THE SAME AUTHOR

Test of Time: Travels in Search of a Cricketing Legend

John Lazenby is a freelance journalist and author. He began his career in Sussex before joining the Press Association in Fleet Street in 1990, where he covered rugby union and cricket. He has worked for national newspapers including *The Times*, the *Sunday Times*, the *Daily Telegraph* and *The Independent*. His first book, *Test of Time: Travels in Search of a Cricketing Legend*, published in 2005, was selected as a finalist for the MCC/Cricket Society's Book of the Year award and chosen as *Wisden's* Book of the Year.

THE STRANGERS
WHO CAME HOME

The First Australian Cricket
Tour of England

JOHN LAZENBY

B L O O M S B U R Y

LONDON · NEW DELHI · NEW YORK · SYDNEY

John Wisden & Co Ltd
An imprint of Bloomsbury Publishing Plc

50 Bedford Square   1385 Broadway
London   New York
WC1B 3DP   NY 10018
UK   USA

www.bloomsbury.com

First published 2015

This paperback edition published 2016

© John Lazenby 2015

John Lazenby has asserted his right under the Copyright, Designs and Patents Act, 1988,
to be identified as Author of this work.

www.wisden.com
www.wisdenrecords.com
Follow Wisden on Twitter @WisdenAlmanack
and on Facebook at Wisden Sports

British Library Cataloguing-in-Publication Data
A catalogue record for this book is available from the British Library.

Library of Congress Cataloguing-in-Publication data has been applied for.

ISBN: PB: 978-1-4088-4397-0
         ePub: 978-1-4088-4288-1

Printed a   Y

To find out more   d extracts,
author interviev   sletters.

Contents

Prologue
Sydney Harbour, 29 March 1878

It might have been just another mail steamer leaving Sydney Harbour for San Francisco on Friday, 29 March, but for the presence of the 11 eager-eyed men who were grouped together on the hurricane deck. They were taking in the busy scene unfolding around them in the final moments before the sounding of the departure bell, when the air is clutched by a sudden sense of urgency and confusion, and the barked instructions of the crew mingle with the plaintive calls of goodbye from passengers and well-wishers alike.

For the 11 men it was to be their last sight of Sydney for eight months, perhaps longer. They had enjoyed a rousing farewell dinner with friends the night before at Punch's Hotel, behind Circular Quay on the corner of Pitt and King streets – the scene of many a Sydney revelry – and some of them were still feeling the effects. Their average age was no more than 23, and as they lifted their hats and smiled in quiet acknowledgment at the crowd who had come to bid them farewell, or talked and joked among themselves, it was obvious they were a tightly knit group and one that was already the focus of all attention. Uniformly trim, athletic looking and sun-bronzed, they were easily distinguishable from their fellow passengers – many of whom had made it their business to find out who this band of brothers were. At first glance they might have passed for venturers on some perilous quest, pioneers, discoverers, gamblers, fortune-seekers perhaps, or sportsmen off to conquer distant fields: in fact they were all of these things, and more.

At 3.30pm, at least half an hour behind schedule, as the last flotilla of watermen's boats crammed with well-wishers, friends and relations was still making its way back from midstream, the RMS *City of Sydney* finally weighed anchor. To the sound of more cheers she glided out into the open expanse of water, where the steamships *Bellbird*, *Britannia* and *Prince of Wales* waited to escort her in a convoy of smoke and sirens to the harbour entrance. A sturdy iron-screw vessel of 3,017 tons and 360ft in length, with one funnel and two masts, elaborate rigging and just a hint of sail, the *City of Sydney* was comfortably capable of carrying over 500 passengers and numbered almost 70 crew. Safely stowed among her precious cargo of despatches and the orderly piles of trunks and sea chests, was a giant canvas bag, as heavy as it was unwieldy. It was the bane of all 11 men who took it in turns to heave it around with them wherever they went. The "caravan", as it was aptly known, concealed the tools of their trade. It already looked as if it had been dragged to the ends of the earth and back, and splashed across it in whitewash were the unmistakable words, "Australian Eleven".

As the small armada approached the mouth of the harbour, the band of the New South Wales Permanent Artillery, positioned beneath the yellow sandstone cliffs near South Head, struck up a stirring rendition of the popular American Civil War song "Cheer, Boys, Cheer!". The heroic sentiment of it would not have been lost on the 11 men. The notes flew across the water towards them like the white wings of the yachts in the harbour. The men waved their hats in the air and called out in response, and, as the *City of Sydney* steamed on alone between the Heads to the poignant strains of "Auld Lang Syne" and a fanfare of sirens, the soldiers returned three lusty cheers to send them on their great adventure. "The water was beautifully smooth outside," a reporter for the *Sydney Morning Herald* filed, "and the *City of Sydney* left here with every prospect before her of a speedy and pleasant voyage."

While the other passengers retreated to their cabins or the saloon, the men remained on deck feeling the steady pulse of the steamer's mighty compound engines beating beneath their feet and watching the landmarks of Sydney shrink slowly into the distance. The sound of the band had soon faded away on the breeze, and their thoughts turned, inevitably, to the families and friends they were leaving behind and their long journey ahead. They expected to accomplish the voyage to San Francisco in a little under a month. There would be much playing of cards to while away the idle hours in between. The *City of Sydney* would call at Auckland en route, to pick up more passengers and mail, and then briefly in the tropics at Honolulu. After departing Auckland, however, they were venturing into the unknown. From San Francisco the 11 men would ride the Transcontinental Railroad across another vast and dangerous ocean – the Great Plains – travelling at a rate of almost 500 miles every day for a week until they reached New York. There, all being well, they were scheduled to board an Inman Line steamer, the *City of Berlin*, bound for the port of Liverpool, their final destination. These weary journeyers had only the haziest notion of what they might find once they reached England – nearly seven weeks and more than 12,000 miles since clearing Sydney Heads. Except that they were finally coming home.

One
15 March–19 April 1877

"The pupils were quite as good as their masters"

The story of the Australian Eleven began almost exactly a year earlier on a breezy sunlit afternoon in mid-March at the elm-fringed Melbourne Cricket Ground. The occasion was the Grand Combination Match, and was billed as the first representative game to be played on even terms between an English touring team (James Lillywhite's All-England XI) and an Australian side (the Combined XI), a bold fusion of the most talented players from Sydney and Melbourne. Before then English XIs had routinely contested their matches in Australia against the odds, usually against teams of fifteen, eighteen or twenty-two men. The Grand Combination Match lasted four days, resulted in a 45-run victory for the inter-colonial XI and was designated, retrospectively, as the first Test to be played between England and Australia.

Although the term "Test" had already been coined, it was not yet recognised in the modern sense, and no one could have foreseen the history that was in the making that Thursday afternoon. Certainly not the Melbourne *Argus*, which described the unusually truncated four hours' play as a "spendthrift waste of an autumn day"; nor the meagre 1,500 crowd – there were almost as many non-paying spectators perched in the gum trees in Yarra Park – who watched Sydney's Charles Bannerman cut the second ball of the match, bowled by Nottinghamshire's Alfred Shaw, past point for an easy single.

Bannerman went on to score a glorious unbeaten 165, and the colonial press and public quickly dropped their indifference. Indeed, the *Argus* reported that no batsman in the world, not even W. G. Grace himself, could have played with "more resolution and greater brilliance". Bannerman would more than merit his subsequent elevation as Test cricket's first centurion. However, his influence in Melbourne was not confined purely to the field of play. It was in the full flush of victory that the idea for a tour of England by an Australian team was conceived, and, according to the Sydney fast bowler Fred Spofforth, it originated with the players: "D. W. Gregory was the first to suggest such an experiment, in which he was supported by Charles Bannerman." The Englishmen, in the shape of the entrepreneurial James Lillywhite and Alfred Shaw, were not slow to offer their support. "Our defeat on level terms in Melbourne was the last encouragement that our Australian friends needed to embark upon a first visit to England," Shaw recorded. "Lillywhite and I had done our best to induce them to tackle the enterprise ... which we had confidence would be a success." That, though, is how it might have remained – the glimmer of an idea – had it not been for the actions of one man.

As the organiser of the Grand Combination Match, and the sole selector of the inter-colonial team (he was also liaison officer for Lillywhite's team), Jack Conway had already made a persuasive case for the job of manager and promoter of the first Australian Eleven. Shrewd, assertive and single-minded, Conway wore his various hats – sportsman, journalist, agent, entrepreneur and maverick – with equal facility; he also had the ear of the players and commanded their respect. "I had a long conversation with the principal members of the Combined Australian Eleven over the matter [of a tour to England]," he wrote, "and I resolved to undertake the task of the formation of an Australian Eleven despite the many difficulties." The difficulties, in fact, would prove multitudinous. But Conway had long demonstrated an unerring ability to get things done, even if his uncompromising style and methods were not to everyone's taste. During the organisation of the Grand Combination Match, for instance, he had made a point of bypassing the Victorian and New South Wales cricket associations and approached the players directly – an act which provoked considerable ire from the Sydney authorities in particular. Excluded once again from the selection process and denied any input into the proposed tour of England, the often-warring associations joined together in a rare show of unity, and publicly distanced themselves from the project. Conway remained resolutely unconcerned. In the coming months, however, he would learn to become the most skilled of negotiators, resourceful in the extreme. He would need to be.

A formidable fast bowler and a quick-scoring batsman (he played for Victoria from 1861 to 1874, when he was described as the "best colonially taught" cricketer of his generation) and a fearsome Australian Rules footballer whose muscular frame was ideally suited to the bruising nature of the sport, Conway was the embodiment of uncomplicated toughness. He was also an able sporting journalist, "renowned for his pugnacity of style and wit" and, for all his brawn, a cultivated man. His grandson, the author Ronald Conway, relates that on one occasion, "after being castigated by the press for having a few brandy nips, and using 'canine' language against his own fumbling men of the East Melbourne Cricket Club, he astutely decided that any further intolerable feelings would be served by profanities in Latin!"

If the players, acting on an impulse, had proposed a tour of England, then it was Conway, Spofforth readily acknowledged, who made the "first definite move in the matter". David Gregory, a forthright captain of the Combined XI, would go further and award Conway all the credit for the venture. "We shall ever be grateful to our friend John Conway," he later wrote, "but for his idea the majority of us probably would never have seen Old England." It was a view seconded by the Victorian batsman Tom Horan, who described Conway as the "presiding genius of the concept". Conway immediately went to work and set about assembling his team, with, in the words of James Lillywhite, "his usual dash and energy". He already possessed the nucleus of a talented XI: the fearless strokemaker Charles Bannerman, Tom Horan, Nat Thomson, Billy Murdoch and David Gregory provided the core of the batting; Jack Blackham was a wicketkeeper of great nerve and skill, of whom it was said there was no equal in the world; Billy Midwinter, a genuine all-rounder; and Harry Boyle, Tom Kendall, the 18-year-old Tom Garrett, Frank Allan and Fred Spofforth, the fastest bowler in the colonies by some distance, formed a potent and varied bowling attack. Indeed, so fast was Spofforth that during an inter-colonial match for New South Wales against Victoria, he claimed to have not only shattered two stumps but broken the bat of B. B. Cooper, the former Kent and Middlesex amateur, on three occasions. There would be other names in the hat, too, and there would be players who, for whatever reason, would be unavailable or who would decline the invitation to tour. Conway promised that the team would be "thoroughly Australian in character" and no stone would be left unturned in his quest: "It was the desire from the first to select the best cricketers in Australia without respect to colony."

There was a new optimism and vigour – a swagger, even – about Australian cricket. Not even revenge for Lillywhite's men in the return combination match at Melbourne, played over 31 March–4 April (and later recognised as the second Test), could slow the momentum or divert the Australians from their mission. In any case the margin of defeat was "so little", Tom Horan declared (in fact the All-England XI won convincingly enough by four wickets), "that competent judges were satisfied that Australian cricket had reached a level of excellence equal to that of the English game". According to Horan, a similar expedition to England had been proposed three years earlier "by several gentlemen in Melbourne who intended to commence in New Zealand", but they had discarded their plans as "the time was apparently not propitious". The assured display by the Australians in both combination matches, and their determination to undertake a tour to England, was the perfect confluence, and no one would have known that with more certainty than Conway. Throughout the late 1860s and early 1870s he had held "stubbornly to the view that random 'tries' against the old country were of little value until the standard of local and inter-colonial play was raised to a more professional level". The inter-colonial matches were the showpiece of Australian cricket, where the best players in the land sharpened and paraded their skills, often in front of crowds of 15,000. It was first-class inter-colonial cricket, he reasoned, to which Australians must "devote our utmost energies. England can wait awhile!" The time for waiting was now over.

The colonial newspapers were eager to reflect this refreshing new conviction in Australian cricket, and to promote the undoubted merits of a tour home, although not all were as sanguine in their views as *The Australasian*:

They wish to show John Bull that we can play cricket here as well as the old folks at home can. They are proud of their skill, as they ought to be, and wish to prove at Lord's and The Oval and other grounds in England that the colonials are worthy descendants of the good old stock from which they have come. The visit of an Australian eleven will be productive of immense good, both to the colonies and the old country … Eleven stalwart Australian natives will be seen at Sheffield and Manchester and Birmingham and other places, in the cricket field, and people will say that the country that can produce such fine men and good cricketers cannot be a bad one by any means. Their hitting powers will testify that the beef and mutton of the country that they represent is the right sort, and their activity in the field will be the best argument that the climate is conducive to energy and muscle.

For too long Australians had been told that their climate did not favour such muscular pursuits as cricket, and that Anglo-Saxon blood was degenerating in the hot sun. The mood of the land was shifting, however, and newspapers, writers and columnists – Conway among them – were no longer prepared to accept such outmoded views. Indeed, the Combined XI's victory over All-England, *The Age* declared, had served as a "crushing reminder to those unpatriotic theorists who would have us believe that the Australian race is deteriorating … or that lengthened resistance under the Australian sun must kill the Briton in the blood". Here were the first discernible stirrings of nationhood. The Australian novelist Marcus Clarke, a close friend of Conway's, put it rather differently. He argued that the gold rush years had brought with them riches and resources of another kind: "the best nerve-power of England, the best bone of Cornwall, the best beef of Yorkshire, the keenest brains of Cockneydom …" In his 1877 pamphlet, *The Future Australian Race*, he invited readers to "Sail up Sydney Harbour, ride over a Queensland plain, watch the gathering of an Adelaide harvest, or mingle with the orderly crowd which throng to the Melbourne Cup race and deny, if you can, that there is here the makings of a great nation".[1] Australia, of course, would have a cricket team before it became a nation: one which *The Australasian* had no doubts would prove victorious against their English opponents on their own grounds and, in doing so, "will have rendered good service to the colonies, and enhanced the prestige of that 'Britain of the South' … which every one of the Eleven can claim as his native land".

Excitement down under was, naturally enough, turned on its head back in England, where news of an impending tour by an Australian team, and talk of a new cricketing power in the firmament, would be met with ridicule. As *Lillywhite's Cricketers' Annual* later confessed in its review of the 1878 season, "the idea of a visit from an Australian team, it may be safely stated, was at first treated as something of a joke". It was a view also held by many Anglophiles in the colonies, who regarded the enterprise as a reckless endeavour – "a jumped-up piece of conceit" – doomed to defeat and failure; others predicted the team would disband before it even left Australia. Lillywhite's men, however, did their best to advance the claims of the colonial cricketers on their return to England, but their attempts for the most part fell on deaf ears. Indeed, the Australian victory in the Grand Combination Match might have taken place on the other side of the looking-glass for all the interest shown in it. *The Times* only condescended to inform its readers of the match details two months after it had been played, and then conveniently buried it in its "Melbourne Letter" column where no one would find it. Not even All-England's victory a fortnight later in the return match could raise a head of steam. Australia was just too far away to be of any consequence. *Wisden*, in what amounted to a rare dereliction of duty, failed to carry an account of either match. Meanwhile, reports in the press of the announcement of an Australian tour were notable only for their brevity – almost all saw no reason to devote more than a single paragraph to it – although *Sporting Life* did at least concede that the Australian team was "very strong in all departments". Nearly six decades later Pelham Warner, reflecting on the airs and graces of his countrymen at that time, concluded, "We were, it would appear, sunk in complacency, and could not imagine that anyone but Englishmen could really play cricket."

However, even before they had sailed for England, the Australian cricketers could at least lay claim to having achieved one momentous "victory". It had been rumoured by the end of the 1877 season that W. G. Grace, the Leviathan of English Cricket, was seriously considering retiring from the first-class game. He had certainly arrived at a crossroads in his career, and was at a point where he needed to re-evaluate his life. He was approaching 30, had completed two years at the Westminster Medical School and had a young family to support. He had thickened noticeably during the past few years, and, although he was no longer the supreme athlete of his early twenties, he was at the zenith of his powers as a cricketer: one who, despite being an amateur, was also excessively well paid for it. It is hard to imagine the game without him. In 1876 – a heady season for him – Grace scored 2,622 runs in 26 first-class matches, including a stupendous 344 for MCC against Kent at Canterbury. By his own standards he scored only a modest 1,474 first-class runs the following year, but still proceeded to top the bowling averages with 179 wickets; hardly the stuff of a man who was about to hang up his boots. How close he actually came to doing so we will never know. Bernard Darwin, his biographer and good friend, wrote that "the decision trembled in the balance"; but the event which "tipped the beam in favour of cricket was the coming of the Australians", and the inaugural first-class tour of England by an overseas opposition.

Grace was no great lover of Australians in general, it has to be said, and it seems that the opportunity to lord it over them in his own backyard was one he found too tempting to resist. He would have also felt that he had some unfinished business with them – the legacy of an ill-tempered and divisive tour down under four years earlier – a consideration that was likely to have appealed to his highly competitive streak and proved equally as enticing.

———

Surrey's H. H. Stephenson captained the first English touring team to Australia in 1861. The sponsors, Felix Spiers and Christopher Pond, the proprietors of the Café de Paris in Melbourne, had originally intended to bring Charles Dickens out on a lecture tour, but when he declined their offer they turned their attention to cricket instead, and sought to engage 12 of England's leading professionals. Stephenson's team was by no means reflective of the strength of the English game. Several of the northern professionals considered £150 a head, plus expenses (Dickens had been offered £7,000), an inadequate sum for a journey of 12,000 miles to the other side of the world and back, and preferred to stay by their firesides. Nevertheless, Stephenson's hardy band received a huge welcome on their arrival in Australia, where they were forced to conduct their first practice session in the bush to escape the crowds. Among their opponents in the opening match, against a Victorian eighteen, was a schoolboy by the name of Jack Conway. They played 12 matches, all against the odds, winning six and losing two. One of those defeats came against a twenty-two of Castlemaine, when *Bell's Life in Victoria* reported that the tourists had consumed so much alcohol "it was a wonder they made any runs at all". They returned to England on 12 May 1862 with only 11 men. Charles Lawrence, the Surrey all-rounder, had been persuaded to stay behind as coach at the Albert Club in Sydney on a salary of £300 per annum. In 1868 he returned to England as the captain-coach of an Aboriginal team. His men held their own on the field, and entertained the crowds off it with such antics as ball-dodging and spear- and boomerang-throwing. But the enterprise – it has been described as a curiosity of history – did nothing to improve the general ignorance in England of Australia's inhabitants, or, indeed, its cricketers, and wreaked much confusion when the first Australian Eleven arrived ten years later.[2] Spiers and Pond's venture into cricket, however, realised a profit of £11,000. The boat had been well and truly pushed out.

Nottinghamshire's George Parr – "the Lion of the North" – took the second England team to Australia a year later; it was also the first to visit New Zealand. Parr's twelve (these pioneering sides rarely numbered more), included the fire and brimstone fast bowler George Tarrant, of Cambridgeshire – who stirred the imagination of a ten-year-old Fred Spofforth – the dapper Surrey batsman William Caffyn, and the wondrously named Julius Caesar, another Surrey man; Gloucestershire's E. M. Grace, W. G.'s elder brother, was the sole amateur. They were a superior team to Stephenson's and went through the tour unbeaten. "It was seen that very little progress had been made during the interval between the first and second visits," Conway reflected, "and offers were made to induce some members of the English team to take up their residence amongst us, to polish up the abundant supply of raw material in the colonies." This time Caffyn stayed behind, taking up a post with the Melbourne Cricket Club as "coach and general instructor to its members". He moved to Sydney a year later, where he became coach and mentor of the Warwick Club, played for New South Wales and was the owner of a "remunerative hairdressing business".

Cricket was thriving in Australia, unrivalled in its popularity in a land where sport already mattered greatly. By the early 1860s Victoria alone could boast 70 clubs. For many, cricket reinforced their Englishness and bound them tighter to the country they still called home. Australians adopted a deferential attitude towards the English game, and it was not considered unusual for crowds at that time to cheer for the touring team. However, as the imperial game advanced in the colonies (the Australians were nothing if not fast learners), so perspectives changed. One of the players who blossomed under the watchful gaze of Caffyn was the princeling Charles Bannerman. "The best bat I ever coached or saw in Australia was undoubtedly Charles Bannerman," Caffyn remarked.[3] When W. G. Grace arrived with the third English team, after a gap of ten years, it was to discover that Australian cricket had not only improved out of all recognition, it had acquired a new attitude.

Grace's tour, at the invitation of the Melbourne Cricket Club, was to prove a distinctly unhappy one, "a turbulent pilgrimage". His team contained a proportionate mix of amateurs and professionals, and therein lay part of the problem. The professionals were engaged on £150 (the rates had not improved in 12 years), plus £20 expenses, travelled second class and stayed in inferior accommodation to the amateurs – a policy which was strictly enforced at all times by their captain. The newly-wed Grace was paid an extortionate ten times more than the professionals, brought his wife, Agnes, with him and treated the tour like a honeymoon junket, which in effect it was. The touring party included the Gloucestershire coterie of Fred Grace, W. G.'s hard-hitting younger brother; his cousin, Walter Raleigh Gilbert, a capable all-rounder; and the wicketkeeper, Arthur Bush, his best man. Egalitarian Australia was shocked by the class divide and treatment of the professionals, and offended by Grace's often boorish conduct, in which he stomped around the country like a John Bull in a china shop. He had regular run-ins with umpires and opposition players – Jack Conway was said to be an "especial *bête noire*" – displayed a very tenuous grasp of diplomatic niceties and generally succeeded in making himself deeply unpopular. Simon Rae, the author of *W. G. Grace: A Life*, asserts that "Grace's manner and behaviour both on and off the field would, in today's climate, have landed him in front of a disciplinary tribunal on charges of bringing the game into disrepute".

When he was not upsetting his hosts or riding roughshod over the rules, however, he displayed a quality of batsmanship which had never been witnessed before in the colonies. Grace scored

711 runs, with a highest score of 126, at an average of 35.11, captured 72 wickets and claimed 42 catches. In 15 matches, his XI won ten and lost three – no mean record. The nub of it all, though, was that Australian cricket was gathering strength – a point which Sam Cosstick, the English-born Victorian medium-pacer, could not resist making at the conclusion of the tour: "Bar W. G. we're as good as they are, and someday we'll lick 'em with eleven." They were prophetic words.

As one of the seven put-upon professionals who toured under W. G. Grace, James Lillywhite was anxious not to repeat the same mistakes, when, as captain, promoter and manager, he led the fourth English team to Australia two years later. *Lillywhite's Cricketer's Companion* had already noted, wrongly, as it turned out, that it was unlikely amateurs and professionals would combine again on tour. Lillywhite's all-professional team were paid £200 plus expenses, although Alfred Shaw, the doyen of medium-pace bowlers who doubled up as vice-captain and assistant manager, received £300 for his additional responsibilities. More pertinently, though, they would travel first-class. No one could pretend that the team was in any way representative of English cricket, but neither was it short on talent: Lillywhite, Shaw, the Yorkshire hard 'uns George Ulyett and Tom Emmett, and the Surrey triumvirate Harry Jupp, James Southerton (who remains, at 49, Test cricket's eldest debutant) and Ted Pooley, were the pick of the professional crop. However, before they departed Australia they would be dubbed, somewhat unfairly perhaps, as the weakest English team to have visited the colonies.

They lost to Victoria and suffered successive defeats to New South Wales, disastrously so in the second of these when they were dismissed for only 35. It was in the light of this that Lillywhite's men were challenged to a match against a New South Wales XI. Lillywhite accepted – the first time an English team had played on level terms against a colony – and the game, held over two days, culminated in a draw. This acted as an immediate spur to Victoria, which, not to be outdone by its great rival, threw down its own challenge on even terms, and it was agreed that the Englishmen would take on a Combined XI of the best players from New South Wales and Victoria, once they had returned from an eight-match tour of New Zealand.

They arrived back in Melbourne on 14 March, the day before the start of the Grand Combination Match, having had to leave Pooley, their only specialist wicketkeeper, behind. An inveterate gambler – in keeping with most of his team-mates – Pooley had been arrested on a charge of assault and causing malicious damage for his part in a betting scam carried out during a match against an eighteen of Canterbury. Pooley used an old ruse by which he predicted he could correctly forecast the score of each member of the Canterbury team; having found a willing victim to fleece, he offered to play a shilling for each wrong prediction, provided he was paid £1 for each one he got right. He then wrote nought against each name; as more than half of the 18 recorded ducks (these teams invariably included their fair share of "rabbits", as Pooley knew they would), he stood to make a tidy profit. He further loaded the dice, it was claimed, by umpiring in the match. When the local man refused to pay up, Pooley struck him and was held responsible for the bar-room brawl that ensued.

The Australians, however, were not without problems of their own. The 23-year-old Fred Spofforth had refused to play in Melbourne after Victoria's Jack Blackham was selected ahead of Billy Murdoch, the New South Wales wicketkeeper, with the fast bowler insisting that he was "the only one who knows how to take me properly". It was a misjudgment put down to the folly of youth. Frank Allan, who had been called up in Spofforth's place, preferred to attend his local agricultural show instead, where the crowd hissed at him for his insouciance. The Englishmen, meanwhile, had endured a torrid voyage across the Tasman Sea, and most of them, according to Shaw, had been seasick: "Not one of us was fit to play cricket ... I was simply spun out of myself." He might have been singing to a very different tune, though, had Tom Armitage, fielding at mid-on, not shelled the simplest of catches off his bowling before Charles Bannerman reached double figures. Bannerman proceeded to play one of the most destructive innings of his or any other era, hitting more than two-thirds of his team's runs out of a first-innings total of 245; the next highest score was 18 made by Tom Garrett, batting at No. 9. Bannerman's exhilarating charge was eventually terminated on 165 when a short-pitched ball from the hostile George Ulyett struck him on the right glove, splitting his middle finger to the bone and forcing him to retire hurt. Requiring 154 to win on the fourth day, the Englishmen appeared to be still in contention at 61 for four but were routed for 108 in a little over two hours by the left-armer Tom Kendall, who captured seven for 55. There is no doubt the defeat came as a shock to the tourists; they were the overwhelming favourites and many had bet heavily on themselves to win. It had been just 15 years since the first tour of Australia by H. H. Stephenson's team, and "the pupils," Conway wrote, were now "quite as good as their masters".

The Englishmen earned their revenge two weeks later when they defeated what was arguably an even stronger Combined XI, in which Spofforth had been forgiven for his earlier indiscretion, and Murdoch played as a specialist batsman. Nonetheless, Conway added, "The closeness of both of these interesting contests showed that there was very little if any difference between the strength of the opposing elevens, but there were many who were prepared to back the Australians if they were to play matches together like the Englishmen." By the time Lillywhite's professionals steamed away from Adelaide for England on 19 April after an epochal five months, preparations to reverse the tide of traffic between the two hemispheres were already under way.

Two
19 April 1877–28 March 1878

"In all probability we shall go to war"

One of the first essential elements of the Australian venture to fall into place was the agreement by James Lillywhite to act as agent for the Eleven in England. Lillywhite was to play an indispensable role, both in terms of the reciprocal encouragement and support he offered to the project during its inception, and in the colonials' ultimate progress through Britain. It was Conway, after all, who had persuaded Lillywhite to bring an all-professional team to Australia. The two men were hewn from the same rock. They were both in their mid-thirties, trusted and liked each other and quickly established that they could do business. They were not dissimilar in appearance – thickset and dark-haired – although Lillywhite, at about 5ft 7in, was shorter than Conway, who sported a long, curly moustache and looked like a gunfighter in his photographs. They were entrepreneurs and initiators off the field (among other things both men were successful publishers of their own cricket compendiums), and former opponents on it, who shared a healthy regard for each other's abilities. Their mutual respect was sealed by a locket, which Lillywhite presented to Conway, "on behalf of the eleven", during the professionals' farewell dinner at the Globe Hotel in Adelaide.

Lillywhite came from a famous cricketing family and was the nephew of the great William Lillywhite, a slow bowler of such repute for Sussex that he was known as "the Nonpareil". James Lillywhite was a wily left-arm medium-pacer who varied his flight, and a useful lower-order batsman who was quite capable of scoring centuries. He made his debut for Sussex at 20 and would go on to play in consecutive seasons for his county between 1862 and 1882, consolidating his reputation as a tough, dependable cricketer. If he lacked Conway's brazen and assertive nature – he had failed to keep the more rowdy members of his professionals on the straight and narrow in Australia – he certainly made up for it in other areas. Home Gordon, in *Background Of Cricket*, claims that on tour in 1876–7 Lillywhite thought nothing of consuming two bottles of champagne every morning.[1] But he also knew the ropes, and was not without influence. His all-professional tour had been a private speculation, and despite journeying to Australia without an official invitation from the Melbourne Cricket Club – it also did so without the endorsement of the English cricketing establishment – the enterprise was said to have made a handsome profit. Exactly how much will never be known: as Lillywhite himself put it, "Bowling and not figures is my line."

Before leaving for England, Lillywhite told Conway he had every confidence that he could provide the Australians with a full itinerary, including a requisite number of first-class matches. Perhaps he sensed that the counties would be only too keen to exert what they assumed to be their natural superiority. He promised to write as soon as he had news to report, and the two men shook hands, vowing to meet again in just over a year's time in England. Staunch advocate of the Australians that he was, Lillywhite nevertheless had a nagging worry. He feared that the internecine rivalries between the colonies – the Victorians and New South Welshmen had managed to keep their differences to themselves during the combination matches – would spill over again on tour, and at some stage he admitted as much to Conway. However, he was also delighted to be proved wrong – emphatically so, as it turned out. "In that regard no difficulty whatever was experienced," Conway later wrote of the matter, "and in the course of a few months the best players of Victoria, New South Wales and Tasmania had consented to take service under the Australian flag." It should, in fact, have been two Tasmanians, and therein hangs a sad tale.

———

On 19 April, after seeing off Lillywhite and his professionals on the mail steamer *Bangalore* from Glenelg, Conway wrote to the Tasmanian batsman John Arthur:

> It is intended if possible to send an Australian team to England, taking in India en route after playing a series of matches in the Australian colonies. Would you form one of the team if sufficient inducement is held out? It is intended to make all the colonies interested in order to ensure the economical working of the team. I may state that Charles Bannerman, Spofforth, the Gregorys, Thomson, Murdoch, Garrett and Coates have already promised their cooperation, and have sanctioned my actions in this matter. Would you favour me by asking Bailey (Launceston) if he would like to join the party?

Conway had intended to include Arthur in the eleven for the Grand Combination Match, but had been unable to agree financial terms. A tall, bearded opening batsman, Arthur was admired for his "straight bat, his off hitting and the patience with which he waited for the bad ball"; he was described as "Tasmania's first home-grown star". He had announced himself three years earlier when W. G. Grace brought his All-England team to Tasmania, striking a flurry of successive boundaries – seven in all – during a brief but whirlwind innings of 32 against the bowling of Grace, Lillywhite and James Southerton. Tragically, two days after receiving Conway's letter at his home in Longford, near Launceston, Arthur died in what was reported as "mysterious circumstances". The Launceston *Examiner* stated that his death was the result of a "short attack of brain fever"; the Hobart *Mercury* that he had contracted pleurisy. His death certificate, however, confirmed that he died of inflammation of the brain, aged only 32 years and 19 days. He had complained of acute sciatica in the last match he played, and the newspapers recorded that despite scoring a half-century, he was barely able to run between the wickets. Before Arthur died, though, he ensured that Conway's letter was passed on to the 23-year-old George Bailey, a wristy and accomplished middle-order batsman.

As the letter indicates, Conway had already planned a preliminary tour of Australia, which would also take in New Zealand, before the Eleven journeyed to England. The tour would serve two purposes: to put money in the kitty to help finance the expedition home and to meld the various colonial factions – a bonding exercise, in modern parlance. The conditions in New Zealand were also expected to replicate those they might find in England. However, the proposed tour to India en route, and the labyrinthine arrangements it would have entailed (reports in the Australian press suggested that Conway intended to play matches in Colombo, Madras, Bombay and Allahabad), was pioneering in the extreme and did not come to fruition. Although cricket had been slow to take hold among Indians – it was still predominantly played by the British – the game was well advanced in the Parsee community of Bombay. Indeed, the Australians might not have been the only touring team in England during the summer of 1878 had a proposed expedition by the Parsees not fallen through at the last minute.[2] It would be another 11 years, though, before a first tour of India was accomplished, when G. F. Vernon, of Middlesex, took out an all-amateur side from England.

During the coming weeks speculation in the press over the composition of the Australian Eleven was rife, with each colony keen to promote the claims of its own representatives. The names of such experienced cricketers as Ned Gregory (David's elder brother), Joseph Coates, Nat Thomson and Edwin Evans would appear, disappear and reappear with unfailing regularity. At this stage, the tour was still in the early planning stages and Conway's enquiries to players were no more than exploratory; players were either expressing their willingness to tour – or not, as in the case of the New South Wales batsman Ned Sheridan, who declined an invitation after the death of his mother. No contracts had been signed, no pledges drawn up, and the tortuous negotiations involving leave of absence from work were still weeks off.

Yet it was clear from Conway's letter that he already possessed the rudiments of a strong eleven. David Gregory, Charles Bannerman, Tom Garrett, Billy Murdoch and Fred Spofforth were among the first to show their hands, soon to be joined by George Bailey. Before the end of the southern winter, Conway would have his team.

———

Perhaps the easiest decision Conway had to make was the appointment of David Gregory as captain of the Eleven. He was the natural choice, much as he had been on the morning of the Grand Combination Match in Melbourne, when the Australian players elected him as their leader, despite the fact that he was a Sydneysider and the Victorian contingent outnumbered New South Welshmen by six to five. He was presented with a gold watch for his part in the Combined XI's rites-of-passage victory. An accountant in the Sydney audit office, and a father and step-father to 16 children, he was a tough-minded, often inventive captain, who at 32 was the oldest member of the Eleven. An authoritative figure, over 6ft tall with a bushy black beard, he was said to have borne a close resemblance to the bushranger Ned Kelly; as such he rarely needed to impose his personality on his players. He had few superiors as a short slip, but as a batsman he had no great pretensions to style. He was what the English players and press liked to call a "rustic thumper". Naturally, the Eleven would hear nothing against him and were prepared to follow him through thick and thin. "He is a rugged individualist as skipper and fears no one," Tom Horan wrote. "A true Australian."

He would be accompanied on the four-month colonial leg of the tour by Jack Blackham, "The Prince of Wicketkeepers", who would share the gloves with the stylish strokemaker Billy Murdoch; Charles Bannerman, the sturdy Tom Horan, George Bailey and Alec Bannerman, a defensive player of inexhaustible concentration – the tortoise to brother Charles's hare – provided the rest of the batting. Alec Bannerman was the beneficiary of

Nat Thomson's failure to agree terms with Conway, although, according to Horan, his place in the Eleven was not assured until two weeks before they sailed for England. A cadre of bowlers – easily the team's strongest suit – comprised the lean, 6ft 3in Fred Spofforth, the lively Tom Garrett, the two left-armers, Tom Kendall and Frank Allan, and Harry Boyle, a crafty medium-pacer who had not been picked for either of the combination matches. Besides the sole Tasmanian, Bailey, there were six New South Welshmen – Gregory, Murdoch, the two Bannermans, Spofforth and Garrett – and five Victorians, Blackham, Horan, Boyle, Kendall and Allan. "The other colonies would have been consulted in the matter had there been any players proficient enough to make up the Eleven, but it was admitted on all hands that there were not," Conway declared. Nevertheless, he was satisfied that the team reflected the optimistic fervour and vibrancy coursing through the colonial game. Only four of the 12 were not Australian-born: Charles Bannerman and Kendall had been born in Woolwich and Bedford respectively; Horan in Midleton, Ireland, and Bailey in Colombo, Ceylon. In addition, it was arranged that the Eleven would pick up the Victorian all-rounder Billy Midwinter on their arrival in England.

Midwinter's family had emigrated to Australia from Gloucestershire in 1861, when he was nine, lured to Bendigo, the Eldorado of the colonies, by the promise of gold. Like those of so many would-be prospectors, the dreams of discovering a fortune did not materialise, and the family eventually settled in Bendigo, where Billy's father took a job as a butcher. Billy returned to England in May 1877 determined to try his luck as a professional cricketer. He had disembarked at London docks with only 30 shillings to his name; ten of them quickly disappeared on a cab fare to the Kennington Oval where the North were playing the South – the price was such that a somewhat naive Midwinter had at first assumed the cab driver was attempting to sell him his entire business – and a further seven shillings on "a real good tuck-in meal". Nevertheless, he had wasted no time in offering his services to W. G. Grace. No doubt, 'the Champion' recognised him as the strapping all-rounder who had disturbed his stumps three years earlier, while playing for eighteen of Victoria against All-England; and, presumably, Midwinter had not been backward in playing the West Country card. Within a few days he was earning money, turning out for the United South of England XI and agreeing professional terms to play for Gloucestershire. Conway had no doubts that Midwinter's experience of the conditions, allied to his ability as a highly rated all-round cricketer, would make him an invaluable asset. "Though English by birth he is a thoroughly Australian cricketer and will greatly strengthen the Eleven," he confidently asserted.

As ever, Conway had been busy. His efforts in securing his players one year's leave of absence from their jobs (six were civil servants, three engaged by banks and a solicitor, Murdoch, who had only recently qualified) proved a triumph of negotiation, of which he was rightly proud, and removed perhaps the most serious stumbling block to the advancement of the tour. Assurances were given that there would be no loss of status and that the players would be reinstated on their return from England. "Conway wrote dozens of begging letters to Ministers," his grandson, Ronald, revealed. "He cajoled, flattered and dined out scores of colonial potentates before he was able to get the desired response."

He also appointed an assistant manager and secretary, William Gibbes, a clerk in the Sydney audit department, and organised a cooperative association in which the members of the team each paid a £50 stake, with all profits or losses from the tour to be shared equally among them.[3] "Articles of Agreement were signed," Tom Horan recorded, "placing players on an equal footing and guaranteeing harmony." There was one exception to this arrangement, Alec Bannerman, who agreed to a fixed sum of £200. He and his brother would also tour as professional cricketers, although they were not professionals in the strict sense of the word, as defined by their English counterparts. The rest classed themselves as amateurs, a perception which would generate much suspicion and no little rancour on their travels in England.

In setting out their mission statement, however, the Eleven made it clear that any thoughts of profit were entirely subsidiary. Their objective, Horan explained, was simple enough: "to measure themselves against English players on the classic grounds of the Old Country", and no more. Of course, should money come their way, all good and well, but, as Horan acknowledged, they would have their hands full just achieving their goal. "There were not wanting in speculators in Sydney or Melbourne willing to back the Eleven and ready to advance the money necessary to the proper carrying out of the project," he added, "but the players preferred to take all the risk themselves, as it left them more independent."

Now all they had to do was play some matches.

―――――

The self-styled Australian Eleven opened their tour in Brisbane on Thursday, 9 November against an eighteen of Queensland. Their departure from Sydney Harbour on the *Balclutha* six days earlier had been a strangely low-key affair, with Fred Spofforth noting that "there was no particular demonstration by the friends of the team". The same critics who had so strongly opposed the venture when it was first announced seized the opportunity to repeat their taunts that it would bring nothing but shame to the colonies and financial humiliation to the players. Their claims prompted Conway to quip that the Eleven "would have to return to Australia in an emigrant ship". It was not perhaps as far-fetched as it sounded. By paying their own expenses up front and investing purely in their talents to recoup the money through gate receipts, the Eleven were taking a huge gamble, a veritable leap in the dark. It was later claimed that some of them took their own money with them to England to cover their return fares. Characteristically, Conway made capital out of the critics. "These false prophets", as he dubbed them, were "splendid advertising mediums for the Eleven, but they did not know it". Their slingshots had the "very opposite effect from that which might have been expected. They bound us together as tight as wax."

Among their fellow passengers as they steamed away from Sydney was the journalist Julian Thomas, or "the Vagabond" as he was better known. Thomas claimed to have a vested interest in the Eleven's venture. "It was a happy accident which caused me to take passage on the steamer *Balclutha*," he wrote in the Melbourne *Argus* of 19 November, "as I consider myself the father of the scheme to send an eleven of Australian cricketers to meet Englishmen on equal terms on their own ground." It was after Victoria's defeat of James Lillywhite's XI in December 1876, "the Vagabond" revealed, that he had stopped at the White Hart in Melbourne to "mingle with the cricketing and betting throng".[4] There, he fell into conversation with Lillywhite and put it to him that "a combination eleven of the best players in the colonies would beat more than half your best English teams. There'd be heaps of money in it, too". Lillywhite agreed, "Yes, it'd pay, no doubt of that, if you could get New South Wales and Victoria to stop their jealousies." Their conversation, Thomas recounted, was overheard by "that entertaining journalist and cricketer, Mr. John Conway", and "a month or two after this [he] opened negotiations with the players of the colonies for the present proposed excursion to England".

An incurable name-dropper and social climber, Thomas's popularity as a cosmopolitan observer of Australian life relied almost exclusively on an aura of mystery, and when he was unmasked as "the Vagabond" not long after, his star quickly waned. Nevertheless, he was in full flow during the voyage and full of himself, too: "I'm always dropping hints and ideas which will make any man's fortune if he knows how to use them. When our boys return from England with their thousands, I shall expect a handsome souvenir for my troubles in this matter."[5]

The Eleven received an enthusiastic welcome on their arrival in Brisbane – they were "feasted and *fêted*", in the words of "the Vagabond" – but were alarmed by the state of the pitch at the Eagle Farm racecourse. Tom Horan, who was reporting the tour for the Australian press under the *nom de plume* "One of Them" (a role in which he would prove a complete natural), described the portion set apart for the match as "unmade ground". It was hardly surprising, he added, that "the batsmen had a lively time of it". So much so that the eighteen were dismissed for 58 and 68 – Tom Kendall was virtually unplayable in collecting 19 wickets – and the Eleven opened their account with an easy victory, by an innings and 23 runs, inside two days. "As regards cricket in Queensland, it may be said to be *in embryo*," Horan observed. "They have no good grounds to play on, and therefore they cannot turn out good batsmen." The wicket at the Toowoomba racecourse, where they played their second match, beating twenty-two of Darling Downs by 170 runs, was, Horan wrote, even worse: "Indeed, it is astonishing that I have not to chronicle a serious accident or two, considering the extraordinary flights the ball took. Sometimes a good ball would be pitched which would fly off at a tangent to short leg. At other times the ball would strike a hillock and bound clean into the hands of long-stop!" He was not exaggerating: fielding there to the terrifying Spofforth, he received a succession of blows all over his body before a fearful crack on the chin necessitated his transfer to another part of the field. Spofforth captured ten wickets in the second innings, splaying stumps, rattling ribcages and shredding the nerves of batsmen and fielders in equal measure.

Their stay in Queensland over, the Eleven returned to Sydney to test themselves against a fifteen of New South Wales at the Albert Ground over 23–26 November. The fifteen included Edwin Evans, who was considered by many as the outstanding all-rounder in the colonies. Although Evans had turned down an initial invitation to tour on "business grounds", Conway remained hopeful he could persuade him to change his mind. In the opinion of the *Sydney Mail*, Evans was the single player whose presence would make the Eleven "complete in every respect". His contribution in this game was negligible, however, and the Eleven achieved an impressive four-wicket victory. Spofforth completed a 19-wicket haul while Charles Bannerman struck the ball with remorseless power in an innings of 83. Further victories followed in Maitland, Bendigo and at the Adelaide Oval, against a South Australian eighteen, where Spofforth continued on his "destructive path through colonial cricket", stacking up another 17 wickets. Despite the colony's failure to secure a representative in the Eleven, interest in the tour in Adelaide was considerable. Too often, though, the Eleven's matches during the Australian leg of the expedition suffered from poor advertising, and as a consequence gate receipts were significantly lower than they should have been. "Square Leg" in the *Sydney Mail* did not shy away from blaming Conway for this oversight: "In travelling shows of all kinds (and the Australian Eleven may, I think, be included in this category) a great deal depends upon the manner in which they are brought before the notice of the public. 'Give us bold advertisement' ought to be an instruction to every agent whose duty it is to see that everything is done to promote the success of any entertainment which appeals to the public for support."

There was certainly no lack of entertaining cricket. Before leaving for New Zealand, the Eleven were involved in an extraordinary tie with a combined New South Wales and Victoria fifteen at Melbourne. Chasing 113 to win in front of a sparse crowd, the tourists had three wickets in hand with the scores level when Evans started his 43rd over, but they somehow contrived to lose Boyle and Kendall (both comprehensively bowled) and Murdoch (run out) without addition to the score. Bizarrely, Bailey had played out a maiden the over before, assuming that victory for the Eleven was a foregone conclusion.

The seven-match tour to New Zealand started on 9 January against a twenty-two of Invercargill after a "very rough and disagreeable" passage to Bluff, the southernmost settlement in the South Island. "Most of us were terribly knocked up by the trip across the Tasman Sea from Melbourne," Horan wrote. It was to be the precursor to an exacting month of cricket – the first by an Australian team in New Zealand. Not the least of the Eleven's problems was "the caravan", their cumbersome canvas bag of equipment. The Eleven could not run to a baggage man, and Spofforth recalled that "we used to draw lots to decide who should look after the bag from match to match". It was a back-breaking chore. On one occasion, he and Billy Murdoch drew the short straw and dragged it for a mile and a half during which "we had to climb fences, and scramble over gates with the huge thing in tow". Spofforth added that the team carried it to England, and "landed it safely in Nottingham; but in London it was lost, and no one knows its burying place". At that time, Spofforth pointed out, only "the very best cricketers owned pads or even bats". They also carried a strong box everywhere, in which they kept their match takings and which, unlike "the caravan", they never let out of their sight.

The Eleven complained bitterly about the weather during their stay in New Zealand – Horan remarked that they experienced only four genial days throughout – and the often primitive conditions they encountered. In Dunedin, for instance, their clothes were saturated by a "pervasive Scotch mist" before a violent hailstorm finally halted play, while their match against a twenty-two of Oamaru was contested on what Horan called a "worn-out potato paddock on which the lovers of the noble game endeavour to play to the detriment of their legs, body and head". The highlight of the expedition was undoubtedly Charles Bannerman's unbeaten 125 against Invercargill – the first century by an Australian on New Zealand soil, and the first of the tour. His innings included two towering blows: one of them landed in an orchard at square leg "50 metres from the ground", and the other in a cottage at long-on. However, it was also in New Zealand that the Eleven suffered their only defeat of the Australasian tour, losing by six wickets to a fifteen of Canterbury at Christchurch's splendid Hagley Park. Perhaps the Eleven should not have riled the local cricketers by insisting that they field 22 men, as was the custom. As the stronghold of New Zealand cricket, Canterbury's players were confident they could give the Australians a run for their money with either 12 or 15, and warned that they would pull out of the match if their request was not met. A compromise was eventually reached at 15. The Eleven were promptly bowled out for 46 in their first innings, and never recovered. The impact of the Eleven's collapse was no more acutely felt than in Australia, where "Square Leg" of the *Sydney Mail* likened the news to "an electric shock". Despite a battling 58 from Horan, the fifteen required only 55 to win on the third day and achieved their target for the loss of eight wickets in front of a rapturous crowd of 6,000. All told, as many as 18,000 visited the ground, but as the park was a public recreation area and no entrance fees were charged, a collection had to be raised for the Eleven, an amount that was said to have realised a "goodly sum". Nonetheless, it did not prevent the tourists from grumbling about the conditions or the umpiring, although Horan's claim that the pitch was "about the worst we met during the tour" was probably more attributable to the chagrin of defeat. The Eleven concluded their tour of New Zealand with victories in Wellington, Hastings and Auckland, and departed for Australia on 12 February.

———

Not long after their return Conway received a letter from James Lillywhite containing important news. "I have fixed your first match against the county of Nottinghamshire for May 20, 21 and 22," he wrote, "and this will give you a week's clear practice." Lillywhite had been as good as his word. There was a match against MCC at Lord's on 27–29 May, followed by a visit to The Oval to play Surrey on 3–5 June: "The 5th is Derby day, and you will be able to please yourselves whether you will play cricket or go to the Derby. London will be full, and Monday and Tuesday ought to be good days." There were matches against the odds, too, at Batley and Longsight – "both populous places in the North" – and then a return to London to play the Gentlemen of England at Prince's Ground on 17–19 June. "This will be hard work for you," he admitted. There was then a lull in proceedings until the end of June, when there were more matches against the odds: at Leeds, Stockport, Crewe, Keighley and Rochdale. The programme was still a work in progress. Some club secretaries had baulked at Lillywhite's request for a game and considered the Australians to be too much of an unknown quantity; others were reluctant to commit themselves. The counties of Yorkshire and Derbyshire had yet to confirm fixtures, but Lillywhite had tied down dates with Lancashire at Old Trafford on 15–17 August; Gloucestershire, the dominant force in the land, had promised a game later in the season, as had "many other large towns against the odds". He was even holding out the tantalising prospect – it was no more than that – of representative games against an England XI "on the Oval and probably at Canterbury".

Lillywhite then turned his hand to more grave affairs: the impending threat of war with Russia. "In all probability we shall go to war, but you need not trouble yourself on that score," he reassured Conway, somewhat glibly, "as it will not make any difference in this country – the first year at least – and I expect Russia will have quite a bellyful after one year at us. They think we won't fight, but if they find we will (and we shall), they will cave in. Why, Nottinghamshire and Yorkshire could lick them before breakfast!"

Anti-Russian feeling was in full spate in England. The Tsar and the Ottoman Empire were at war, and had been since 24 April 1877. On 10 December the Turkish fortress of Plevna had fallen after a long and bloody siege, and a month later Russian troops were occupying Adrianople. When it was reported that the Tsar's army was in sight of the minarets of Constantinople, Disraeli had ordered the fleet through the Dardanelles and into the Black Sea, ostensibly to protect British interests in the Mediterranean but also to act as a show of support for Turkey. Queen Victoria's eagerness for war, and her displeasure at the dithering of her cabinet, was such that she had even proposed her abdication only days before. Her zeal was mirrored by the man on the street. The American author Henry James wrote to a friend that "London smells of gunpowder" – there were anti-Russian demonstrations – and the music halls of England rang to the words of "Macdermott's War Song", the ditty which famously introduced the word "jingoism" to the English language:[6]

We don't want to fight;
But by Jingo if we do,
We've got the men, we've got the ships,
We've got the money too.

Lillywhite's excessive boast that the counties of Nottinghamshire and Yorkshire could lick the Russian Bear before breakfast perfectly caught the temperature of the nation. He concluded his letter to Conway, "You will soon find if we are in a row – that is, if you don't know before you start – you will have an escort in the shape of a big ironclad."

Before the Eleven left for England, however, they were forced into a hurried and unexpected change of plan. The wrecking of the Orient steamer the *Chimborazo*, which was to have carried them to England from Adelaide, left them with no choice but radically to redraw their schedule and depart from Sydney, via San Francisco, instead.[7] Conway would sail in advance of the main party on the Suez mail packet a week earlier. The Eleven pulled out of the fixtures in Warrnambool, Victoria, and Mount Gambier, South Australia, and played their final game against eighteen of Victoria in Melbourne over 22–25 March. They would then travel overland to Sydney to catch the San Francisco mail steamer on Thursday, 28 March. In his last letter Lillywhite had impressed upon Conway the importance of the Eleven arriving in England on time. There was now no margin for error. The unreasonable demands of the Melbourne Cricket Club – it insisted on 20% of the gate and 60% of the grandstand revenue – compelled yet another change, and the Eleven pointedly switched the game against Victoria across town to the East Melbourne Club, where they were offered cheaper rates. "The Yarra Club sought to justify the increase in its charge by saying that this new rate would apply to all future matches at the Melbourne Ground," Horan reported. "But that explanation begged the question: why make an Australian Eleven, which was risking its own money on the England venture, the first side to be asked to pay the elevated rates?" They completed the tour with a convincing 155-run victory, packed their bags and set off post haste for Sydney.

The journey, which involved two trips by rail and one by coach, turned into a frantic race against time after a heavy rainstorm turned the road into a quagmire, and left the Eleven soaked to the bone. The downpour did not let up for 18 hours, and at every stage of the journey by coach they found themselves falling further behind. There was only one train connection from Bowning to Sydney, which was another 180 miles away. "If we missed the train we could miss the boat, and the whole of our English programme would be disorganised," Frank Allan recalled. "Hoping against hope, we promised our driver a ten-pound note if he caught the train. You can guess how he worked his elbow, and the time he gave his horses!" The train from Bowning, in fact, turned out to be two and a half hours late, which still allowed them enough time to reach Sydney and board the steamer. They arrived in the city the following morning on the 28th, weary and bedraggled, only to be informed that the departure of the *City of Sydney* had been put back a day.

One player did not take his place on that grim journey, however. The Eleven had already made the contentious decision not to take Tom Kendall with them to England, omitting him from their last three matches, against Geelong, Ballarat, and Victoria. No one in the Eleven doubted his talent – he was a left-arm spinner with an easy, graceful action who could turn the ball prodigiously – but his increasing fondness for the bottle had made him a liability. Only a year earlier he had produced the outstanding figures of seven for 55 to skittle All-England in the Grand Combination Match, and had been rated as the best bowler of his type in the colonies. "He appeared to have quite lost the splendid bowling faculty he exhibited against Lillywhite's Eleven," Conway stated in the *South Australian Advertiser* on 24 April. "The Eleven, feeling they had the representation of the

Australian colonies in their hands, could not afford to be delicate in the matter, though each one regretted to lose the companionship of the left-hander … They unanimously decided to leave Kendall behind. They will thus journey with eleven men, the vacant place being left open for Midwinter, who is now in England waiting to join."

The banishment of Kendall – he had finished the Australasian leg of the tour with 102 wickets; only Spofforth (281) and Garrett (103) took more – met with a mixed response from both press and public, many of whom thought the Eleven would come to regret their decision. Horan even appeared to suggest that the resolution had not been as unanimous as Conway claimed. "Altogether he has not shown such a marked falling off in form as to justify his exclusion from the place in the Eleven he had earned by his previous doings," he wrote, "and his absence will be felt in England." The message, though, could not have been clearer: Kendall was the weak link, and there was no place in the Australian team for backsliding or indolence. If there had still been any doubt about their desire to make a success of their venture to England – or, indeed, the ruthlessness to see that outcome through – it had been expunged at a stroke.

Three
29 March–13 May 1878

"We arrived in New York all very much knocked up"

The Eleven did not know it at the time of their departure, but there was bad news on the breeze. They had received a rousing send-off from Sydney on the afternoon of Friday, 29 March, the armada of steamers and the military band adding to the unmistakable aura of adventure and expectation that filled the air that day. "A large number of persons collected to wish success to the cricketers, who are now on their homeward voyage," the *Sydney Morning Herald* reported, "and success and good luck were wished to them times out of number." All appeared to be set fair after the commotion of the past few days. But, as Horan would later write, "Little did we know ... Midwinter's English commitments were to prove a severe embarrassment to the Australian Eleven." The bad news would pursue them for 12,000 miles, before finally catching up with them in England.

"We learned later that, even before the *City of Sydney* cleared Sydney Heads, our playing strength in England had been reduced to eleven," Horan explained. Midwinter had jumped ship. It seemed that on 22 March – seven days before the Eleven sailed from Sydney – a letter had been received by a friend and correspondent of Midwinter's in Bendigo. According to Horan, the friend subsequently passed it on to a Melbourne newspaper columnist, who disclosed the incendiary contents in his "Cricket Gossip" page:

> *When the Eleven left Sydney on Friday last they were under the impression that Midwinter would play with them, but in this it seems they are mistaken ... I am informed that a letter was*

> *received from Midwinter last mail in which he states Grace had*
> *told him if he played with the Australian Eleven, Gloucestershire*
> *would have nothing more to do with him. He could take his choice*
> *of playing with the Australian Eleven, or of remaining and*
> *playing with Gloucestershire; and that if he remained with them*
> *he could form one of an All England Eleven to visit the colonies*
> *next season, to include the Graces, with W. G. as captain …*
> *Midwinter further wrote that the Englishmen had treated him*
> *well and he had decided to stay with them and would positively*
> *not play with the colonial team.*[1]

The columnist appeared to have some sympathy for Midwinter's predicament, although, as he admitted, the news could not have been more ill timed, or injurious to the Eleven, having already taken the decision to discard Kendall. They would be hard pressed to keep eleven men fit and in the field during four months of continuous cricket. "One can hardly help wishing he [Midwinter] would assert his independence by joining his colonial brethren – for a player held in the estimation he is, would always command a market – but still, if he has good prospects, and is actuated by so praiseworthy a motive as gratitude, he cannot be blamed for not casting his English patrons aside," the columnist wrote. The fault, if any, he perceived, lay with Grace: "Whether Grace is acting a manly and chivalrous part in putting Midwinter into a corner, as he appears to have done, is another question entirely, and one about which there is not much to be said in his favour."

Accompanied by their secretary and assistant manager, William Gibbes, the Eleven pressed on with their voyage of discovery, unaware that the mutinous Midwinter had left them high and dry. They had run into strong headwinds soon after leaving Sydney and, in an effort to make up for lost time, spent only two hours in Auckland before setting off again. There, they took on another 60 passengers, including a group of theatrical entertainers called the Troubadours, who were travelling en route to Los Angeles. "This brought the number of cabin passengers to 128: the largest number a Pacific Mail boat had ever carried at one time," Horan recorded. However, all was far from well on board. The source of this dissatisfaction was the food, most of which was so badly cooked, Horan complained, that it was often inedible: "The water was also very bad, and the tea smelt like bilge water. Meal time was a thoroughly unpleasant experience." Several of the passengers had threatened to write to the newspapers, he added, "advising intending travellers for England not to go via America if they desired to keep their health".

The Eleven stayed fit and alleviated their boredom on the voyage with an hour or two's cricket practice every day, "using a piece of wood, a little thicker than a stump as the bat … the field scattering around everywhere". The hurricane deck soon proved inadequate for such purposes, and within a few days they had lost several valuable balls over the side. They pitched their wicket on the spar deck instead, where they were offered more protection, but no matter how hard they tried the balls continued to disappear into the vast, tumbling outfield. As a last resort they borrowed potatoes and turnips from the galley for catching practice, but with the same result. Eventually the cook refused to part with any more, fearful he might be cleaned out before they reached San Francisco. One thing was certain, Horan remarked: the Eleven would not grow fat on this voyage.

Nineteen days out of Sydney they sailed into Honolulu, where they stayed for six hours picking up despatches for the American mainland. The Eleven stretched their legs, sent messages back to Australia and were "quite captivated by the beautiful vegetation and lovely scenery of this gem of the tropics". Finally, on Friday, 26 April, they sighted the coast of California, and after navigating more than 3,000 miles of ocean (or what Horan described as "29 days of tedium") they steamed through the Golden Gate into San Francisco Bay, with its thicket of masts and funnels. They were only too glad to find themselves back on dry land, and were soon reclining in the Palace Hotel, a spectacular white and gold eight-storey edifice, which stretched for two and a half acres along New Montgomery and Market streets. Opened two years earlier as a symbol of San Francisco's rapid transformation from raw boomtown to prosperous, polyglot city, the hotel contained 800 rooms, "complete with all the conveniences and comforts the most fastidious person could wish for". It would be their last glimpse of the inside of a hotel for two weeks, and each man made the most of his last night of luxury for a while. The following day the Eleven would catch the ferry to the Oakland terminus and begin the seven-day journey by railroad to New York.

———

The Transcontinental Railroad was one of the technological wonders of the 19th century. It took six years to construct and connected San Francisco with the existing eastern railroad terminus at Council Bluffs, Iowa, in the MidWest. A journey from the Pacific coast to the Atlantic – all of 3,310 miles – that might once have taken six months or longer could now be accomplished in seven days, or five without stops. It was a truly American feat: both epic and heroic in its scale, and brutal in its execution, by destroying one way of life and creating another it changed the landscape of a continent for ever. It was also a commercial venture, and a race between two railroad companies – the Central Pacific in the West and the Union Pacific in the East – to see who could lay down the most tracks. The Union Pacific advanced rapidly west from the Missouri River through the prairies towards the Rockies, fighting off the Sioux as they went; while the Central Pacific, building east from Sacramento, hurdled and tunnelled their way over or through the granite of the High Sierras and beyond. At first, there was no designated end of the line; the two companies would build full-tilt and meet head-on, wherever that place might be. Eventually, however, it was agreed they would meet in Utah at Promontory Point, where, on 10 May 1869, Leland Stanford, the Governor of California, drove the ceremonial golden spike into the last sleeper. In what has been described as the world's first "live" mass media event, the hammer and the spike were both wired to the telegraph line, and the sound of the blow would register as a click at various telegraph stations across the nation. It barely mattered that Stanford missed with his first swing and struck the rail instead – the telegraph operator had already sent the news announcing the "annexation of the United States", and the great race was over.

In their anxiety to reach England on time and to keep to Lillywhite's strict schedule, the Australians were in their own race against the clock. After departing Oakland on the Silver Palace cars of the Central Pacific line, their journey had taken them in a north-easterly direction through Sacramento and the snow-capped peaks of the Sierra Nevada towards the Great Salt Lake, averaging 500 miles a day. At Ogden, having completed almost 900 miles since leaving the waterfront at Oakland, they transferred to the cars of the Union Pacific Railroad without pause. They crossed the Rockies and plunged through the vast, wide-open prairies of Nebraska, the halfway point of their journey, sometimes touching speeds of 40mph. Robert Louis Stevenson, who travelled through the prairies on his way to California from New York a year later, recalled "a world almost without a feature; an empty sky, an empty earth; front and back, the line of railway stretched from horizon to horizon, like a cue on a billiard-board". Here, in 1866, the Union Pacific crews had passed the "100th Meridian Line", guaranteeing them the ir-refutable right to continue pushing westward. The company had celebrated by throwing a huge extravaganza among the wild buffalo grass, which included the mock ambush of a locomotive by Pawnee and Sioux braves in front of assembled bigwigs and guests. By 1878, however, the threat of an attack by Plains Indians on a Union Pacific locomotive had all but vanished into the ether. Two years after the massacre of General Custer and the Seventh Cavalry at the Little Big Horn in June 1876, a warrior force of primarily Cheyenne and Sioux was fragmented and scattered, the majority forced onto reservations by a lack of food and ammunition and a relentless army offensive; Sitting Bull had escaped to Canada and Crazy Horse was dead.

A much more imminent threat to the equanimity of the railroad barons, and their passengers, was the train robber. On 18 September 1877 the Texas outlaw Sam Bass acquired legendary status when he and his gang held up an eastbound Union Pacific train in Big Springs, Nebraska. It was described as one of the "boldest train robberies that had ever occurred in the United States". They lifted more than $60,000 of freshly minted twenty-dollar gold coins from the express car, and another $1,300, plus four gold watches, from the passengers. Bass's notoriety was such that he became the "most famous outlaw in the United States after Jesse James", and the Union Pacific summoned the full might of the army to bring him to justice. Bass, though, remained on the loose, leading his pursuers a merry dance, and by April 1878 he had robbed two stagecoaches and a further four trains.

For all its promotion as a grand adventure – and no one advertised with as much prodigality as the Americans – the journey by railroad was one still fraught with unpredictability and potential danger. The unflinching Harry Boyle (he would have been more than a match for any desperado) remained singularly unmoved. Writing home to his brother in Bendigo, he described the trip as "very tiresome", and found little to report other than the acute discomfort: "We had seven days and seven nights in the train, and it is not like riding on our lines. All American lines are lightly made, and not being properly ballasted they cause the cars to rock about. We arrived in New York all very much knocked up." The return trip in six months' time would at least prove more eventful, and provide the Eleven with a taste of the real Wild West. For Tom Horan, who found it almost impossible to sleep on trains – an affliction which would bedevil him and his team-mates throughout the tour of England – the journey was a particularly excruciating experience. He would not pick up his pen again until Omaha and Chicago were left well behind them, and they had safely alighted in New York City.

"We were met at the station by several prominent members of the St George Cricket club," he wrote, "who wished us every success in England and hoped that we should be able to return to our own country through America and play a few matches there. After walking through Broadway for an hour or two, admiring the handsome buildings, we went on board the splendid Inman Line steamer the *City of Berlin*, bound for Liverpool."

The *City of Berlin* was the lap of luxury after the rigours of the San Francisco mail packet. Indeed, Horan christened it a "veritable floating palace". Her two-cylinder compound steam engines were capable of achieving speeds of 16 knots, making her the fastest liner in the Atlantic; three years earlier she had won the Blue Riband, completing the Queenstown–New York run in only seven days. In a year's time she would be lit from stem to stern with electricity. However, the *pièce de résistance*, according to the *Illustrated London News*, was a sumptuously decorated 44ft saloon, panelled in walnut and fitted with gilt mirrors and decorative columns; "the ceiling was white and gold, with an elegant cupola skylight". The Eleven even had the company of some fellow pioneers on board: the 60-strong Gilmore's Band from New York, who were undertaking their first tour of Europe. The musicians cut a dash on deck with their blue suits, military caps and loud American accents.[2]

The next nine days passed quickly, and on Monday, 13 May, having spotted Holyhead off the north coast of Wales at six that evening, the *City of Berlin* finally slipped into the darkness of the Mersey where she anchored at 10.30pm, within sight of Liverpool docks. "Everyone slept on board for the night," Horan recorded, although sleep was the last thing on their minds. They were home.

Four
14–23 May 1878

"They bean't black at all; they're as white as wuz"

On Tuesday, 14 May, in a paragraph tucked away beneath the runners and riders for the Chester Cup and a report of the first day's play between MCC and an England XI at Lord's (in which W. G. Grace and Billy Midwinter found themselves on opposite sides), the *London Standard* wrote:

> *The City of Berlin, which reached our shores yesterday from New York, brings the team of Australian cricketers, whose arrival has been looked forward to with so much interest by the English cricket public, and whose doings during the present season will doubtless be followed most attentively and criticised most keenly. The tour begins at Nottingham, on Monday next, with a match against the famous Notts Eleven.*

The Australians had been reluctant to leave the comforts of their floating palace on the morning of the 14th. It was a damp, chilly start on the Mersey, with dark roiling clouds and no prospect of sun. The clamour on the landing stage had all been for Gilmore's Band, the Americans having gone ashore first thing at 7am in their blue suits to enthusiastic cheers and a fanfare from the band of the first Liverpool Rifle Volunteers. The local newspaper, the *Liverpool Mercury*, had awarded the New York musicians top billing in its edition that morning, relegating the Australians to nothing more than a footnote at the bottom of the column; and even then the team had been incorrectly named. Most of the newspapers had included the unfortunate Kendall in the touring party. "Until they played at Nottingham, it was not even known that Kendall had been left out," *Lillywhite's Cricketers' Annual* later remarked. Midwinter's defection, though, had been noted by all.

However, the Eleven were much cheered by the sight of the stolidly reassuring Jack Conway, accompanied by James Lillywhite, who had come aboard with a small delegation of local cricketers to greet them. There were handshakes and back slaps all round, and news and stories to exchange, before they finally disembarked and the majority of the Eleven set foot on English soil for the first time. It was a momentous step for all, but especially so for Charles Bannerman, who had left behind the country of his birth as a small boy, and George Bailey, who had been educated at Lichfield Grammar School in Staffordshire, and Elizabeth College, Guernsey, where he captained the first XI for two years.

The jostling parade of masts and funnels, the noise and smoke, the grand rows of warehouses and wharfs left the Australians in no doubt that they were now in one of the great mercantile ports of the world. The American novelist Herman Melville had marvelled at Liverpool after seeing it for the first time as a young man, nearly 40 years earlier, and wrote hauntingly of the "long China walls of masonry; vast piers of stone; and a succession of granite-rimmed docks … In magnitude, cost and durability, the docks of Liverpool … surpass all others in the world." The grandeur of the grey stone buildings, crammed in around the docks, was equally striking and could not have failed to impress the Eleven: the lofty domes and porticoes, the monuments and columns, the shipping offices and treasure houses of the Empire radiated power, influence, prosperity and wealth. In another 15 years the world's first overhead electric railway (the plans for which had been rejected only months before in 1877) would run the six and a half miles of the waterfront, from one end of the docks to the other, the thunder and lightning from the tracks lending a futuristic air to those noble landmarks.

After their luggage had been cleared by the customs officer, the party hurried to Central Station by coach, where they just managed to catch the 9am train to Nottingham by the proverbial whisker; little suspecting, perhaps, that a piping hot welcome awaited them there.

There was some confusion at the other end of the line, too, where a large crowd, including the Sheriff, the local aldermen, representatives of Nottinghamshire Cricket Club, and the Sax-Tuba Band, had assembled at the Midland Station in anticipation of the Australians' arrival. The cricketers were expected at 12.15 and when a train steamed in close to the time, many of the crowd, having been "on the tip-toe of expectation", burst into spontaneous applause – "much to the surprise and astonishment of the passengers who were about to alight" – before discovering that it was the wrong train. "Some amusement was afforded at the expense of the enthusiasts," the *Nottingham Express* reported. Five minutes later the Liverpool train carrying the Australians pulled in, and the Eleven, who looked still fresh from their sea voyage, stepped on to the platform to a cheer so tumultuous that the band's rousing rendition of "Auld Lang Syne" was all but smothered. After spending the past nine days at sea wondering just what sort of a welcome, if any, lay in store for them in England – the greeting in Liverpool was restrained by any standards – this was a reception to gladden their hearts. As the *Nottingham Express* put it, they were "received with open arms. The ovation … must have been very encouraging."

Their arrival was not without incident, however. The Eleven had to be ushered through a side entrance to prevent them from being mobbed by a certain section of the crowd, "who on most days would have found something else to do", in the opinion of the *Nottingham Express*. An omnibus, drawn by four splendid greys, was waiting to transport the team to their hotel, and it was as they were preparing to board it, according to Tom Horan, that one of the onlookers, having elbowed his way to the front of the throng to gain a closer look, delivered his withering assessment of the strangers. "Whoy, Billy," he called out, "they bean't black at all; they're as white as wuz!" The remark clearly left an indelible impression on Horan and the reporter for the *Argus* – as it did on all the Eleven – because both men attempted to capture it exactly as it had sounded to them, complete with the hard vowels of the distinctive local dialect. However, the *Argus* suggests that the incident took place, not at the railway station, but as the Eleven were arriving at their hotel: "Many of the lace spinners and hose weavers expressed disappointment at the colour of the visitors, whom they expected to be black." It is also possible, though, that both Australian scribblers chose to omit a few details (the local press ignored it altogether), or at least felt the need to play the matter down; for their accounts appear almost tame by comparison with that of Benny Green, who, writing in *A History of Cricket*, recounts a much more salty and vivid version of events:

> *The team went straight from Liverpool by train to Nottingham, where a huge crowd … greeted them as they stepped on to the platform. Murdoch and Spofforth, who had been sleeping at the back of the train, slipped out unnoticed and mingled with the crowd. One burly, bare-armed man wearing a blacksmith's leather apron exclaimed, "Well, I'm damned! They aren't black at all. If I'd knowed, I wunna come." Dave Gregory then alighted from the train and the man studied his black beard and skin browned by the Australian sun. "Ah, 'ere's one's a arf-caste any ow," he commented.*

What is not in any doubt is that the Australians were shocked by what they heard – doubtless, the reaction of several in the crowd was equally clumsy and boorish – and they were said to have resented the remark, to a man, "until they were reminded of the visit that preceded them". As Charles Lawrence's team of Aborigines had been the first cricketers from Australia to tour England, and played at Trent Bridge in 1868, many among the crowd expected David Gregory's men to be no different. Indeed, the *Daily Telegraph* wrote of that 1868 expedition, "Nothing of interest comes from Australia except ˙gold nuggets and black cricketers" – a view that was actively propagated by the newspapers of the time.

Although the world had undoubtedly become a smaller place by 1878 – as the eminent cricket writer Frederick Gale somewhat optimistically pointed out, "now people think nothing of going to the north of India, to Australia, Africa, the prairies of America ... for sport or money-making, and naming the day and almost the hour of their return, which, humanly speaking, is almost as great a certainty as running down to Brighton and back" – opinions of Australia had not altered significantly in those intervening ten years.[1] If Australia was the land of "golden nuggets and black cricketers", it was also the stark, inhospitable place "down under" where people were sent, and from which they rarely, if ever, returned. Charles Dickens, until his death in 1870, had done much to try to enlighten and alter people's perceptions of Australia, but ignorance of the country, its geography and its ethnicity, as displayed by the average Englishman, remained widespread. Wild, outlandish rumours regularly circulated about the Australian visitors during those early days of the tour – many did not even expect them to speak English – and were mercilessly exploited by the ever-ravenous gossip columnists. "As usual there has been the old confusion in the uninformed, though, by no means uninfluential circles, as to whether the men are black or white ... but all fear of a cannibal outbreak has been dispelled by the assurance that they are men of like complexion and degree with ourselves", was one such observation. While another, *The Lounger's* gossip column, was almost consumed by its own sarcasm:

> *The gentlemanly appearance of the Australian cricketers has taken English society by surprise. It was reasonable, of course, to expect that this land of cattle and sheep, kangaroos and savages, should send home a troupe of yokels and clodhoppers to represent its cricketing prowess. Well, it is something after all to find that a*

> *man may be born and educated in Australia, and yet manage to*
> *preserve the appearance and acquire the manners of the ordinary*
> *English gentleman.*

As if that was not bad enough, the colonials had to contend with the public's profound lack of knowledge and comprehension of the sheer size and scale of Australia, and would regularly field questions during their travels on whether they knew a "Mr Blank, a farmer in Ipswich, or Mr Dash, a storekeeper, in Western Australia". Melbourne, Sydney and Adelaide may have been cities as rich in culture as any in Europe, but more often than not they were seen as a collection of small towns "only a few miles apart" in which the "inhabitants of one of these cities should know the inhabitants of the other three personally!" Jack Blackham recalled how he was once asked by an "expensively dressed woman" to deliver a parcel to her sister in Adelaide; after informing the woman that he lived in Melbourne, she responded by offering to pay his return cab fare. As Horan was fond of relating, "When the inquirer is told that Sydney is 600 miles, and Brisbane over a 1000 miles from Melbourne, his astonishment is as great as when he learns that New South Wales is not a town, but a country larger than England."

To this end the Eleven regularly found themselves acting as ambassadors for the new world, often in the face of what they would have regarded as old world indifference and condescension. The desire to hold their own against England's best may have been their lodestar – the only standard by which they knew they would ultimately be judged – but their enthusiasm to promote all things Australian, even if at times they allowed it to get the better of them (their cricket grounds were bigger and better, their cities more capacious), burned just as brightly and added significantly to their sense of mission.

Their journey from the station to the hotel, with the band blazing the way "playing inspirational airs", passed off without further alarm, in what the *Sporting Gazette* described as a "triumphal procession". An estimated crowd of 8,000 lined the streets as the omnibus carrying the Australians wound its way through Station Street, Lister Gate and Market Place, beneath the old overhanging timber frames of Long Row, towards the Maypole Hotel, where they would spend the next nine days of their stay in Nottingham. The band had taken up their position outside the hotel by the time the omnibus clattered into the yard and, "in response to the strains of the national anthem, every member of the eleven uncovered loyally", before alighting to take up his quarters. Two hours later, after the completion of the obligatory speeches "over bumpers of champagne" – Gregory thanked those assembled for their generous welcome, and trusted that his team would make a good fight of it against Nottinghamshire – the Australians were practising on the Trent Bridge ground. Without so much as a sniff of a cricket field for almost two months, the Eleven were understandably anxious to pick up a bat and ball again, to stretch and coax their sore muscles and, more intriguingly, to test the novel conditions. Special wickets had been prepared for them, but a combination of the dismal, showery weather – one newspaper complained that it was even colder in May "than it generally is with us at Christmas" – the exertions of their long journey, and the slippery turf, meant that they "all shaped very badly".

Their first sight of an English cricket ground, for the most part, made a favourable impression on them. Although Fred Spofforth was surprised by the proximity of the houses, and by the size of Trent Bridge, which he had expected to be on a grander scale: "The ground itself was quite different from those which we were accustomed … it seemed much smaller than any of the principal grounds in Australia, and the turf much greener, while the red roofs of the surrounding buildings gave the whole enclosure a quaint and unusual appearance to our eyes." Horan was also beguiled by the verdant green, and the "small inn situated close to the entrance gate … which I am informed was built by William Clarke, the celebrated slow bowler".

Clarke did not build the homely Trent Bridge Inn but he did marry the landlady, and before long he set about turning the meadow at the rear of the inn into a cricket square. The founder of the highly profitable All-England XI, which travelled the length and breadth of the land – an enterprise made possible by the advent of the railways – Clarke and his cohort of players popularised cricket, blazing a trail that would lead, ultimately, to overseas tours and Test matches. As such, he was inextricably linked to David Gregory's Australians. Described as a man of "solemn, deceptively parsonic expression under his tall hat", Clarke was an extravagantly talented underarm bowler, who plundered more than 300 wickets a season between 1847 and 1853, extracting vicious lift and imparting "a baffling spin" on the ball which was delivered from above hip level. He staged the first game on his new pitch next to the Trent Bridge Inn on 28 May 1838, against Sussex, and charged an entrance fee of 6d.; three months later he registered its first century. By 1878, 22 years after Clarke's death at the age of 57, Trent Bridge had emerged as a ground that was talked of in the same breath as Lord's or The Oval, with a wicket as trustworthy and reliable as any in the country.

The Australians spent the rest of the week attempting to put in some hard practice. Their initial session, so soon after making landfall, had succeeded only in aggravating the aches and pains acquired on their travels, and their efforts (often in front of several hundred inquisitive spectators) were constantly interrupted by the freezing showers and arctic winds, leaving them woefully undercooked for their opening match. They could be forgiven for thinking, as some of them undoubtedly did, that they had arrived in the midst of the football season; and as they felt the turf turn to mud beneath their boots, or another shower sent them scampering back to the shelter of the pavilion, they wondered how on earth they would ever start a game of cricket – let alone finish one – in such conditions.

———

One of the first things the Eleven did on their arrival in England was to assert their right to be called amateurs. "They desire to be regarded as an amateur XI and intimate that with the taking of expenses of the trip they will be amply repaid and rewarded," *The Sportsman* reported a few days into the tour. Accordingly, they would be granted the courtesies of Mr or Esq on match scorecards and in newspaper reports. It was not, however, quite so straightforward. As the guardians of their own destiny in a profit-sharing enterprise, the Eleven (with the exception of Charles and Alec Bannerman) did not consider themselves to be professionals, the artisans and tradesmen of the game. Nor, though, as civil servants, junior bank clerks and a solicitor (or speculators, for the purposes of the tour) did they fit the archetype of the true amateur, who played the game for a pastime. The ambiguity was instantly seized upon by the *Sporting Gazette*, which, in attempting to answer "what constitutes the difference between an amateur and a professional?" (under the salient headline "Paid Amateurs"), argued:

> *Time was when the question was easily answered by saying that the one was paid, and the other was not, and that, therefore, the mere passing of money constituted the difference. But that answer will no longer meet the exigencies of the case. The paid amateur is a creation of the last few years, and he stoutly maintains that the fact of his accepting money does not take him out of the category of amateurs. We propose showing … that the real test of difference between an amateur and a professional still exists in the acceptance of money, and it is desirable that the old distinction should be rigidly adhered to.*

The Australian statement of intent could not have come at a more critical or challenging time for the game: the remuneration of amateurs – or, to put it another way, the abuse of the system – was the burning issue of the day. MCC, roundly condemned for dragging its feet, had at last bowed to public pressure and appointed a subcommittee to investigate the matter. The Eleven, by positioning themselves under the amateur banner, were further muddying the water, however, and laying themselves open to the resentment of the English professional cricketer, many of whom were treated little better than hirelings by their counties.[2] Indeed, it was the visit of the Australians, the *Sporting Gazette* claimed, which had compelled it to reopen a debate "which apparently has not been yet satisfactorily answered". For, "if the Australians were to be accepted as amateurs, then it is obvious that our English definition of the term," will be widely stretched it reasoned, before continuing:

> *This is not a matter of social status; it makes no matter what a man's position in society may be – if he consents systematically to receive money for his services in any capacity, he ceases ipso facto to be an amateur, and becomes a professional. Judged by this standard, the only one we can submit, the Australian players have no claim whatsoever to be considered amateurs. They are playing for money – each of them has a share in the speculation, and a division of profits will ensue ... Let us not be misunderstood; we do not blame them in the least for looking after the main chance – we find no fault with them for exhibiting their skill for gain, and making profit out of their prowess. There is nothing derogatory to man's dignity in making money by his proficiency in any art or sport – he has a perfect right to do so if he is so disposed; only he must allow himself by so doing to be classed among professionals, not amateurs.*

In fact, the Australians were guilty of doing no more than travelling on the same well-trodden path as W. G. Grace, and many others besides, whose claim to amateur status was nominal at best. Not for nothing has Grace been described as the "greatest shamateur of the lot": he unhesitatingly commanded a match fee of £20 when playing for Gloucestershire; he managed the itinerant United South of England XI as a profit-making concern, charging a match fee of a shilling rather than the standard 6d. a head; and demanded, and was paid, £1,500, plus expenses, to tour Australia in 1873–4 – an outrageous sum of money for the times. Grace, it can be confidently stated, during his career coined money with the same ruthless intent as he accumulated runs; next to which anything the Australians were expected to pocket on their tour – that is if they managed to break even at all – would be small beer indeed. It might also be argued in defence of David Gregory's team that they were a convenient target, a symptom, nothing more, of a far deeper and divisive problem, one which the *Sporting Gazette* made only passing reference to in its column: "But it will be asked, how many of our so-called English amateur cricketers, then, deserve to be termed amateurs pure and simple? We answer, those only who can say that from one end of the season to the other not a single penny has been paid to them for playing."

It would be November by the time MCC, having studied the subcommittee's findings into the vexing question of the "Definition and Qualifications of Amateur Cricketers", resolved, "That no gentleman ought to make a profit by his services in cricket". The decree was, it pointed out, nothing more than a consolidation of its original position on the matter. However, the club added, "That for the future, no cricketer who takes more than his expenses in any match shall be qualified to play in the Gentlemen versus Players at Lord's; but that if a gentleman faces difficulty in joining in the match without pecuniary assistance, he shall not be debarred from playing as a gentleman by having his actual expenses defrayed."[3]

Before then the Australians' "desire to be regarded as an amateur XI" would, predictably, some might say, have come to a head.

———

It was also in Nottingham that the Eleven reacquainted themselves with their old friend Billy Midwinter, and, much to the surprise of all, named him in the team for their opening match.

By throwing in his lot with W. G. Grace and Gloucestershire, it was assumed that Midwinter had thereby severed all ties with the Australians. The press, many of whom believed that the question of Midwinter's loyalties "had been settled long ago", were taken aback "to find the Gloucestershire county player working with the Australians". The *Sporting Gazette* made the point that although

Midwinter was a "*bona fide* Australian by residence", he was "by birth and qualification a Glo'stershire player", and "cannot well be both". Perhaps Conway brought his considerable personality to bear on the situation by reminding Midwinter of his responsibilities to the Eleven, or perhaps the all-rounder simply made himself available. As it was, Midwinter's old mucker from Bendigo, Harry Boyle, was severely handicapped by a stiff neck and in no fit state to play at Trent Bridge, thus reducing the team to only ten men. It was just as well, then, that of the many characteristics attributed to the mercenary Midwinter, a thin skin was not one of them.

The Eleven, however, clearly believed that they still had a genuine claim to Midwinter, who was match-hardened and in robust form with both bat and ball. More significantly, as the County Championship did not get under way until late June (Gloucestershire opened with a match against Surrey at The Oval on 20 June) and concluded after an all too brief reign in August – Championship fixtures were by no means plentiful in those days – Midwinter would have had more than enough time at his disposal, and ample opportunity, to keep a foot in both camps. As his undoubted paymaster, though, Grace would have prior claim on his services for all county matches.

It was unlikely that when Midwinter stepped on to the pitch at Trent Bridge he had yet conceived a way in which he could juggle this to the satisfaction of both parties, if indeed he gave it any thought at all. Perhaps he just expected the matter would take care of itself. As he was one of the most enigmatic of cricketers ever to have buckled on a pair of pads, it is impossible to know with any degree of certainty what his thoughts were. In fact, opinion of Midwinter is divided in almost equal measure: he is depicted by some as "recreant", a vacillator, who was wracked by his own indecision, unable to make his mind up from one day to the next; to others he was a "phlegmatic character", calmly confident, duplicitous even – an individual, in the opinion of Benny Green, with a "temperament more serpentine even than W. G. Grace". There is even a degree of mystery about the exact whereabouts of his birth place. Although it is generally accepted to be St Briavels, a village in the Forest of Dean, near Lydney, Gloucestershire, there have also been claims that he was born in Yorkshire, or as far afield as Australia or Canada – a confusion which Midwinter appears to have done little to discourage.

The author Eric Midwinter, of whom Billy is reputed to have been an ancestor, perhaps comes closest to pinning down the errant "Mid", in *W. G. Grace: His Life and Times*, when he writes, "His career was intertwined with Grace, and, in his financial opportunism and cocking of snooks, he reflected, in subdued hues, some of the flamboyance of Grace's character." The author adds, "Possibly Midwinter was later content to appear under one label or other as it suited his purpose." There is no doubt that by taking up with the Australians at Nottingham (it is possible he had not even consulted with Grace on the matter) he was playing a potentially dangerous game. Yet, as Eric Midwinter suggests, "It is reasonably likely that Midwinter might have expected that Gloucestershire – with only thirteen county fixtures in 1878 – would have easily reached some compromise with the Australian management, always considering how many teams people like Grace and several of the professionals served." And so it might, had anyone other than Grace and Conway – who harboured such a mutual dislike and mistrust of each other, and had a trunkful of old scores to settle – been pulling the strings.

Whatever Midwinter's shortcomings off the pitch, however, there was not a scintilla of doubt that he was the genuine article on it. He was, in the words of Conway, "a good medium-paced bowler, with a high delivery", who exhibited "a fair command of the ball". As a batsman "he enjoyed the reputation of being the hardest hitter in Australia", a quality he combined with the soundest of defences. Moreover, he had successfully tailored his skills to English conditions, having been taken in hand by Grace, and been "thoroughly well coached since coming over here a year ago", the *Sporting Gazette* noted. He had been in typically muscular form during the run-up to the Australians' opening game, too: playing for an England XI at Lord's, he had taken five for 52 to help bowl out Grace's MCC for 93 in their first innings, a match MCC duly lost by three wickets. Exchanging Lord's at the conclusion of the first great match of the London season for Nottingham – where the focus of all cricketing attention had switched with the arrival of the Australians – was pure Midwinter. Nonetheless, he would prove an invaluable asset against a Nottinghamshire team of all the talents.

Buttressed by a core of gifted and tough-minded professionals, including the likes of Alfred Shaw, Fred Morley, Richard Daft, Arthur Shrewsbury and John Selby, Nottinghamshire were in the middle of a golden age in which they would win the County Championship nine times between 1873, its inception, and 1887. The bowling attack was led by Shaw, who, as a member of James Lillywhite's 1876-7 tourists, needed no introduction to the Australians – least of all to Fred Spofforth, who had closely studied the Nottinghamshire exemplar's methods at first hand. Known as 'the Emperor of Bowlers' – a sobriquet that might just as easily have applied to his portly, well-fed appearance – the 5ft 6½in Shaw operated off a short run at around medium-pace, with what has been described as a "beautifully easy action". His great weapon was his remorseless accuracy, allied to flight, spin and variation of pace: "ball after ball looked the same, yet no two balls were precisely the same". His command of line and length was such, it was said, that he did not send down a single wide – indeed, he barely bowled a bad ball – more than half of his overs were maidens, and he bowled more overs than runs were taken off him. It is worth recording that during a career in which he reaped 2,207 wickets from 404 matches, 49 of those dismissals included W. G. Grace, whom he clean bowled on 20 occasions. Shaw's principal henchman was the left-arm fast bowler Morley, who was regarded for a time as the quickest in England. Both men were gluttons for hard work, and during the wet summer of 1878 bowled unchanged on numerous occasions. If the ball could be prised off either, Wilf Flowers, a future England all-rounder, provided useful support with his slippery off-breaks.

At 42 years old Daft, the captain, remained supremely fit and the county's principal batsman still. He was a rare beast in that, formerly an amateur, he had been honest enough to admit he could not sustain a cricket career on expenses alone, and in 1859 took the decision to cross the divide. For the next 15 years or more he was acclaimed as the most complete professional batsman in the land. Tall and elegant at the crease, he was, like Grace, a ruthless executioner of fast bowling. Shrewsbury, at 22, was at the opposite end of his career: having first played for Nottinghamshire in 1875, he was a comparative novice, and his infinite patience and technical dedication to run-making – he would become the acknowledged master of back play – was still in the process of being honed. The wiry Selby, another member of Lillywhite's tourists, added to the batting riches of an eleven that would have been more than a match for any battle-tempered team, quite apart from one that had only just stepped off the boat barely a week before.

—

The morning of the opening match on Monday, 20 May dawned bright and sunny, but it seemed that no sooner had the Australians arrived at Trent Bridge (they looked like business in their dark blue and white striped blazers, blue pillbox caps and matching handkerchiefs round their waists) than the rain started to fall again. It had poured heavily for much of Sunday night, and with the state of the ground already in a "sorry condition" – the outfield was virtually awash with mud – doubts were cast on whether there would be any play at all during the day. "It might have been fancied that the Gods would have at least smiled on the colonial cricketers," *The Sportsman* reasoned in its match report the following day, "if only to give something like a fitting welcome to a band of players whose visit to England may fairly be considered as the biggest thing ever recorded in cricket." However, it took more than a smattering of mud and rain to stop a cricket match in those days – especially one that had been the "all-absorbing topic of conversation" – and the umpires, anxious no doubt to accommodate the expectations of several thousand spectators who had already taken their seats, determined that play would start on time at noon.

Gregory won the toss and elected to bat first – with some advice, it was said, from Midwinter – but as if on cue another burst of rain swept across the ground, preventing any hope of a prompt start. Some 45 minutes later, however, "the monotony of the dull leaden sky" having cleared, the Nottinghamshire XI finally emerged from the pavilion, to be followed moments later by the Australian openers, Charles and Alec Bannerman. The appearance of the players was "the signal for a hearty round of applause" from a crowd of "between four and five thousand", *The Sportsman* estimated; the cheers "did not cease until the two batsmen had reached the wickets". Charles Bannerman wore a white flannel helmet with blue stripes, the newspaper noted, "an excellent notion for a head-dress for a cricketer, for the shade it affords to the face as well as for the protection it gives to the neck"; although an ambitious one, it might have added, considering the Eleven had yet to see the sun since setting foot in England. Their innocent notion of an English summer was such that they had neglected to pack any woollen sweaters – an oversight which, in light of the Nottingham weather, deserved to belong on the pages of the latest penny dreadful. Their cream silk shirts and thin jerseys were no match for the elements.

Alec Bannerman received the first ball of the tour from Shaw, and proceeded to play the rest of the over – a maiden – with his usual meticulous care. Charles Bannerman then scored the first run, pushing Morley's second ball purposefully away off the front foot past point. The contrast in style and character between the two batsmen could not have been more apparent, and Charles Bannerman repeated the stroke at the start of Shaw's second over to add another single. Nottinghamshire cricket crowds were known to be among the most discerning and appreciative in the country, and there is little doubt that they would have been keenly aware of Charles Bannerman's great reputation. "It was immediately evident that he possessed a very neat style, and also considerable freedom, as he played forward very hard, and with plenty of confidence", *The Sportsman* reported, an impression he quickly enhanced by twice driving Morley through the off side. The last of these two strokes brought three runs, although Alec Bannerman would have been run out attempting to complete the third had the wicketkeeper, Fred Wild, not fumbled the throw. The slowness of the outfield – the ball trickled through the long grass or often came to an abrupt halt in the mud, no matter how hard it was struck – made running between the wickets a hazardous occupation for the Australians. However, Charles Bannerman continued to shape well, and it came as a surprise when, with the score on nine and his brother yet to get off the mark, he drilled Shaw straight into the hands of Flowers at mid-on.

Another ten runs were added by Alec Bannerman and Horan, with the former registering the first boundary of the tour before Morley sent his middle stump skidding along the turf with a fast shooter. Horan became Shaw's second victim, smartly caught and bowled, and when the same bowler trimmed Spofforth's stumps, the Australians were 27 for four, by which time Midwinter had come to the wicket. The all-rounder soon lost Gregory, summarily bowled by Morley for a duck, and Murdoch – run out after some electric work in the field by Shrewsbury – but he found an obdurate ally in Tom Garrett. The pair had added a further 24 runs when Morley finally broke the stand, inducing Midwinter into a rash shot outside off stump to have him caught at cover-point for 13. Garrett followed soon after for 20, and by 3.30 the Australians were all out for 63, Shaw finishing with five for 20 and Morley four for 42.

There was a further delay after the termination of the Australian innings – this time for an hour – while another downpour lashed the uncovered wicket and the spectators, of whom there were now some 8,000 in place, "a thick ring several deep encircling the ground". The stoicism of the much put-upon crowd clearly intrigued the Australians, who observed that "no matter how heavy the rain may be they never stir, but hoist their umbrellas and wait until the storm abates". When it did eventually blow over, and the Nottinghamshire reply got under way, Gregory promptly dropped Daft off the bowling of Spofforth. It was hardly surprising that the chance went begging: Horan, writing as "One of Them" in the *Bendigo Advertiser*, remarked that, "our hands were so cold and our bodies so chilled that we could scarcely feel the ball". It was particularly demoralising for the bowlers, who had not only to wrestle with the conditions – none felt more muzzled in that regard than Spofforth – but to contend with a ball, "which, after a few overs became swollen and soft", and was more often than not caked in mud. Fortunately, for the Eleven, Gregory's miss did not prove costly, and an over later Frank Allan trapped the Nottinghamshire captain leg-before for three. Shrewsbury fared little better, having his leg stump plucked out of the ground by the same bowler for eight, and at the close Nottinghamshire were 61 for four, with Selby and Wild the not out batsmen.

Rain intervened again on the second day. It started well before noon and "continued to descend in torrents", blown in all directions by "a blustering boisterous wind" which threatened to tug the flags off the poles, turned umbrellas inside out and snatched hats off heads. By one o'clock, the *Argus* claimed, the umpires had agreed that the wicket was unplayable (the Eleven certainly thought as much), although a crowd of almost 10,000 – "the largest turn-out ever seen on the Trent Bridge Ground" – were not so easily deterred; and as soon as the rain relented, the umpires made an inspection of the wicket. "The ground was hardly in a fit state," *The Sportsman* wrote, "but there was a round of applause from all sides of the ground as the bell rang to announce the preparation for the resumption of play." Whatever the thoughts of the Australians, they kept them to themselves, and as *The Sportsman* noted, "they were ready to appear at the first signal".[4] It was "horribly cold and very windy," Spofforth recalled – so windy, in fact, that at one stage the telegraph board blew over, to the great amusement of the spectators.

Selby (66) went on to complete the only half-century of the match, putting on 70 for the fifth wicket with Wild, before the county were bowled out shortly after four o'clock for 153. Particularly severe on anything loose, and quicksilver between the wickets, Selby – a crack sprinter – gave the Australians an object lesson in how to bat in such conditions. The Eleven reached 46 for four in reply at the close, with Midwinter, pushed up the order to open, undefeated on 13. His innings was anything but a sprint, and by stumps he had already spent one and a half hours at the crease: a marathon effort, in the context of the match.

There were barely 400 present on the third day to witness what Horan termed the "last rites". However, Nottinghamshire were delayed for a further 90 minutes by Midwinter, who carried his bat for 16 – the first Australian batsman to do so in England – and played the greybeard role for all he was worth. If it was intended as a show of loyalty to the Eleven, it could not have been bettered. According to the *Argus*, Midwinter "had at this time arranged to play as much as possible with the team, except when his professional engagements with Gloucestershire interfered". When the last wicket fell at 76, a few minutes before two o'clock, Midwinter had added just three runs to his overnight score while batting for a total of three hours in all. Richard Daft described it as a "remarkable display of endurance", although one newspaper was not so enchanted, referring to Midwinter as the "slowest of slow punters [who] paddled about for three hours ... the last three runs being made at the rate of one in 30 minutes".

None of which, of course, could disguise the fact that the Australians had lost their opening match by an innings and 14 runs. It was, perhaps, no great shock, coming as it did so soon after their arrival, in such adverse conditions and unremitting cold, and against a bowler of Shaw's stamp, whose six for 35 in the second innings earned him the outstanding match figures of 11 for 55. However, the magnitude of the defeat may even have been partly offset by the gate receipts, of which the Australians received 80%: the proceeds amounted to £120 on the first day, £160 on the second, and £80 on the third.

No defeat was complete, though, without the pantomime of excuses in which the vanquished team, or individual, ritualistically indulged. The excuses of the 19th century sportsman were often a wonder in themselves – the more fantastical and outrageous the better, it seemed – and the Australians were no different; except that in this case it would be hard to quibble with a single reason they gave for their defeat. "Our loss to Nottinghamshire was understandable," Horan declared. "We were considerably out of practice after our long voyage and the cold wet weather we encountered in the midlands was not conducive to our playing well." For those back in Australia "who will be very much surprised to learn we have received such a hollow defeat … that feeling would quickly vanish after an inspection of the wicket on which we played. A batsman used to the fast grounds of Australia could not make a big score on it in a week without extraordinary luck". Nonetheless, he reassured them, "It may be that after three or four matches we shall be quite as effective batsmen in the mud as Englishmen are."

The Eleven even found an unexpected ally in the *Sporting Gazette,* which, when it was not throwing more mud at them for their amateur status, questioned whether a cricket match of importance should ever take place in such conditions, if all it achieved was to reduce the sport to a form of slapstick. "The Australian cricketers must have formed a cheerful notion of an English May," it ventured. "Cricket in Australia and cricket in England must seem to them two totally different things; for cricket is usually associated with fine weather and dry turf – two *desiderata* which have been conspicuous by their absence this season so far. In fact, cricket has been a mere farce as yet." The newspaper cited a recent encounter between Yorkshire and Derbyshire at Sheffield as an example of why a match should not be played under those circumstances, reprinting an extract from its match report:

> *The ground was now a perfect quagmire, and was quite unfit for cricket. We can only imagine what Wright's (the custodian of Bramall-lane) feelings were to see the ground in front of the pavilion trodden into a puddle. It would have required tons of sawdust to cover it up. The ball was so dirty that Lockwood kicked instead of throwing it back to the bowler. Mr Smith, in hitting, bespattered Pinder with mud. Emmett being unable to stand, Lockwood went on in his stead...*

The newspaper continued, "That sort of thing is not cricket, and it is a pity that a match should be allowed to proceed under such conditions." It did not bargain for sunshine – "that would be too much to expect in England" – but cricket should never be played on "a marsh". Under those circumstances, it concluded, it becomes "a nondescript aquatic pastime, to which you may give any name you like so long as you don't call it cricket".

———

Nottingham may have rolled out the mud, wind and rain for the Australians – in fact almost everything the elements could throw at them – but there was not a man among them who could have complained that they had been anything other than royally treated. On the evening of the 22nd they attended a grand banquet in their honour at the George Hotel, delighting in the protocol, "which included the presence of a loving cup and a toast master dressed in scarlet". An excellent evening was had by all, with Conway and Gregory demonstrating that they lacked for nothing when it came to diplomacy or good manners.

A vigorous and entertaining speaker (as he was in all things), Conway praised the reception given to the Australians in Nottingham, confiding that it had far exceeded any they could have expected. There was praise, too, for the county ground, and "the splendidly critical audience of Nottingham" which, he added, amidst much laughter and applause, he would "like to import into Australia". There were also warm words of encouragement for the Australians, notably from Richard Daft, who, in bringing more than 20 years of experience to bear as a top-class cricketer, predicted that they would "come out at the end of the tour with flying colours" and their reputations embellished. Their display, he insisted, should not under any circumstances be taken as a true reflection of their strengths.

There were visits to the town's two ice-skating rinks, the Marble and the Alexandra, where the Eleven witnessed the craze known as "rinkomania" (London alone boasted some 50 rinks at that time). There was also a trip to Sherwood, although the Eleven were disappointed to discover that it was no longer the great forest of legend. "Scarcely a tree can now be seen," Horan recorded. Instead, they were "astonished to find two hundred of the rising generation of Nottinghamshire practising vigorously at cricket" in the clearing. "It struck nine before they drew stumps," a charmed Horan added. They were much taken with Nottingham, from its expansive parks and "neat little country gardens which meet the eye in every direction", to its narrow and winding streets, "all models of cleanliness", and the towering lace factories of gleaming red brick.

The reaction of the press after their defeat by Nottinghamshire, however, did not make for particularly comfortable reading. "The majority of the team played on the dead ground just as they would have done on the faster wickets of the season, and to this alone must they attribute their bad defeat," was the verdict of the *Nottingham Daily Guardian*. "Against any bowler it would have been dangerous in the extreme but against Shaw and Morley, perhaps the most dangerous slow and fast bowlers respectively on bumpy wickets in England, it was suicidal." The *Sporting Gazette* also drew attention to their "limited batting powers": "No doubt some of their little failings will be readily accounted for by the want of practice and the long journey; but there are some things which a good bat would scarcely, under any circumstances, do …" Their running between the wickets, it added, had left much to be desired. The prevailing view was that they would struggle against all but the weakest opposition.

On the morning of the 23rd the Eleven called in at Trent Bridge for one last practice. "The ground was still soft, but infinitely better than when the match was played, and we only wish we had had to start the match that day, as we would have done very much better," Conway wrote. Their time in Nottingham was almost at an end and they would leave "the good old town" behind for London, on the 24th. There, three days later, they would play their next match, against MCC at Lord's, and rejoin battle for the first time in four years with their old nemesis, W. G. Grace.

Five
24–27 May 1878

"Lord's is to cricket what Rome is to the world"

A crowd of little more than five hundred watched David Gregory lead out his Australians against MCC at Lord's on 27 May in almost apologetic sunshine. It had rained on and off in the capital for the past four days, during which the thermometer barely nudged 10°C; in fact, it had hardly let up since the team's disembarkation at Liverpool 13 days earlier, uncertain whether they had arrived in the deep of an English winter. This was not, as some of them might have suspected, a cruel and elaborate hoax – an illusionist's clever trick – designed to throw them into confusion: this was the land of which Tom Horan would later reflect, "cricket matches were watched by women wrapped in furs and by men in heavy top coats".

They had caught the train from Nottingham to St Pancras Station – the London terminus for the Midland Railway Company – on the morning of the 24th, pulling into its great vault of wrought iron and glass, some three hours later, in the early afternoon. If St Pancras was the city's cathedral of steam, the station's Midland Grand Hotel – built by Sir George Gilbert Scott in 1868, but not fully completed for another eight years – must have looked to them like a Gothic phantasmagoria soaring above the street. Behind its granite arches and turrets, its limestone columns, there were walls of gold leaf and a crackling fire in each of its 300 rooms to warm their cold, aching limbs. However, a room at the Midland Grand would have cost as much as fourteen shillings – an inordinate amount of money for the time and one, no doubt, that would have left them sorely out of pocket.

The Eleven's destination for the next five nights was the Horse Shoe Hotel, a short carriage journey away, on the northern junction of Tottenham Court Road and New Oxford Street. They would get to know the commodious Horse Shoe well over the next four months, transforming it into their base, a home from home, during their numerous visits to the city. Opened in 1875 and built in the ornate French Empire style, with a slate mansard roof and yellow brick with terracotta and Portland stone dressing, it was a shining example of the new "monster" hotels, which were reaching out beyond the railway stations and replacing the inns and taverns of old London.

Next door was the smoking, sprawling four-acre Meux's Horse Shoe Brewery, an establishment with a history as dark and potent as the porter it brewed.[1]

———

At 4.30 on the afternoon of 17 October 1814, George Crick, a storehouse clerk in the brewery, noticed that one of the iron hoops girdling a gargantuan, 22ft vat of porter had snapped off. Crick thought nothing of it and returned to his work; as he would tell an inquest two days later, this happened "frequently" and had not been "attended by any serious consequence" in the past. By all accounts it was not even the brewery's biggest vat. In 1790 Richard Meux invested £5,000 on one which was 23ft tall and 60ft in diameter, and ostentatiously filled it with 200 dinner guests as a demonstration of its behemothic proportions. This was topped five years later by his son, Henry, who created his own monstrosity: 25ft high and 195ft in circumference, and capable of holding the equivalent of some 20,000 barrels of beer.

About an hour after Crick had discovered the splintered hoop, the vat in question – this one contained almost 4,000 barrels' worth of ten-month mature porter – burst apart with such explosive force that it ruptured another huge vat in the cellar while, at the same time, smashing open several hogsheads and casks in the storehouse. The impact released a wave, approximately 15ft high, which instantly took out the brewery wall, demolished two houses in New Street and poured into the St Giles Rookery, a rotting vipers' nest of courtyards, narrow alleys, passages and crumbling, cheek-by-jowl houses. The black torrent engulfed basements, cellars and backyards, brought ceilings crashing down and filled ground- and first-floor rooms, where terrified occupants clambered on to furniture to save themselves from being washed away.

In all, eight people lost their lives in the Great London Beer Flood, six of whom drowned; among them a mother and her daughter, who were swept to their deaths while taking tea after the porter burst through a partition of the first floor of their house in New Street. A barmaid at the Tavistock Arms in Great Russell Street was killed outright when part of a wall collapsed on her; rumours even circulated of a ninth victim who had perished of alcohol poisoning, attempting to consume as much of the ebony liquid as he or she could hold. For several weeks afterwards the area resembled a giant shipwreck, above which the stale, noxious odour of beer hung as heavy as a storm cloud – a lingering reminder of one of London's "most melancholy accidents". Crowds flocked into the area to pick over the flotsam, gape at the destruction or just spectate in such numbers that, according to the *Morning Post*, they were "beyond calculation". The verdict of the inquest, suggesting that the coroner's jury might have imbibed more than their fair share of porter, was to absolve the brewery of any trace of culpability, ruling that the flood had been an "act of God". Meux and Co. estimated a loss of £23,000 – a conservative figure, in their opinion – and successfully petitioned Parliament for a refund of the duty it had paid on the beer.

Two years later the brewery came under siege from a mob protesting against the despised Corn Laws of Lord Liverpool's Tory administration – although why they should have singled it out for particular attention remains unclear – before it closed and bolted its doors for the last time in 1921, the demand for porter having run to a trickle.

By the 1870s Tottenham Court Road had earned a reputation as London's "Furniture Street". Heal's, at number 196 – a site it still occupies today – was already a household name: it had not only opened its first purpose-built store by 1854, and one of the finest in the city, it was a pioneering exponent of advertising, with its brass beds and four-posters appearing regularly on the pages of Charles Dickens's serial novels. Tottenham Court Road was also one of London's busiest thoroughfares, and, viewed from its garrets and attics, or even the fourth floor of the Horse Shoe Hotel, it would have been creaking at the seams, crammed with commercial traffic, horse-drawn trams, hansom cabs and carriages of every description; the constant ebb and flow of pedestrians swollen by an innumerable army of street vendors and hawkers, selling anything from lemonade and ginger beer, penny pies and pickled whelks to Union Jack paper flags and boxes of matches.

The Australians did not appear particularly comfortable with their new surroundings at first. "The immensity of London almost oppressed us," Horan noted, shortly after their arrival, "and we dare not venture to walk more than a mile from our quarters, lest we should be lost in the maze of streets." Or the smoke and steam from the brewhouse, he might have added. Perhaps their mood was merely in keeping with many who witnessed the mighty metropolis for the first time and longed for the open spaces – "the roar of London is ever in your ears," wrote one chronicler of life in the capital during the 1870s – or, more pertinently perhaps, the overwhelming margin of their defeat at Nottingham was still playing on their minds; for as Fred Spofforth recalled, "We were not very confident."

There was more rain in the air on the morning of the match, when their carriages wheeled away from the Horse Shoe Hotel and splashed through the puddles for the pastures of St John's Wood.

We do not know the route the Australians took on their three and a half mile journey to Lord's: whether they turned left off Tottenham Court Road and then headed north along Albany Street, which bounded the stuccoed frontages and verdant expanse of Regent's Park, past Sir Felix Booth's renowned gin distillery, and the Albany Street Cavalry Barracks; or whether they drove west towards the Metropolitan Railway station, on the junction of Baker Street and Marylebone Road, where the world's first steam-powered underground line had been in operation for 15 years (the "Underground", as a term, was already part of the London lexicon). There, maybe, they swung right, taking in the exotically named Baker Street Bazaar at number 28, which in those days housed Madame Tussaud's, whose hugely popular Chamber of Horrors fed the voracious Victorian appetite for all things gruesome and macabre; or perhaps they took the next right instead and turned down Gloucester Place towards Dorset Square, where Lord's cricket ground first pitched its tents in 1787.[2]

As a branch line from Baker Street station to St John's Wood had been in service since 1868, it would also have been possible for them to travel to Lord's below ground, had they felt so bold. Although it was just as well they did not, if an account by the American journalist R. D. Blumenfeld, who made the journey from Baker Street to Moorgate in 1887, was anything to go by. For they would almost certainly have been subjected to an airless compartment – the windows remained tightly shut to keep out the smoke from the engine – the dense aroma of tobacco and "a mixture of sulphur, coal dust and foul fumes from the oil lamp above". Their very own chamber of horrors, perhaps. Blumenfeld concluded that, on finally reaching his destination, "I was near dead of asphyxiation and heat". One thing is certain, though: whatever route the Australians took that morning they would have witnessed the largest and richest city on earth, the powerhouse of the British Empire, going about its business with its usual hustle and bustle – or, with what one observer identified as "a determination distinctly London".

The newspapers that Monday morning were full of the latest developments between Britain and Russia. The conflict, which had earlier that year threatened to spill over into war, now appeared to be nearing its endgame. Invitations were understood to have been issued to the powers involved for a congress to take place in Berlin during the first week of June. However, the risk of war had not been entirely expunged: the British Mediterranean fleet remained anchored off Constantinople, and there were not yet "sufficient grounds for announcing the Congress as assured". On the home front, the grey and chilly weather of a "very unfortunate and cheerless May" failed to dampen the ardour of the crowds who had turned out in their thousands for Trooping the Colour. "We will not stop to inquire why the martial spirit of London was more excited than usual on the occasion of the 59th birthday of her Majesty. But it was so," the *Daily Telegraph* remarked. Feelings, meanwhile, continued to run dangerously high in Lancashire, where cotton workers were striking against reduced working hours and a 10% pay cut imposed by the mill owners. In Blackburn, the home of one mill owner had been looted and burned to the ground, and there were fears of further riots, the newspapers reported.

The Eleven, who included Midwinter, drove in through the Lord's gates on St John's Wood Road – unnoticed and unrecognised, it was said – to discover a ground that was virtually deserted. Even W. G. Grace was moved to describe the conditions that greeted them as "depressing", recording that "there were not 500 persons present when the Australians arrived". Perhaps they should not have been surprised: after all, there had been no one to meet them on their arrival in London at St Pancras three days earlier. In fact, their appearance in the city had not been looked forward to with any "unusual excitement, and indeed was very little spoken of", according to one newspaper. A few small posters along the walls of St John's Road may have advertised "a grand match" on the 27th, but they neglected to name the two teams taking part. There was a general air of uninterest: "People strolled round the ground, or rested themselves on the benches bounding the match reserve quite apathetically. To a visitor there was nothing whatever to indicate that anything beyond an ordinary match between second-rate players was about to commence."

Lord's at that time bore little or no resemblance to the ground that we recognise today, and it would no doubt have appeared rather primitive to modern eyes. However, a grandstand was in place by 1867 – a low, single-tier construction, above which the neighbouring three-storey villas still commanded their lofty views; opposite were the Tavern Hotel and the ivy-clad real tennis courts, which dominated the south side of the ground. A little farther along stood the greenhouses of Henderson's nursery and market garden, where pineapples and tulips flourished; the three and a half acre plot was purchased by Lord's in 1887, when it became known famously as the nursery end. Facing Henderson's at the other end of the pitch was the old pavilion, which had been extensively enlarged in 1865; once described as "cottage-like" – an impression augmented by the patch of shrubs which grew around the entrance – its red brick was now "almost black through the effect of metropolitan smoke". The structure would eventually be demolished in 1899 to make way for Thomas Verity's landmark brick and terracotta pavilion. A telegraph and scorer's box had also been added in 1865, although it would not be until the eighties that a telegraph, capable of registering the batsmen's scores run by run as they were made, was installed.

Middlesex were also in residence, having migrated from their Prince's Ground headquarters, near Sloane Square, at the close of the 1876 season. The arrival of the county side had done much to add a touch of panache and variety to a fixture list that was becoming increasingly dull and elitist. According to Edward Rutter, a former Middlesex player and a member of the MCC committee during the 1870s, the crowds were often negligible and the matches "were mostly of no interest except to the players themselves". Of course, there were exceptions, notably in 1874, when attendances were so large before the start of the Varsity match that the gates had to be opened at five in the morning. Rutter, though, painted an unashamedly doleful picture of Lord's as it was during the early to mid-1860s – a period when a "deplorably lethargic and out of date" committee were guilty of allowing the grass to grow under their feet, both physically and metaphorically: "There were no boundaries – except the pavilion – no stands or fixed seats of any kind, nothing but the small old pavilion and a line of loose benches running part of the way round the ground, and these were but little occupied save at the most important games."

However, some substantial advances had been made by 1878, and the Australians, comparing it to their own burgeoning Melbourne Cricket Ground – the yardstick by which they measured all of England's premier grounds – clearly liked what they saw. "Lord's is to cricket what Rome is to the world," Horan enthused. "The Laws of cricket are made by the Marylebone Club and to the committee of it all anxious questions are referred. Here are played three or four of the great matches of the year. Here Oxford play Cambridge; here Eton is pitted against Harrow; here the Gentlemen contend with the Players and here the North tries if it is better than the South." You could almost feel them breathing in the rarefied air. Lord's appeared "a little larger than the Melbourne Ground", while the members' pavilion was "comfortable in the extreme; there are dining rooms, reading and writing rooms, and a bar". Only the grandstand, which Horan considered inferior to its Australian counterpart, failed to match expectations. As Melbourne's "reversible" £4,700 edifice was the *stately pleasure dome* of grandstands – it "allowed summertime viewing of the cricket to the immediate west and winter viewing of the football in Richmond paddock, adjacent to the east" – it would have proved a hard act to follow at the best of times.[3] The practice wickets, though, won admiring nods and Horan declared them to be every bit as impressive as the one in the middle.

There was a time, certainly until the 1880s and perhaps even beyond, when no batsman – and especially not one in his right mind – would have had anything complimentary to say about the wicket at Lord's. The majority of batsmen who regularly risked life and limb on what was undisputedly the most dangerous surface in England, did so against a pack of wild and erratic, but often terrifyingly fast, round-arm slingers who bowled with the scent of blood in their nostrils. During the 1860s, when W. G. Grace first came to prominence, the wicket was regarded as "unnecessarily rough"; it was "not chalked out, but cut out; the markings were an inch deep [and] the batsman could amuse himself by picking up a handful of gravel when a wicket fell". Such were its vicissitudes that the batsman could also expect to receive two or three shooters an over and at least one ball which, if it did not kick into his ribs, would fly over his and the wicketkeeper's head to be caught by the fielder at long-stop, often on the full.[4] The position became such an indispensable part of a captain's armoury that every team had at least one man who excelled there. It was only after the Australian buccaneers Blackham and Murdoch emerged in 1878 to take wicketkeeping skills to unimagined levels that long-stops were more or less rendered an "obsolete functionary".

The wicket at Lord's was so bad that Surrey, in 1859, and Sussex, four years later, refused to play there, while Frederick Gale felt compelled to record during a match between the Gentlemen and the Players in 1868 that, "Had I been a wicketkeeper or batsman at Lord's I should have liked (*plus* my gloves and pads) to have worn a single-stick mask, a Life Guardsman's cuirass, and a tin stomach-warmer." Gale added, "I have no hesitation in saying that in nine cricket grounds out of ten within twenty miles of London, whether village green or county club ground, a local club could find a better wicket … than the Marylebone Club supplied to the Players of England." The wickets were equally grim in 1869 and 1870, when only two of the scheduled three-day matches – both against Nottinghamshire – lasted the distance. Why MCC exhibited such a stubborn disregard for the state of its square, or the safety of its cricketers, particularly when rivals such as The Oval, Trent Bridge, Fenner's and Canterbury were gilding their reputations, defies any logical explanation. Pelham Warner, who knew more about these things than most, suggests that the prevailing, "What was good enough for my father is good for me" attitude of the MCC committee of those days was as much responsible as anything. In that case, they were fortunate indeed that they did not have to bat on it themselves.

However, one man, as fearless as he was matchless, took it upon himself to tame this wild beast and to redress the balance between bat and ball. That man was W. G. Grace. Welding an ironclad defence – he unerringly kept out the shooters and was not afraid to take the bouncing ball on his redoubtable chest – to a prodigious stamina, an unassailable confidence and a seemingly limitless repertoire of shots (he could cut to his heart's content and was a ferocious driver of fast bowling), Grace turned the fire back on the bowlers. So successful was he, in fact, that he did not just restore the equilibrium, he treated a legion of bowlers to such a display of contempt that it was said they "were almost afraid to bowl within his reach". But then Grace would probably have made runs on the craters of the moon.

It took a fatal accident to finally bring MCC to its senses. It had surely been only a matter of time before disaster struck: a tragedy that one such as Frederick Gale – who made no attempt to disguise or dilute his criticism of a wicket that left many a batsman counting his wounds – might in his darkest moments have dreaded above all else. The incident when it came, though, was no less shocking for that.

On the morning of 15 June 1870, George Summers, batting first wicket down for Nottinghamshire, was struck a sickening blow on the head by a short, rising delivery from Jack Platts, a young fast bowler from Derbyshire who was making his MCC debut. Platts was described as a bowler with a "rather laboured action, [who] pounded the ball down with some pains, his deliveries always bumpy, and at times dangerous". Some claimed, in fact, that the ball had struck one of the many loose pebbles, which from time to time worked their way up to the surface, causing it to deviate alarmingly off a length. The fielders quickly gathered round the stricken Summers, one of whom, W. G. Grace, a 22-year-old medical student, immediately assumed control. The batsman came round and was eventually helped to his feet, and although he returned to the pavilion and took no further part in the match, "the story goes that he was given brandy, the last thing to do in the circumstances, and, further, sat in a hot sun". The next man in, Richard Daft, considered the wicket so treacherous that, despite having scored 117 in the first innings, he emerged from the pavilion with a protective towel wrapped around his head – an act for which he was openly ridiculed by several members of the fielding side. Seemingly none the worse for his experience, however, Summers travelled back on the train to Nottingham that night, a journey where parts of the track were so rough and uneven in places (a trait not dissimilar to the wicket at Lord's) that luggage was flung from the racks and passengers often complained of dizziness. He collapsed and died four days later of a fractured skull, aged 25. Platts was described by Grace as being "terribly cut up" over the incident, and despite developing into an outstanding all-rounder who served Derbyshire with distinction for 14 seasons, he could never find it in himself to bowl fast again.[5]

MCC at last took some action and appointed a groundsman of the "modern type", Peter Pearce. Pearce had performed wonders transforming the Sussex county ground at Hove into a run-heavy wicket – it was said that, among other things, he top-dressed the soil with road sweepings – and he wasted no time in attempting to exorcise the demons from the Lord's pitch. Many on the committee probably thought his methods quixotic at best, but few could quibble with his results. He introduced the regular use of the heavy roller, drained and relevelled the pitch, and even procured some soil from nearby Kilburn "in which there was much iron" to help quell and sweeten the wicket. By 1876 it was said that he had achieved such a remarkable improvement that the pitch was deemed to be in "faultless condition". Indeed, some accounts went as far as to claim that it had become too good, and that Pearce was under strict instructions from the committee not to improve it any further. While it was certainly true that Lord's had "lost its proverbial reputation of being the most dangerous ground in the country", we should perhaps take Pelham Warner's more considered summation of the Lord's wicket at that time as being a little closer to the mark: "The wickets gradually began to improve, but they could hardly be described as perfect, or anything like perfect, until we came to the eighties. Even then the heavy clay and the inadequately drained ground produced sticky wickets of the type that bowlers dream of."

He might have been describing to a tee the pitch that awaited David Gregory's Australians on the morning of 27 May 1878.

––––––

The miserable, wet start to the summer had no doubt contributed to the sparse attendance at Lord's that day, although the resounding defeat of the Australians at Nottingham, coupled with the newspapers' patent lack of enthusiasm for their cricket, appeared to have exerted a more persuasive influence on the public. Whatever the exact number of the crowd that morning – Horan and the *Argus* both put it at a thousand, though they would have had good reason for not wanting to err on the side of caution – it was still a disappointingly small gathering. The truth was that no one gave the colonials a chance. "So much so," Horan related, "that, as an instance of the prejudice which is felt against us, I may mention a certain gentleman who was in one of the leading clubs in England – not a cricket club – who was talking about our boys. He was interrupted by a party who could have known very little about the game, as he said he would bet 180 pounds to 20 that we did not win a single game in England playing eleven a side!" The odds were stacked four to one against the Australians at Lord's and such was English cricket's overweening sense of superiority that many were prepared to wager that the contest against MCC would be won by an innings, and concluded well within its allotted three days. They would be proved right about that at least, if nothing else – although not in a way they could have ever imagined.

Little or no allowance had been made for the Australians' lack of practice, for the fact that they were still recovering from the rigours and dangers of their long journey, or for the soreness of their limbs. They were equally disadvantaged by the bitterly cold weather and the relentless rain which, to their eyes, rendered the conditions unplayable, made the ball as heavy as lead and played havoc with their attempts to acclimatise. They yearned for the sun, for their own quick wickets, muttered darkly to themselves about the weather, and wondered whether they would ever chase a ball across an outfield which was not ankle deep in thick, squelching mud and would have tested the resolve of footballers. It was anything but the homecoming they had envisaged.

To suggest that the MCC team was an England XI in all but name, as has often been claimed, might be straining the truth more than a little. However, any side that included the Champion of England himself, W. G. Grace, and the thunderous Lancastrian hitter A. N. Hornby, alongside the great Nottinghamshire firm of Alfred Shaw and Fred Morley, could hardly be portrayed as anything other than powerful. Certainly, the selection of Grace and Hornby meant that in batting alone it was vastly superior to James Lillywhite's All-England XI of 1876–7, while *Wisden* declared there were enough marquee names for it to be described as "one of the strongest MCC elevens ever put out by the famous old club".

Nonetheless, by arranging such formidable opposition for their opening two matches, Lillywhite, perhaps in his anxiety to attract the best fixtures, had permitted the Australians few favours: this was no gentle bedding in, but an ordeal by fire, and rain. Another defeat, on a similar scale to the one at Nottingham, would have had dire consequences, not just for the financial prospects of the tour, but for the very future and validity of such colonial-run ventures. Indeed, even, for the "destiny of Australian cricket". Richard Cashman, in his book *The "Demon" Spofforth*, argues that, "It was a match of far greater importance than what are now recognised as the first two Tests, played in Melbourne in March 1877." The Australians, though, were up for the fight. "Our detractors say that this MCC side is not as strong as it might be and the club has fielded an under-strength eleven on the evidence of our showing at Nottingham," Horan recorded on the eve of the match, "but frankly we do not believe them."

There was a heavy downpour 30 minutes before the start of play, but by the time MCC had won the toss and elected to bat, Lord's was bathed in a pallid, watery sunshine. The rooftops of the surrounding villas were still glistening wet as Grace and his opening partner, Hornby, followed the Australians down the pavilion steps and out into the middle. The dissimilarity in appearance between the physically imposing Grace, with his piratical black beard, and the diminutive Hornby, who wore a neat military moustache and a trademark centre parting in his hair (unusually for the times, he never batted in a cap), could not have been more striking.

The pitch was described as being in a "sodden state", the outfield dotted with puddles, when Frank Allan prepared to bowl the first ball from the nursery end to Grace at three minutes past twelve. Even then, one reporter noted, "there was a drowsiness over the spectators, who seemed as if they had made up their minds that Grace and Hornby would knock the ball about for an hour or two; and the only amusement, if any, would be that of 'leather-hunting' by the Australians".

Sure enough, Grace struck Allan's first ball through square leg to the boundary with such consummate ease that the crowd's first reaction was to laugh at the predictability of it. However, at this point, Midwinter took the decision to steal a few yards back from short leg to square leg while the bowler was running in. Allan pitched his second ball in exactly the same spot and Grace, in attempting to repeat the shot through what he assumed was still the vacant square-leg area, spooned it straight into the hands of Midwinter. Years later, Spofforth would refer to it as a "shocking bad stroke". Grace's anger at his swift dismissal was no doubt exacerbated by the fact that Midwinter was the fielder: perhaps he half expected the Gloucestershire player to put his loyalties to his county captain above those of the Australians. "The snide laughter turned to amazement," Horan recalled, and when Grace tucked his bat under his arm and started to stride towards the pavilion, "the astonished crowd erupted into cheering".

Harry Boyle – happily recovered from the stiff neck that kept him out of the game at Trent Bridge – saw Hornby receive the benefit of the doubt for a catch behind at the start of an eventful second over, before clean bowling the new batsman, Clement Booth, with the score on five. Arthur Ridley joined Hornby at the wicket, and despite innumerable near misses – Hornby led a particularly charmed existence, somehow surviving a stumping chance and a run-out – the pair moved the total on to 27 without further loss. It was at this stage in the game that the tall, sinuous figure of Spofforth entered the attack.

Charging in off an oblique run-up of some 12 paces, "starting several yards to the offside of the batsman", Spofforth, at full-tilt, cut a fearsome aspect. The superlative action photographs of him taken by George Beldam provide a tantalising glimpse of what it might have been like to face him: his long left arm pointing down the pitch like a javelin, the formidable final bound at the moment of delivery, his high, scything right arm and sweeping follow-through, in which he appeared to hurl himself after the ball and run unchecked down the wicket. Beldam's images take on an even more impressive hue for the fact that they were shot in 1904, when Spofforth was 51, "long after his days in the sun were over", yet still convey the full-blooded hostility of the man.[6] Spofforth also liked to spike his fast bowling with the occasional choice word, and a glare that could crack a safe. But "the Demon" was not all fire and brimstone; he derived just as much pleasure from out-thinking a batsman as he did from blasting him out. He was a master of deception, who would recalibrate the deadly art of fast bowling to such a degree that he could vary his pace, length and flight, bowl an off-break or unleash a venomous yorker without any discernible change in his action. Opinion is divided as to just how quick Spofforth really was; indeed, some claimed that he was no more than medium-pace (and so he might be to modern eyes). However, the Hon. Edward Lyttelton's assertion that facing him was like standing "on the brink of the tomb", or Grace's less picturesque but just as convincing testament, he was "terrifically fast", should be enough to scotch any argument in that regard. England, certainly, could muster no fast bowler to compare with him, and would not do so until the emergence of the Surrey thoroughbred Tom Richardson in the 1890s. "Before Spofforth appeared, bowlers were either fast, slow, or medium; seldom indeed, did they think of varying their pace," Pelham Warner later wrote. It was this unrivalled skill, and his high arm, of course, that was to mark him out as the first great modern bowler.

Spofforth struck an instant rhythm, and after Boyle's medium pace had removed Ridley for seven, "the Demon" announced himself by flattening Hornby's leg stump for 19 with the second ball of his second over. One Australian reporter observed that Hornby appeared to take no guard at all, while playing with his bat "fully four inches from the leg stump", and appeared less than impressed with the opener's methods: "[he] hits at everything". But those who knew his batting and admired him for his pugnacity and "passion for taking a risk", held him in the highest regard. In the words of Neville Cardus, Hornby belonged to a "great company of 'originals' [who] grew around" Grace – cricketers such as his fellow Lancastrian Dick Barlow, and the Yorkshireman Tom Emmett – "all men of ripe comedy, home-spun and fresh, each of them as vivid as characters on a page of Dickens". A true Corinthian, Hornby was an England rugby international, who excelled at athletics, football and boxing, and was good enough to step into the booths of some of the most feared prizefighters in the land. It was also said that he was responsible, albeit inadvertently, for having persuaded Lord's to establish fixed boundaries at the ground, after injuring a spectator while giving chase to the ball. Before then batsmen ran until the fielder found and returned the ball. However, aside from one mighty blow when he smote Boyle through the skylight of the billiard room, causing a spectacular shower of glass – the only shaft of batting supremacy throughout the match – Hornby was no different from any other batsman in that he failed to master the stickiest of wickets, and the consistently high quality of the bowling.

Spofforth was virtually unplayable by this time and he quickly accounted for the prolific Middlesex batsman A. J. Webbe with the score on 29, before becoming the first Australian bowler to claim a hat-trick on English soil, in his fifth over. As testimony to the potency of his black art, two of the hat-trick victims – Shaw and G. F. Vernon (the first, G. G. Hearne, had been conclusively bowled) – were lured from the crease and stumped by Murdoch, who had replaced Blackham for this match. It was not unusual for Murdoch, like Blackham, to stand up to the timbers when Spofforth bowled – in fact, the bowler usually insisted on it – and it would have been as much of a revelation to the Lord's crowd as the sight of Spofforth's extravagantly high arm. As English audiences still expected their bowlers, with very few exceptions, to be round-arm, there was an undoubted whiff of magic about his action. Blackham and Murdoch possessed lightning reactions, bags of courage and an innate confidence in Spofforth's powers. They would have needed them: not only did they stand up to the greatest fast bowler of the time – who performed more tricks than a magician at Piccadilly's Egyptian Hall – they carried it off with some style and aplomb, on substandard wickets, armed only with flimsy pads and threadbare gloves; the latter may have been perfectly sufficient for pruning the roses, but were wholly inadequate for juggling the flaming coals propelled their way.

Wilf Flowers was the last wicket to fall, caught and bowled by Spofforth for a duck, and exactly 70 minutes since Grace had taken guard and imperiously cracked Allan's first ball to the leg-side boundary, the MCC innings was over: all out for 33, the last eight wickets going down for six runs. Spofforth, a "whirlwind of destruction", had captured six of them for four runs in 5.3 overs. Bearing in mind that these were four-ball overs, so Spofforth bowled only 23 balls, the figures make devastating reading:

...2/ .W.. / W... /1 ... /W W W . / .1 W

Among the heavy fallers of the MCC top order, only the doughty Hornby managed to reach double figures. Boyle, an estimable foil for Spofforth, bowled 14 overs for three wickets and 14 runs, while Allan's one wicket (the most highly prized of all) came at a cost of 14 runs from nine overs. The crowd – many of whom had paid their 6d. entrance fee to mock and jeer the Australians – swarmed on to the field, all but mobbing them as they made their way back to the pavilion. "The applause was immense, and when we reached the gate we had to pick our way through as best we could," Horan recalled. "Of course, Spofforth was the lion," the reporter for the *Sydney Mail* wrote. "Lads peered up into his face, men looked up and down at him, cheering lustily all the while, and pushing him into the pavilion, when they cheered and cheered again."

Runs were every bit as hard to come by when the Australian reply got under way ten minutes later, and Charles Bannerman and Midwinter renewed their battle with Shaw and Morley. The Nottinghamshire professionals immediately went to work, bowling with "mean intent" and giving the batsmen absolutely nothing to hit. Shaw's immaculacy of line and length was such that he did not concede a single run until his 12th over. It was Morley, though, who made the breakthrough, having Bannerman superbly caught by Hearne at long-off in the fourth over after a desperate attempt to put the first runs on the telegraph. It was an ill-considered shot under the circumstances, for a batsman who rarely hit the ball in the air. The Eleven relied heavily on Bannerman for runs, and there was a feeling among several of them that his impetuosity led him to give his wicket away too cheaply on occasions. Horan and Alec Bannerman were also back in the pavilion – two more victims for the fast left arm of Morley – when the lunch bell rang to conclude a breathless and quite improbable session of cricket, with the score on 17 for three.

Midwinter had drawn on his not inconsiderable experience of English conditions to survive until lunch, but after becoming only the second batsman to record double figures, he edged Shaw to the wicketkeeper, Wild, shortly after the resumption. Whatever Shaw had feasted on during the interval it had done nothing to blunt his appetite for wickets and, at 20 for six, the tourists were in danger of being bowled out for even fewer runs than MCC. Two more wickets went down in rapid succession – including the dismissal of Gregory, bowled by Shaw, for his third consecutive duck – by which time Allan had joined Murdoch. Allan batted with the air of a man who had wandered by accident into the wrong sport; indeed, Horan went as far as to describe his fellow Victorian's eccentric crouching style as "grotesque". But somehow he managed to keep the bowling at bay, amusing and frustrating the spectators in equal measure, while inching his team ever closer to a first-innings lead. Perhaps even Shaw and Morley's fabled powers of concentration faltered in the face of his crude and comical strokeplay, and the "deprecatory laughter" that invariably accompanied it. Shaw finally rattled Murdoch's stumps for nine, 11 runs later, but Allan "clung tenaciously to his bat" and was last man out, caught and bowled by Shaw for six, with the score on 41. Shaw and Morley had shared all ten wickets while bowling unchanged again, for 66.2 overs. The lead was only eight, but for the Australians each one must have felt as precious as gold dust.

Meanwhile, another kind of whirlwind was sweeping through the streets of London – one that moved by word of mouth, and bore Spofforth's name. News of the Australian fast bowler's hat-trick and the state of the match had "spread like wildfire", bringing with it a procession of hansom cabs, carriages and pedestrians hastening towards St John's Wood. The city's five evening papers would not hit the newsstands until after three o'clock and, with the exception of the highly efficient telegraph system, this remained the quickest and cheapest means for news, good or bad, to travel. Doubtless, this way many of the tales grew in the telling, although in Spofforth's case his feat would have required no further embellishment.

By mid-afternoon the turnstiles were doing a brisk business, and almost 5,000 spectators would pass through them before the day was done. That was still some way below the huge numbers that regularly attended contests between the Gentlemen and the Players, or the Varsity match, but at least a sizeable crowd was building, and one worthy of the occasion. The grandstand and the pavilion hummed with conversation and opinion, as did the benches and seating areas around the boundary. The talk was still fiercely partisan, Horan reported: Grace would put the colonial bowlers, and Spofforth in particular, in their rightful place after his first-innings aberration; and Shaw and Morley would administer the *coup de grâce*, just as they had done at Nottingham five days earlier. On a wicket still heavily stacked in favour of the bowlers, and on which only two batsmen had managed double figures thus far, it was presumptuous in the extreme to expect 'the Champion' to flay the Australian attack to all parts; but expect it they did. It mattered little that he had made a miserable start to the season by his own inimitable standards, or that he was still inconvenienced by a thumb injury sustained while playing for MCC against an England XI two weeks earlier. This was his turf, his fiefdom.

The Australians returned to the middle for the start of MCC's second innings at four o'clock, and for what must have been the first time since walking down the gang-plank at Liverpool, they had a bright sun on their backs; *Wisden* confirms that it "shone out in good old fashioned early summer form". Although Spofforth remembers it rather differently: according to him, they spent most of the day shivering in their silk shirts, swinging their arms in the field to keep warm whenever the sun disappeared behind the frequent clouds. However, there was clearly an inner fire coursing through the great fast bowler's veins, and he would bowl the first over to Grace: from the end where he had wrought such havoc in the first innings, with the greenhouses of Henderson's nursery and the tall trees of Wellington Park behind him. The crowd watched while he paced out his run-up and waited expectantly and noisily for the umpire's outstretched arm to drop. As it did so, the chatter died away until there was only the sound of horses' hooves on the streets outside, and the tinkle of harnesses from the ring of carriages inside the ground. Grace stood perfectly still, his bat poised at the ready in the pendulum position, as Spofforth, his silk shirt billowing like a sail, surged towards him. The spectators could not have known that they were witnessing the opening of hostilities between the two men who would become the first great duellists of international sport, but they might have sensed in the sudden and alchemic shift of mood that something dramatic was about to happen.

They did not have long to wait. If 'the Champion' was dumbfounded by Spofforth's first ball – his "uncertainty was quite apparent to the spectators" after he got an edge to it only for Murdoch to spill the chance as it cannoned into his gloves – he would be left thunderstruck by the second. It was described by Horan as a "slower ball", but it was so perfectly disguised that it ripped past his bat, almost before he had time to react, hitting the stumps with such a clatter that – slower ball or no – the leg bail went flying 30 yards in the direction of the pavilion. A scream of "Bowled!" from the exultant Spofforth triggered what Horan remembered as "a perfect storm of applause" and, seconds later, "the leviathan … was retracing his steps".[7]

The Australians had quickly become accustomed to the way even the most one-eyed spectators cheered and roared when "anything brilliant was done", but this was nothing short of miraculous. There were even suggestions that Grace had been undone by a ball which had come back sharply from outside his leg stump. Spofforth's best ball was the fast off-break, and while there is no reason to suppose he had not devised a subtle variation, namely one that broke back from leg, there is little evidence that he ever put it into practice. However, Lord Harris, who faced "the Demon" on numerous occasions, most notably in the hothouse of the Melbourne international a year later, when Spofforth performed the first hat-trick in Test cricket, told *Wisden*, "He could break slightly from leg, I believe, though I cannot remember him doing so; and the rumour went round amongst us who had to face him for the first time, that if he was going to break from the off, he held the ball at the tips of his fingers; if from leg, the palm of his hand." In his recollections of "the first great match that an Australian team played in England", Spofforth sheds no light upon that particular mystery, other than to convey his pure and unabashed delight at castling the world's greatest batsman for a second-ball duck: "This gave me more pleasure than any ball I bowled."

Spofforth removed Webbe with his next delivery, and although Booth denied him his second hat-trick of the match, the Hampshire batsman was promptly bowled by Boyle's second ball to "another hurricane of cheers", after Hornby had managed to get the first away for a single. Boyle then completed the over by ripping out Ridley's middle and leg stumps, at which point MCC were four wickets down for one run. Hornby aside, the cream of England's amateur batting had been eviscerated in the space of only eight balls. There was worse to come: Hornby, having found himself trapped at the non-striker's end for all but two overs – a predicament that did not suit his combative nature – was struck "a severe blow" by Spofforth and forced to retire, without further addition to the score. As Horan and Spofforth, along with every other match account, seemed almost at pains to exclude any specific detail of the injury – the Lancastrian was described as having the "misfortune" to be "cut over" but little else – it was more than likely that he took the blow in the most delicate part of his anatomy. Hornby, in all probability, was not wearing a box (a primitive form of protector had been available since the 1850s), but in keeping with most, if not all of the amateur leading players of the time, who trusted implicitly in their nerve and skill, he would have considered his bat his most effective means of defence.

The MCC batsmen, though, could barely lay one on a single delivery, and while there is no doubt that the humiliating collapse of the top order – not to mention the sight of Hornby *hors de combat* in the dressing-room – would have had a debilitating effect on the innings, nothing should be allowed to detract from the bowling of Spofforth and Boyle. As *The Times* commented, "It signified little who went in, for Messrs. Spofforth and Boyle were determined upon their speedy dismissal."

Flowers became the third batsman to reach double figures, and in company with Wild he added another 15 runs, dragging the score to 16 before he was bowled by Boyle for 11. Flowers' departure, however, was the cue for another flurry of wickets – Hearne and Wild were accounted for by Spofforth and Boyle respectively – and with the cricket taking on an almost trance-like quality at this stage, "the innings disintegrated in the space of three runs". Fortified perhaps by several restorative swigs of brandy – the cure-all for an ailing batsman – Hornby had returned to the firing line, with Grace as his runner, but was quickly cleaned up by Boyle. The last man Morley had not detained the Australians long either, though at least he was the only batsman not to be dismissed by having his stumps rearranged, being caught instead at mid-off by Horan off Boyle. In all, the innings had lasted 55 minutes. Horan relates that the total of 19 was "the lowest score ever recorded by an MCC team"; in fact they had just achieved the somewhat scant consolation of beating their previous lowest all-out score – recorded against Surrey six years earlier, on another murderous Lord's wicket – by a mere three runs.

This time it was Boyle, the former gold miner from Bendigo, who struck pay dirt, finishing with the remarkable figures of six for three from 33 balls. However, despite virtually matching Spofforth wicket for wicket and conceding fewer runs (Boyle's match figures were nine for 17 from 22.1 overs, as opposed to "the Demon's" ten for 20 from 14.3) his part in Australia's success at Lord's has always been overshadowed by that of Spofforth, a trend that would endure for as long as their careers intertwined. It has been written that Boyle suffered in comparison with Spofforth because "he partnered one of the immortals". Yet Boyle was no sorcerer's apprentice. Indeed, his bowling sobriquet was "the Very Devil", and, with his exemplary command of line and length and deceptive change of pace – he could break the ball both ways – he was as capable of delivering a match-winning performance and playing merry hell with an innings as "the Demon" himself – just perhaps not as sensationally. What is not in question, however, is that they made the perfect combination, and as such are rightly venerated as Australia's "first great firm" of bowlers.

The Australians needed only 12 for victory, although they knew that Shaw and Morley would make them scrap for every run; that they would have to be chipped out of tablets of stone. And so it proved when, with only a single on the board, the indomitable Shaw bowled Charles Bannerman – the one batsman capable of taking the game away from them with a couple of well-timed blows – with a ball that broke back by as much as a foot. This time he had been powerless to prevent his wicket going down. There was still hope for MCC at that stage, but with Midwinter and the new batsman, Horan, prepared to roll up their silk sleeves and defend their stumps as if their lives depended on it, it would have required a quite remarkable feat of escapology by Shaw and Morley. Horan survived one lapse of concentration that should have seen him run out, when attempting a quick single off Morley, but the fielder, Booth, failed to return the ball to the wicketkeeper's end and the chance went begging. Slowly, but inexorably, the batsmen ticked off the remaining runs – much to the annoyance, no doubt, of the scowling Grace – and when Horan cut Morley to the boundary off the first ball of the 16th over, the game was finally up. Australia needed only one more run for victory, and, with the clock approaching 5.40, it was the Irishman Horan who duly delivered it, repeating the stroke, although with less authority this time, and running two, off the fourth and final ball of Morley's over.

The crowd, having watched every thrust and parry in a "fever of excitement", poured across the pitch to acclaim an astonishing victory by nine wickets: a victory that not a soul among them would have dared to predict before the start of play. This was a triumph made even more extraordinary by the fact that this was only the Australians' second foray in English conditions; they were still rusty, short of a gallop and judged to be nothing more than cannon fodder for the big guns of Grace, Shaw, Hornby and the others. The notion that they lacked the skills, or the nerve, to compete in English conditions, against the pick of the best cricketers in the land, had been comprehensively and irresistibly laid to rest. As Horan put it, "It was generally agreed that English cricket had underestimated our strength ... none had the faintest idea we were good enough to beat the Marylebone Club!"

Rarely, if ever in the history of sport, can a giant-killing of such epic proportions by the visiting team – and one in which the Goliath of English cricket was felled for a total of only four runs off four balls in two innings – have been celebrated so joyously by the hometown supporters. "If the two redoubtables of the Australian team had been objects of curiosity in the first innings, they seemed to be now regarded as bowlers from another world," the *Sydney Mail* exclaimed. Two decades later, Grace, while accepting, "it was, no doubt, a glorious victory for Australia", stubbornly maintained that "the conditions of the ground accounted for the phenomenally low scores". No doubt that was true, but it spectacularly failed to take into account the supreme efforts of Spofforth and Boyle in both innings. The conditions had, after all, been the same for both teams – and adversely so in the case of the Australians who, because of the weather, had managed only a couple of hours "indifferent practice" since their arrival in London.

Not surprisingly, the match was awash with statistics: in all, 128.2 overs were bowled, and only 104 runs scored from the bat; seven batsmen were dismissed first ball; Grace was out to the second ball of each innings; nine batsmen were clean-bowled in MCC's second innings; no batsmen were run out, or adjudged leg-before; and only one chance had been dropped by either side, when Murdoch reprieved Grace off the first ball of MCC's second innings.

Afterwards, as many as a thousand spectators, according to *Wisden*, massed outside the pavilion repeatedly calling the names of Spofforth and Boyle, while "the members of the MCC keenly joined in the applause of that 'maddened crowd', who shouted themselves hoarse before they left to scatter far and wide ... the news how in one day the Australians had so easily defeated one of the strongest MCC elevens ..." A cannon shell, had it landed on the square, could not have rocked the foundations of the home of English cricket with any more force. It was during those wild and unprecedented scenes that Spofforth claims he was first christened "the Demon": "It was in this match I received the sobriquet of 'Demon Bowler' or, rather, in consequence of it." Horan, though, suggests that the New South Wales batsman Nat Thomson may have been the first to call Spofforth "the Demon", "before he went to England", although he concedes, "But others say that Spofforth called himself the 'Demon'... at Lord's ... and at the finish in the dressing-room he said 'ain't I a demon? ain't I a demon?' gesticulating the while in his own well-known demoniac style."

Whatever the provenance of "the Demon", Spofforth – with his burning dark grey eyes, hooked nose and striking 6ft 3in frame – was unquestionably a star, a ready-made drawcard. Whether doffing his cap to the crowd (such showmanship was not for the taciturn Boyle) or prowling the pavilion balcony with the demeanour of a gunfighter, he looked and played the part. In an age when the sobriquet was as much a part of sport as the luxuriant beards and side-whiskers of its protagonists, surely no sportsman has so closely mirrored his as the saturnine Spofforth. Even *Wisden*, whose style of reporting on such occasions was often no more than functional at best, appeared to get caught up in the moment: "The decisive victory of the Australians was earnestly applauded by members of the MCC and tumultuously so by the thousands of other Englishmen present, whose bones will have mouldered to dust long, long before the cricketers of the future – colonial and English – cease to gossip about the marvellous short-time match played by the Australians at Lord's on 27 May, 1878." So short, in fact, that the time the players spent on the field – allowing for lunch and intervals between innings (tea was not yet an accepted part of the game) – amounted to just over four and a half hours.

One can only imagine what Grace, stewing in defeat in the dressing room, would have made of it all. No doubt he was already plotting his revenge.

Six
28–29 May 1878

"The Australians came down like a wolf on the fold"

The Australians woke the following morning to discover that the newspapers had performed a volte-face every bit as resounding as the one managed by the Lord's crowd. They had returned to the Horse Shoe on the evening of their victory to be met by another cheering crowd. The whole of London it seemed was in the grip of the whirlwind, and "our hotel was almost besieged," Spofforth remembered. But even they must have been taken aback by the extent of the praise lavished on them and the speed with which they had been transformed – overnight – from laughing stocks into all-conquering heroes. *The Globe*, for instance, while going out of its way to lionise the colonial cricketers, made no effort to spare the blushes of the MCC players – many of whom must have felt as if they had just plummeted from the stars:

> *A victory won by the strangers against the crack club of this country would under any circumstances, have been a notable and even an extraordinary event. But the peculiarity of the game yesterday was not, perhaps, the mere fact that the Australians won, but that they should have made such a pitiful example of their antagonists. Seldom in the annals of modern cricket has so small a score been made, as by the Marylebone Club yesterday, and never was so severe a humiliation inflicted individually and collectively upon the members of the club. The eleven was as good a one that could be found to represent London and England ... Whatever be the results of future matches, the reputation of the Colonial eleven is made and they will be welcomed with enthusiasm where ever they now appear.*

The newspaper concluded its account with a reference to another sporting occasion – this one had been played out upon the waters of the Thames – when the kangaroo, in the formidable form of oarsman Ned Trickett, administered a similarly decisive mauling to the lion. "Australia is advancing, indeed in sports as in everything else," it proclaimed. "She has beaten the country on the Thames and now she beats England at Lord's. At the present rate, we shall soon have nothing left of our boasted athletic pre-eminence." Whether it was intentional or not, *The Globe* had succeeded in elevating the match to international status.

———

In an almost exact parallel of the match at Lord's, Ned Trickett – a 6ft 3in colossus from Sydney – was crowned the world sculling champion after easily overcoming England's Joseph Sadler on 27 June 1876. The race, over the four and a quarter mile Championship Course between Putney and Mortlake, was watched by huge crowds, who lined the river banks or crammed into the flotilla of chartered steamboats and other assorted craft that followed in its wake. Sadler – a London chimney sweep before he took to vanquishing allcomers on the water – was the clear favourite and widely tipped to retain his title, and "uphold the supremacy of the old country". Rowing was a hugely popular spectator sport and professional scullers stood to earn considerable amounts of money, often engendering bitter and intense rivalries. Trickett, for instance, pocketed £400 in prize money for beating Sadler, although in this case it has to be said there was no animosity between the two. Henley Royal Regatta and the University Boat Race were high spots of the social and sporting calendar, rivalling the Derby, Ascot, Goodwood and the Varsity match at Lord's, and received lavish coverage in the newspapers. The Boat Race of 1877 even finished in a dead heat, for the one and only time in its rich history, "amidst a scene of excitement rarely equalled and never exceeded", according to *The Times*.

At 36, Sadler, already conspicuously grey-haired, was conceding 12 years to his Australian challenger; he was also five inches shorter and almost two stone lighter. The *Sporting Gazette* billed the race as a contest between "the young country's most fitting representative" and "the old champion of the parent stock", but there was little doubt which man the newspaper expected to win.

Sadler was the first to dip his oars when the race got under way. Trickett, though, made the faster start, and drawing on his "immense natural reach", soon opened up an appreciable lead, his six-inch blades slicing impressively through the water. By Hammersmith Bridge, he had stretched his lead to four lengths. Sadler rallied briefly and even clawed back some of the distance between them, but the effort appeared to sap his strength, and, by Barnes Bridge, Trickett had re-established a lead of four lengths and was pulling away. It soon became clear to the crowd that Sadler's race was spent, and he suffered further indignity when he was overtaken by one of the many pleasure boats which had encroached upon his stern like a giant logjam in their haste to gain a better vantage point. In the vessel's attempts to turn around and rejoin the pack it managed to impede the umpire's boat, bringing its progress to an unceremonious halt amidst a cacophony of horns, whistles, trumpets and bells, while almost swamping Sadler in the backwash. Oblivious to the pandemonium taking place in his slipstream, Trickett went on to win by four lengths, in a time of 24 minutes and 35 seconds. In doing so, he became Australia's first world champion sportsman.

Trickett would be greeted by as many as 20,000 people on a triumphal return to Sydney, and even had a ballad composed in his honour. As for Sadler, he went from being "the best of any professional" and showered with approbation by the newspapers before the race, to "evidently not the man he has been … and long past his prime", in the eyes of *The Sportsman*. In emptying several buckets of dirty, cold Thames water over Sadler – the MCC players would receive much the same treatment – the sporting press appeared to demonstrate a complete disregard for what they had written only the day before (behaviour not a world away from today's tabloids). As journalists at that time operated mostly behind a cloak of anonymity – there were no bylines, only the occasional *nom de plume* – the frequency and alacrity with which they changed their minds, often at the drop of a hat, was mind-boggling.

The Sportsman also noted the willingness with which the crowds were prepared to accept and even boisterously cheer Trickett's victory over the hometown favourite, which in Sadler's case – he was born in Putney – could not have been more pertinent. "There seemed to be no symptoms of jealousy on the part of the public ... though the Championship of the World had, for the first time in the records of rowing, been wrested from England," it wrote.

During the summer of 1878 Trickett made it known that he wanted to return to England to defend his title. His message was delivered through the auspices of his fellow Sydneysider and good friend Fred Spofforth and stated that he was willing to row anybody for the championship of the world for a purse of £500. But, for all its financial incentive, the challenge was never taken up.[1]

———

Among the many paeans of praise for the Australian performance at Lord's – naturally, Spofforth received top billing – *The Times*, distinctively, preferred to concentrate on the collective rather than the individual, and singled out their fielding: "The Australians were not very highly thought of after their recent contest with Notts but they showed themselves in a very different light yesterday, for better fielding has rarely occurred." It was a point well made: not only were they infinitely sharper and more athletic in the field – their dazzling one-handed pick-ups would often draw gasps of admiration – the Australians had superior arms, returning the ball on the full to the wicketkeeper or the bowler, whereas English teams tended to throw it in on the hop. It often appeared, too, that they played with an extra man in the field, which in effect they did, having dispensed altogether with a long-stop. They also possessed, in Boyle and Alec Bannerman, two men who could be considered out and out specialists in their positions.

In Boyle's case, he actually invented his – as his contemporary, the South Australian all-rounder George Giffen explained, "Boyley's great nerve not only served him when bowling, but also in the field, for he created a new position, 'short mid-on' or 'silly mid-on', as it is colloquially known, a place where few men have the pluck to stand …" He would often manoeuvre himself as close as five or six yards from the batsmen, "unflinchingly, notwithstanding repeated threats from … Grace and others that he would be killed". The black-bearded Boyle brought off many miraculous catches in that position, and the sight of him there, implacably crouched under the batsman's nose, would have been as much of an eye-opener to English audiences as the spectacle of Blackham standing fearlessly over the stumps to Spofforth. Alec Bannerman, all 5ft 5in of him, was also a cut above anything that the crowds might have been used to, and was considered an exceptional fielder at mid-off. He was, in the words of Horan, "needle-sharp" in his position, "full of dash, clean in picking up, a sure catch, and remarkably accurate in return". The most famous of all stonewallers was, it seems, as electrifying in the field as he was obdurate and immovable at the crease. Horan was no slouch himself either, while it was claimed that more than half the team could throw a cricket ball further than a hundred yards.

Although the newspapers were unanimous in their praise of the Australians, a couple, at least, were at a complete loss to offer a logical explanation for such a crushing victory. "We must wait for another opportunity before we express an opinion on the merits of the new-comers … [as] something must be put down to luck," the *Pall Mall Gazette* wrote, somewhat sniffily. While withering in its condemnation of the MCC players – with the notable exception of Grace, Shaw and Hornby – the newspaper also displayed a marked reluctance to admit that the colonials had been the superior team: "It was apparent that, though several of the Australians bowl well, they have no such master of the craft in their ranks as Alfred Shaw, nor so consummate an all-round player as Mr. W. G. Grace ... Mr. Grace was perhaps a little unlucky in the first innings ... [while] Mr. Hornby alone, in the first innings, seemed to have any idea of how to play the bowling." As for the rest: "They seemed to have conspired together to show the strangers how they could not play ... men who are so nervous or so out of practice that they cannot keep half-volleys out of their wickets have no right to appear in a first-class match." The *London Standard* was equally perplexed: "The only explanation we can offer for the downfall of the MCC is that most of the batsmen were completely beaten by bowling that was strange to them."

Another newspaper, however, had been unable to resist informing its readers that a sizeable portion of Yorkshire grit had in fact rubbed off on the Australians' victory. "The progress of the Australian eleven is dramatic ... Their bowlers have long enjoyed a peculiar sobriquet indicative of their powers ... but Mr Spofforth ... carries off the palm," *Home News* declared, before adding, "Mr Spofforth is a Yorkshireman by extraction. His father was a wicket-keeper as a sportsman, and rode straight and true as the best with the York and Ainsty and other packs." Some newspapers were only too ready in the aftermath of the Australians' success to trumpet the "Englishness" of the team. If they had to be beaten by anyone, it was far more palatable that it be done by a team of Englishmen (and an Irishman), even ones who had come from more than 10,000 miles away to do it: "He [Spofforth] and his colleagues are all of our own flesh and blood, and we welcome their prowess cheerfully as a proof that the old blood is not degenerating in those far off lands." In applauding the Australians, those newspapers, such as *Home News*, were merely taking the opportunity to laud the virtues of the Anglo-Saxon race.

The weekly satirical magazine *Punch* got in on the act by publishing a parody of Lord Byron's popular 'The Destruction of Sennacherib' – a poem based around the biblical version of the

Assyrians' siege of Jerusalem – as its tribute to the colonials' conquest of Lord's:

> *The Australians came down like a wolf on the fold,*
> *The Marylebone cracks for a trifle were bowled;*
> *Our Grace before dinner was very soon done,*
> *And Grace after dinner did not get a run.*

The Australians were suddenly hot property, and everyone it seemed wanted a piece of them: from club secretaries up and down the land – some of whom had been only too eager to bat away any initial requests for a fixture – to MCC. It was amidst the chaotic scenes of Australia's victory at Lord's that the most famous cricket club in the world had sought an immediate rematch, to be played the following day. Doubtless, MCC expected the offer to appeal to the competitive instincts of its opponents, while ensuring a healthy return on gate receipts; a bumper crowd would be guaranteed after their exploits of the first day.[2] However, if MCC also saw it as a chance to repair its honour, and redeem the good name of English cricket into the bargain, it would be disappointed: the Australians, politely but firmly, knocked back the request. The official line was that as "we had many strenuous days of continuous cricket ahead of us we declined to pick up the gauntlet". Certainly, for a team that seemed to be in a state of perpetual motion, the opportunities to relax, let alone indulge in a spot of sightseeing, were few and far between. But perhaps the Australians – having seen the reaction of the crowd and felt the sporting world shift on its axis – had something more important to protect: a new and glittering reputation. After all, it required no great leap of the imagination to predict what the newspapers might have written about them had they accepted the invitation and promptly lost. The *London Standard* reported on 28 May that both parties would, nonetheless, endeavour to arrange a return fixture at a later date in the tour – particularly the Marylebone Cricket Club, for whom the rematch was clearly a matter of some urgency: "The MCC will do all in their power to bring it about, and will if necessary shift their fixtures to suit the Australian convenience."

The strangers had truly arrived.

They basked in the glory for another couple of days, and even found the time to visit the Houses of Parliament, Buckingham Palace and the Tower of London. It was not, they discovered, a treasonable offence to beat MCC inside a day, and they were granted access to even the most sacred of places in the Tower – "a privilege, we were informed, conceded only to distinguished visitors," Conway remarked. This included being locked for "about a minute" in the cell where Guy Fawkes had been imprisoned before his execution. Their guide, a Beefeater with "a loud and sonorous voice seemed happy in the narration of the horrible associations connected with the dungeons and the instruments of torture". Later they drove home through the throng of carriages, horse-back riders and promenaders along the fashionable avenue of Rotten Row, on the south side of Hyde Park, where Londoners came to see and to be seen. Their mood had lightened considerably, and, like any company of young men who find themselves far from home in a strange city, they took more than a passing interest in the "fair occupants" of many of the carriages, which "whirled past us in a continual line". However, the *pièce de résistance*, in the opinion of the cricketers, was "the appearance of splendour of the ladies on horseback" who frequently caught their eye en route to the Horse Shoe. The gimlet-eyed Horan recorded that they must have counted "fully 300" in a distance that he estimated to be no further than the short four-block walk from Spring Street to Elizabeth Street in his home city of Melbourne. That evening they returned to Lord's where they were entertained at a banquet hosted by the Marylebone Cricket Club. "A very pleasant evening was spent among the best gentleman cricketers of the day", which included among others Hornby, Webbe, Ridley and Booth from the beaten MCC eleven, but not, it seems, W. G. Grace.

On Wednesday, 29 May, with the praises of the city still ringing in their ears, they boarded the 12.30pm train from King's

Cross – the hub of the Great Northern Railway – for Huddersfield, and the start of their third match, against Yorkshire, the following day. The journey would take five hours, but as so much of their travelling was done at night they could content themselves with the rare luxury of watching some of the most spectacular countryside in England from their saloon car windows. London may have been connected to Huddersfield by almost 200 miles of modern, smooth track – the "grass-green" liveried locomotives of the Great Northern Railway were even said to be the fastest and most reliable in the world – but, as the Eleven would soon discover, they might have been heading towards another country.

Seven

29 May–5 June 1878

"The wickets could not be seen from the pavilion"

The crowds were out in force to welcome the Australians to Yorkshire. The platform at Huddersfield station was filled to overflowing with an estimated one thousand, all eager to see the men who had conquered MCC in a day. The numbers would have been far greater, the Eleven learned, but for the fact that they had been expected from London on an earlier train. It was tangible proof of their soaring popularity and celebrity; the local newspapers were full of them. Quite apart from anything else, the triumph at Lord's had assured the financial success of the tour. The crowds were boisterous but friendly, the Eleven noted: "We were welcomed with salvoes of cheers and looked upon almost as heroes." And none more so than Spofforth, who quickly found himself the focus of all attention.

The fast bowler was even believed to be descended from nobility, and claimed he could trace his Yorkshire lineage all the way back to the Battle of Hastings: "My father came from a very old Yorkshire family, who fought for their country in 1066, and suffered defeat at the hands of William the Conqueror." His father, Edward, had been born in Howden, a small market town in the East Riding of Yorkshire, in 1805. He migrated to Western Australia some 30 years later, where he became, in the words of the *Leeds Mercury*, "a daring explorer" – a tradition for adventure that was being maintained by his son, Frederick Robert Spofforth.

The Eleven were escorted to the George Hotel by the crowd, which included several members of the Yorkshire Cricket Club. Spofforth was the pied piper, surrounded by a swarm of children who pulled on his coat-tails and trotted eagerly at his heels. The

George, where they would spend the next three nights, was a magnificent four-storey building with an Italianate façade, just a short stroll from the railway station. The hotel would celebrate another famous sporting occasion 17 years later, when 21 northern rugby clubs convened there on the night of 29 August to announce the formation of the Northern Rugby Football Union, and their resignation from the Rugby Football Union. The great schism would lead to the formation of the Rugby Football League and, ultimately, the birth of rugby league.

The third match of Australia's tour of England got under way before another sizeable crowd – there would be as many as 5,000 by stumps – and, finally, some warm sun. "Beautifully situated" at the foot of the tumbling hills which surround Huddersfield, the St John's ground made for a spectacular setting with its cream tents and fluttering flags. There had been a distinct spring in the step of the Australians when they commenced their usual half an hour's practice before the start of play. They did not just want to beat Yorkshire, they wanted to beat them in style. The reason could be traced back to Melbourne a year earlier, when Lillywhite's XI lost the first combination match by 45 runs. Several of the five Yorkshiremen who played in that contest – Tom Emmett, George Ulyett, Allen Hill, Tom Armitage and Andrew Greenwood – had not endeared themselves to the colonials, blaming their defeat on a "surfeit of champagne, beef and Australian hospitality". The slight had not been forgotten. "They shall have no such excuses in their native dales," Horan wrote. "Nor will they be able to claim that they are unused to the wicket conditions, as they did in Australia."

The Yorkshire team were a rough and ready lot; in truth, more rough than ready. They were in good form, having just beaten Derbyshire by five wickets in the mud at Bramall Lane. As their many followers knew, however, that would count for little. They were exasperatingly inconsistent, as befitted the hard-living, hard-drinking roisterers they were, as likely to pull off an outrageous victory as they were to slip to an ignominious defeat. Nowhere perhaps was this more vividly illustrated than in their fielding, where they would routinely spill the easy catches – prompting one of Tom Emmett's many witticisms, "It's an epidemic, but it's not catching" – while miraculously holding on to the impossible ones. They did not, however, lack for brilliant or talented individuals, and Emmett and George "Happy Jack" Ulyett were as good (on their day) as any in the land. Emmett was one of the game's true characters: a popular professional captain, inexhaustibly good-humoured and partial to a drink or two. A fast left-arm bowler, with what has been described as "a near round-arm action", he mixed wayward deliveries – his propensity for wides was legendary – with unplayable ones. His self-styled "sostenutor", which pitched on leg stump and darted away to clip the off stump, was a weapon to be both feared and marvelled at. Ulyett, at 26, ten years younger than Emmett, was the best batsman in the team and another with an irrepressible sense of humour. An audacious strokemaker, he would, in the estimation of *Wisden*, have been worth his place for his lively round-arm bowling and fielding alone. Described by Lord Harris as a "great, hearty, rosy Yorkshireman", it was his batting in the return combination match at Melbourne, when he top-scored in both innings, which had swung the match in England's favour.

The turf was still soggy when Gregory and Emmett walked out to spin the coin at 12.30, and a broken drain had not improved matters by flooding much of the enclosure. Gregory won the toss and, "somewhat strangely" in the opinion of his team, put Yorkshire in to bat. The decision quickly paid off. Boyle tempted Ulyett into an extravagant drive to have him smartly caught at cover-point by Garrett for one, and Horan effected the run-out of the next batsman, Benjamin Lister, without addition to the score. It was a double blow from which the Yorkshire innings never recovered, and they were reduced to 46 for nine in short order by Spofforth and Boyle, who simply carried on from where they had left off at Lord's.

The Yorkshire crowd were far more zealous in support of the home team than anything the Australians had experienced thus far, refusing to greet the fall of each wicket with the same abandon as the spectators at Nottingham and Lord's. They were not averse to expressing their opinions either, and their surprise at the fact that the Australians spoke the mother tongue, or were no different in appearance from themselves, was a constant source of chatter. They reserved their biggest cheer of the day for Allen Hill, who took the long handle to Boyle to strike him high into the grandstand. But Spofforth reduced them to silence a few balls later, scattering Hill's stumps when he attempted to repeat the shot. The last-wicket pair added 26 before Boyle ended the innings by bowling the middle-order batsman Ephraim Lockwood, off his pads, to pick up his fifth wicket, with the score on 72. Boyle would claim that he never bowled to a more fluent timer of the ball than Lockwood: "His style is not at all of the dashing order … But what surprised me most was his timing; he is, without doubt, the best timer of the ball I have seen, bar none." One of the most gifted batsmen of his generation, Lockwood was invited to tour Australia on more than one occasion but, having no desire to leave his native dales, always "resolutely declined".

Emmett improved the mood of the crowd by removing Midwinter with only five runs on the board. But they resumed their stony silence when Charles Bannerman pulled a ball from Lockwood with such ferocity that it sailed clean out of the ground, bounced across a street and fetched up in a neighbouring garden. Conway reported that it did not "elicit any applause from the Yorkshiremen". Bannerman's pyrotechnics were ended by Tom Armitage, who bowled him with the score on 33. The opening batsman would have had good cause to remember Armitage from the first combination match in Melbourne: the Yorkshireman dropped him at mid-on from the simplest of chances early in his innings; he went on to make 165. Armitage's underarm bowling at Melbourne had been equally unforgettable, when an eccentric concoction of donkey drops and lobs – with the occasional grubber thrown in – was launched at such a height that they would have needed a "clothes-prop to reach them". He had since reinvented himself as a round-arm bowler of gentle medium-pace, and it was this perhaps more than anything that took Bannerman by surprise, as he simply missed a straight one. Horan departed just before the close, bowled by one of Hill's fast off-cutters, by which time Yorkshire's first-innings total had been overhauled.

The Australians added only another 31 runs to their overnight score before they were bowled out for 118 before lunch on the second day; Gregory's wretched run of form continued when he collected his fourth successive duck. Ulyett and Lockwood briefly threatened to make a fight of it at the start of Yorkshire's second innings, but when the former holed out to Boyle off Garrett, and Lockwood followed soon after to Spofforth, the county collapsed for 73, leaving Australia needing only 28 to win. They soon lost Midwinter and Charles Bannerman in pursuit of the target before heavy rain caused play to be abandoned for the day at 5.45. The rain, for once, could not have been more timely. The thick evening smoke from the chimney pots, which had started to billow across the pitch from the surrounding houses, quickly enveloped the ground in a blanket of choking smog. It soon became so dark, according to one reporter, that "the wickets could not be seen from the pavilion". The result, which had appeared a mere formality, was suddenly thrown into some confusion and doubt, and "it looked quite possible in such bad light for the Australians to fail in obtaining the required number of runs". The arrival of the rain drove the players from the field, and the two not-out batsmen, Horan and Alec Bannerman, were relieved to return to the pavilion with their wickets intact. The Australians seemed unsure whether the incident was an occupational hazard of cricket in the north, or an ingenious ploy by the townsfolk of Huddersfield to turn the tables on them. However, having already safely negotiated mud, rain and near gale-force winds on their tour, they must have felt as though they had now seen it all.

They attended another grand dinner that evening, held by the Huddersfield Cricket and Athletic Club, at the George Hotel. As gratifying as these functions may have been, it seems they were already trying the patience of Harry Boyle, for one – if he had any for them in the first place. He wrote home to his long-suffering brother, "We had another confounded dinner tonight, making the fourth in eight days." The following morning the Australians knocked off the remaining runs without any further interruptions to record victory by the satisfying margin of six wickets. The Yorkshire players "took their defeat with very bad grace", one newspaper reported, "but many of the onlookers gradually warmed towards the visitors and praised them". The Australians' decision to play a single-wicket competition with the county during the afternoon "to keep the Saturday crowd of 5,000 happy" would not have been without influence in that regard. They won that game, too.

Another huge crowd crammed into Huddersfield station later in the evening – "the cheering was deafening," Horan wrote – to see them off on the 9.10pm train to London. Word had quickly passed down the line, and at the numerous stops along the way hundreds of people congregated on the platform, despite the lateness of the hour, to catch a glimpse of them. One reporter recorded that "the windows to the saloon carriage set apart for their use were darkened by the faces pressed against it". Many years later, Horan could still recall how "at wayside stations in distant counties little country lads – and old ones too – would flatten their noses against the carriage windows, and ask 'which be demon'?" Within days the names of Spofforth, Boyle, Charles Bannerman and Jack Blackham, among others, would become common currency.

The Australians arrived at a cavernous, echoing King's Cross in the early hours of the morning of Sunday, 2 June, and made straight for the Horse Shoe Hotel, where some time before 4am they tumbled into their beds, weary but elated. Their fourth match, against Surrey, would start the following day.

———

It is unlikely that such scenes had been witnessed before at a first-class match in England, and certainly not at one of its "classical grounds", as the *Daily Telegraph* referred to The Oval. Crowds had started streaming in long before the start of play; at one o'clock all the seats in the new stand next to the pavilion were occupied, while the hordes still waiting to get into the ground seemed to stretch for miles in every direction through the narrow streets. By mid-afternoon, the crush was so great at the turnstiles, and the desire to see the Australians so overwhelming, that the crowds simply took matters into their own hands, pouring through the carriage gates or trampling over the wooden fencing to gain access. At least half of the estimated 20,000 spectators who were present that Monday got in without paying a penny. That number might have been even greater but for the ever-resourceful Jack Conway, who, aided and abetted by Harry Boyle, manned the barricades, filling his top hat to the brim with entrance money. "Many a shilling and sometimes even a half-crown went into the hat," Conway declared.

"The excellent form shown by the colonial cricketers since their first reverse at the hands of the Nottingham Eleven ought to have prepared the committee of the Surrey Club for a large attendance at the commencement of this match," *The Sportsman* commented. There were only four or five policemen in attendance, it was reported, and even fewer gatemen. However, the newspaper added, "Such a scene as that presented yesterday could never have been foreseen." The Australians were informed that a bigger crowd had not been seen at the ground, while *Sporting Life* went even further: "On Monday last, at the Oval, there was the largest gathering of spectators that we ever saw assembled to witness a cricket match."[1]

The police presence was entirely inadequate for dealing with the crowds, either at the unguarded entrances where they surged through unopposed in a mass stampede, or for preventing their encroachment in vast numbers on to the pitch during play. "When the second innings of our opponents commenced, the circumference of the playing area had been reduced from something over 500 yards to 250," Horan recorded, "so that the slightest tap to cover or hit to leg would travel to the onlookers for four: a manifest disadvantage to us, if our bowling had been loose." The good-humoured efforts of the Australian fielders to persuade the crowds to move back met with little success. "We were chaffed unmercifully," Horan continued. "I can say, however, that I never saw a more contented and jocular company; the crushing and jostling was in perfectly good faith and not the slightest incident took place to mar the harmony of the day's proceedings." The *Daily Telegraph* also praised the restraint and geniality of what it called "the disordered order of these thousands of sightseers", but pleaded with the Surrey club to establish a boundary rope "for the sake of cricket".

The Surrey captain, George Strachan, had elected to bat first after winning the toss on the brightest day the Australians had experienced so far; "the sun shone with a pleasant warmth," Horan noted. Three of the Surrey team – James Southerton, Harry Jupp and Ted Pooley – were well known to the Eleven. The heavily whiskered Southerton had toured Australia twice, first with Grace's 1873–4 party and then Lillywhite's two years later. An artful slow bowler with a pronounced off-break, Southerton was popular with the Australians, who valued him for his fair-mindedness and good sportsmanship. He was also the convivial landlord of the Cricketers on Mitcham Green. Jupp, another senior member of Lillywhite's team, was a steady batsman who had earned the sobriquet "the Young Stonewaller" for his studied back-foot play and assiduous concentration. He may be best remembered, though, for the occasion when he calmly replaced the bails after being bowled first ball in a local match; when the umpire reminded him that he was out, he replied, "Not at Dorking I ain't". Pooley would have been England's first Test wicketkeeper had he not been languishing behind the bars of a New Zealand jail for his part in a betting scam. Although Pooley was subsequently found not guilty, his career would always be associated with allegations of heavy gambling, alcohol and match-throwing.[2] Sadly, he would end his days in the workhouse. He was, nevertheless, a highly accomplished stumper, who often stood up to the faster bowlers and formed a double act of great renown with Southerton, whom he read with uncanny skill. The glove work of Pooley and Blackham would set new standards of excellence during the match at The Oval, where Blackham's one-handed takes off Spofforth vied with Pooley's ability to remove the bails in a flash.

Surrey made a solid start, but after Boyle dismissed the Cambridge University batsman A. P. Lucas with the score on 21 and Spofforth relieved Allan from the pavilion end, wickets soon tumbled. "They could do nothing with Spofforth," the *Daily Telegraph* wrote. "It was the old story of Lord's over again." Bowling with great penetration and guilefully varying his pace – "he pretended to work himself up to a fury and a mild little ball followed" – Spofforth proved far too inventive for most of the batsmen. Indeed, the Australians went as far as to suggest that several were afraid of him. The ball that bowled Jupp, for instance, was so quick that it sent his off-stump cartwheeling halfway towards long-stop. Only the amateur batsman John Shuter – who fell leg-before to Spofforth for 39 – and Pooley batted with any conviction out of a total of 107. In fact, the faster Spofforth bowled, the more Pooley appeared to relish the challenge, twice pulling him through square leg and then cover-driving him to the boundary in exhilarating fashion, before he was last man out, bowled by Boyle for 29. The 50-year-old Southerton, "the Grand Old Man of English Cricket" pluckily resisted all that Spofforth, Boyle and Allan could throw at him to finish unbeaten on 20. Spofforth's reward for another hard shift – he bowled unchanged for 27 overs – was the superb figures of eight for 52.

There was much interest in how the colonial batsmen would fare on the fastest run-getting surface in England, one that might have been said to more closely resemble an Australian track than any in the land. Although the ground was still soft in parts after the recent rain, the Eleven had been impressed by the speed with which the ball travelled to the boundary, particularly when Pooley was taking up the cudgels against Spofforth. However, they soon lost Charles Bannerman for a single, to Ted Barratt, and Horan, who was expertly stumped by Pooley off the same bowler for 16. A slow left-armer who curled the ball away from the bat, much in the vein of James Lillywhite, Barratt's tactics were to stack the off side with eight fielders and simply wait for the batsman to make a mistake. Midwinter, whose presence in the Eleven now seemed almost taken for granted, alone succeeded in getting to grips with him in an innings of 32; one newspaper described him as being "as steady as a church" – an intriguing simile for the burly all-rounder. Spofforth's attempts to ruffle the bowler's tactics included playing a "left-handed stroke" – what we would call a switch-hit today – sending the ball past a "bemused" Pooley to the boundary, and "occasioning much laughter and applause". Spofforth proved that it was not just as a bowler he was light years ahead of his time. Barratt had the last word, though, drawing him down the pitch for Pooley to complete another stumping. The left-armer finished with eight for 58 from 46.2 overs, but not before Gregory – at the fifth time of asking, and three weeks since disembarking in Liverpool – scored his first runs in England, helping Australia to a first-innings lead of three. Surrey closed on seven for one when stumps were drawn at seven o'clock.

It rained heavily that night and again first thing, making the top surface of the turf sticky when Surrey resumed their second innings at 12.30. The weather was "unsettled and fickle", the *Daily Telegraph* reported, with "thunder-clouds hovering over the gasometers that brooded upon the Kennington Oval". Another massive crowd was in place – well shepherded by a detachment of police – to see Surrey bowled out for a disappointing 80. Midwinter claimed the bowling honours this time with four for 14, while Spofforth completed another marathon spell of 39 overs (he bowled 66 in all), taking three for 42 to record match figures of 11 for 94. He was also hit clean out of the ground by the amateur batsman William Game for a huge six – the ball disappearing over the parapet walls and chimney pots of Kennington. The bowler exacted his revenge, as he invariably did, by ripping out Game's stumps with a yorker a few balls later, removing his cap in a gesture of menacing intent before administering the kill.

Australia needed 78 for victory, but the crowd's interest did not waver for a second; even the busy streets seemed to come to a standstill. "The narrow roadway between the Oval houses and the virtually unenclosed cricket ground is about the idlest place in the world on these great occasions," the *Daily Telegraph* noted. "It is curious to observe how many coal carts, tradesmen's vehicles, omnibuses, and drags of every description find it necessary to call for orders, or to deliver goods by way of the Oval on a match day." The goods were rarely delivered, the reporter pointed out, or orders taken, and the wagons and carts then became "a perambulating grand stand" before they were finally "hustled out of the way by business-like hansom cabs and carriages".

Barratt and Southerton soon had their hands on the ball, but Charles Bannerman – with one eye on the weather – quickly took the game away from Surrey with a series of punishing blows, one of which landed several rows back in the pavilion, while another went "whizzing over the crowd by the racquet courts". The job was all but done when Bannerman was caught at cover-point for 31 with the score on 72, leaving Tom Garrett to complete victory by five wickets – and Australia's third win on the trot – on the stroke of 5.30.

The match having ended early, the Australians attended the Derby the following day, riding in a yellow coach and four in the mass cavalcade from London to Epsom Downs, when the whole of the city seemed to be on the move. They stopped en route for a "friendly glass" with James Southerton at the Cricketers on Mitcham Green and bought pea-shooters from hawkers along the way, "conducting a 'war' with the other coaches". The weather was miserable, though, and the crowds were well down on previous years. The Australians strolled among the shooting galleries and coconut shies, the show tents and merry-go-rounds, happily rubbing shoulders with the great Epsom mob. "It was a grand sight going along the road to the Derby and on the course,"

Horan wrote. "But the race itself was a disappointing experience, since we were only able to see the running of the race for a distance of six to seven hundred yards. Most of us were of the opinion that we would sooner have witnessed the Melbourne Cup." Harry Boyle even managed to sound more curmudgeonly than usual in his assessment of events: "It was a great sight to see the people, but I would never go again."[3]

It is not known whether the Eleven enjoyed a flutter or two, but they certainly raised the stakes a few days later by increasing the standard entrance fee to their matches. If the announcement smacked of opportunism – it was seen by some as nothing more than a blatant attempt to cash in on their fame and wring more profit out of the tour – they were not particularly apologetic: "The size of the gates made us reconsider the sixpence admission charge we had previously asked for. Henceforth we shall ask for a shilling wherever we go." The decision, if nothing else, underlined the Australians' ambivalence towards their amateur station. To the overworked and underpaid professional cricketer, it was yet another example of the hypocrisy of a system that allowed so-called amateurs to bend the rules and line their pockets at will. The Australians would argue that they were merely safeguarding their investment, and no more. Nevertheless, another turning point in the tour had been reached.

Eight
5–18 June 1878

"The unwashed crowds were gazed at in awe and horror"

The Australians endured a rough ride back to Yorkshire after their day at the races. Their compartment on the train that left King's Cross at midnight for Huddersfield was so cramped that not one of them managed to sleep during the entire journey. They were tired and cold as it was, after returning from Epsom by coach and catching the 10.30pm connection from Richmond into the city. Their hearts must have sunk when they saw the accommodation set aside for them by the rail company. It had clearly not been designed for the likes of Spofforth, who might as well have wedged his 6ft 3in frame into a contortionist's box. As none of the carriages were built with corridors at that time, they were quite literally confined to their compartment. Such was the lack of space on this occasion that some of them even attempted to sleep on the floor. Generally, however, the standard and efficiency of the rail companies was much praised by the Eleven, and this was a rare blot on their record. They finally reached Huddersfield at seven o'clock the next morning, where they stumbled on to the platform, bleary-eyed and exhausted. After resting for a couple of hours at the George Hotel – their northern headquarters – they were back on the move again, making the three-mile trip by road to Elland for the start of their fifth match, against a local eighteen, at 12.30 that afternoon.

This was the start of a long, gruelling haul for the Australians, who would play 20 matches against the odds in all during their tour of the British Isles, travelling from one end of the country to the other, mostly through the night, to fulfil fixtures in such far-flung cricketing outposts as Glasgow, Swansea, Burnley,

Scarborough and Hastings. The demands of the schedule were so helter-skelter that it was not unusual for them to finish a match in Yorkshire and be back in London or on the south coast the following morning for the start of the next. *Wisden* referred to it as "railing it by night and match-playing by day". Jack Conway would later admit that they took on too many matches against the odds, but having accepted much of the tour itinerary before they arrived in England, they had little choice but to honour it.[1] For Tom Horan, the travel was a particularly onerous experience: not only did he have to perform his prime role as one of the team's top batsmen, but he was also expected to meet his rigorous deadlines as the reporter "One of Them", while diligently maintaining a diary of the tour. The newly installed telegraph line, or "the imperial connection" as it was known, meant that Horan's reports could be read back in Australia within a few hours of them being written. Conway, among his many duties, was also contributing regular newspaper articles, or his letters as he liked to call them. There was much burning of the midnight oil. Hardly surprising, either, that on one occasion Frank Allan had to be roused from a deep sleep before going in to bat. The matches, against teams of eighteen or twenty-two, were intended to be nothing more than light-hearted exhibition games. In fact, they were anything but.

In most cases the reputation of the Australians preceded them, and they would take the field to find that the locals had recruited a fistful of hardened professionals. These hired guns included such well-known names as Tom Emmett, Allen Hill, Harry Jupp, and three future England Test players, Lancashire's Dick Barlow and Ted Peate and Billy Bates of Yorkshire. Another, Arnold Rylott, a fast left-arm bowler from Leicestershire, turned out against them so many times – eight in all – that he might have been on his own personal crusade. Surrey's Ted Barratt put in six appearances. So familiar did these two become that it was almost a surprise to the Australians to arrive at a ground and discover that neither one nor the other was playing. One club, Yeadon and District, fielded only one local in its encounter with the Australians, but conjured up 17 professionals as though pulling rabbits out of a hat. But it was not just the professionals who were in demand: Fred Grace, W. R. Gilbert (on four occasions), Lord Harris and the Hon. Ivo Bligh were as eager as any man to put one over the colonials.

The Australians were still jaded after their long, sleepless journey from the night before, but enjoyed a bracing ride to Elland, where they were much charmed by the countryside and the town's narrow, winding streets. So narrow, Horan wrote, "that we could almost shake hands with the many people who crowded the footpaths to have a peep at us". The ground was situated in an elevated position above the town and enclosed by a 6ft stone wall. The first thing they had to contend with after being put into bat (bizarrely, Gregory found himself accompanied by three of the opposition at the toss) was a Sheffield chucker by the name of E. Osborne, and a Derbyshire professional, George Hay, who bowled "very quick and straight". The match, though, will be remembered purely for the performance of Boyle who, after Australia had been dismissed for 90, routed Elland for 29, to claim the remarkable figures of 11 for 12 in 18 overs. These were not easy pickings either, as Elland were reinforced by the Yorkshire batsmen Benjamin Lister and Edward Lumb and Derbyshire's Thomas Foster. At one stage Boyle captured seven wickets in eight balls – a feat that was punctuated by shouts of "send 'em in two at a time" and "send the whole lot in at once" from a noisy crowd of 3,000. Frank Allan remarked that if three wickets in three balls was deserving of a hat, Boyle's achievement was worthy of a brand new suit.

Spofforth went on another wrecking spree in Elland's second innings, bagging ten wickets and scattering the stumps eight times to secure victory by 80 runs. In a game dominated by bowlers, Osborne completed match figures of 12 for 78, although his throwing went completely unchecked by the umpires. Horan claimed that he would have been no-balled in Australia, but added pointedly, "In England any style of delivery appears to be allowed without question." On their way back to Huddersfield the Australians were caught in a downpour and were thoroughly disgruntled by the time they reached the George Hotel. It was still raining the following day when they travelled the eight miles by coach to Batley for a game against a local eighteen starting on Monday, 10 June. However, they arrived to find there was room for only seven men at the Station Hotel where they were booked, and the rest had to set off in the rain in search of lodgings elsewhere in town. Horan recorded that the food and accommodation during the three nights they spent in Batley were the worst they encountered on tour: "Midwinter stated that he could get a better and more plentiful supply of food in any shanty in the wilds of Northern Australia."

The old rumours were still doing the rounds, too, and during his stay at the Station Hotel Charles Bannerman was stopped by an old man who asked him whether he had seen "the chaps". "What chaps?" Bannerman asked. "The cricketers, of course," the old man replied. "We are the cricketers," Bannerman told him. The old man looked him up and down quizzically: "I mean *the cricketers* – the black fellows."

The pitch did nothing to alter the Eleven's opinion of Batley. It was little better than a quagmire. There was a pronounced tilt, too, so that long leg was "half-hidden from cover-point". The ground was situated at the bottom of a "gently sloping hill" and overlooked by the ruined battlements of Howley Hall, a Tudor mansion that had come under siege from Royalist troops during the Civil War in 1643. The match started in intermittent rain in front of some 4,000 spectators, who watched from under their umbrellas like an army sheltering from a hail of arrows. Several of the Batley eighteen had failed to show, and, to add to the general air of farce, they were replaced by volunteers from the crowd, who fielded in their "broadcloth" flat caps and working boots. Horan top-scored with 50 out of an Australian total of 160 before becoming one of five victims for Allen Hill, who shouldered the bowling, ploughing through a gargantuan 69 overs. The conditions were so atrocious that bowlers, fielders and even batsmen were spattered from head to foot with mud. The second day was a washout, and although there was some play on the third day – Batley "floundered their way" to 59 for ten on a new wicket; the old one was by now a swamp – the rain returned (mercifully, in the view of the Eleven) to have the final say.

Leaving Batley behind they continued their "procession around England", catching the 9pm train from Huddersfield to Manchester and making the one and a half hour journey across the Pennines into Lancashire. There, they were surprised to find that two of their fellow lodgers at the Waterloo Hotel were Fred Grace and W. R. Gilbert, and even more surprised to learn that they had been recruited to play for Longsight and District against them the following day. On another sodden wicket the Australians were hustled out for 67 – Gilbert doing his bit with four for 40 – a total that might have been even more embarrassing but for Charles Bannerman's 31. However, they fared no better in the second innings, losing their last six wickets for only ten runs to be bowled out for an identical score, leaving the eighteen requiring 72 to pull off a notable victory.

At 47 for 12, Longsight appeared to have missed their opportunity. But Fred Grace, hitting the ball with great power and precision, proceeded to turn the game; like his brothers he enjoyed nothing better than a good scrap, particularly if it was against the Australians. Gregory kept Spofforth going from one end in the belief that he could summon one last thunderbolt, but the exertions of bowling on dead wickets (he chalked up 62 overs in this match alone) had taken their toll. It was Midwinter who eventually whistled one past Grace's bat for 42, with the scores tied and the job still not quite done. The locals held their nerve, and with a crowd of more than 8,000 in full voice and in rapidly fading light, the Manchester club squeezed home with two wickets to spare.

There was no doubt that Grace made the most of the fortune that came his way. He was dropped by Murdoch at long-on when he had made 11 and received the benefit of the doubt with two leg-before decisions, both off the bowling of Midwinter and both "palpably wrong" in the eyes of the Australians. "It appears that some umpires in England are frightened to give certain batsmen out," Horan observed. The same umpire also incorrectly awarded a six when one of Grace's blows failed to clear the ground but struck an outer wall instead.[2] For Spofforth, who returned match figures of 13 for 71 and had already accumulated 60 wickets from six games (he was spared the mudbath at Batley), defeat left a particularly sour taste. There were grumbles, too, over the appearance of assorted mercenaries – especially the West Countrymen Grace and Gilbert – in teams with which "they have no association", and in matches for which, in the case of the amateurs, they were handsomely recompensed.

Hard-headed cricketers that they were, however, the Australians readily accepted that they should still have won the contest and were annoyed with themselves for not having done so when they had the chance. Although, if the batting was "most disappointing" (just five of the Eleven managed to record double figures), it was only to be expected. As Horan pointed out, "In our present exhausted state I wonder that we can bat at all. We are travelling most of the night and when we go on to the ground we cannot get a good sight of the ball at all." There was, however, a consolation: as many as 26,000 Mancunians happily parted with their shillings to watch the match over its three days' duration, guaranteeing the Australians a healthy profit.

Another interminable night loomed ahead of them when they boarded the 9.30pm train for London and their next appointment with W. G. Grace, in a game against the Gentlemen of England at Prince's Ground in Chelsea, starting on Monday, 17 June. They arrived at the Horse Shoe Hotel tired out in the early hours of Sunday morning, and, after snatching a few hours' sleep, were on their travels again, catching a train to Hampton Wick and a steam launch down the Thames to Windsor, where they were guests of honour at a picnic. The caterers were Melbourne's Spiers and Pond, the sponsors of the first England tour to Australia in 1861–2, and now the proud owners of the glittering Criterion Restaurant in Piccadilly. There was also time for a peep at Windsor Castle and the playing fields of Eton. On the launch back to Hampton Wick they recognised the famous sculler Joseph Sadler out on the water; the former world champion saluted the Australians as they passed by and they saluted back, before leaving him in their wake, just as Ned Trickett had done two years earlier.

———

A dispute between the Australians and Grace during and after the match against the Gentlemen of England at Prince's set the tone for much that was to follow in the next three months of the tour. As W. G., Fred Grace and Gilbert each received a sum of £20 to appear for the Gentlemen (there were claims that an additional £120 was also paid to them from the gate receipts), Jack Conway felt strongly enough to raise the matter with the owners of the ground, the Prince brothers. The Australians insisted, somewhat naively given their own position, that since the Graces and Gilbert were each paid to play, they should be "regarded as professionals and therefore ineligible to participate". The protest risked stirring up a hornets' nest, particularly in light of the history between Grace and Conway. The Princes, however, informed Conway that the Gloucestershire amateurs were "invariably paid for their services" and would hear no more of it.[3] W. G., still bristling after the Australians' triumph at Lord's and itching for revenge, now had another slight to add to his tally.

There was more overcrowding before the start of play. Those who could not find anywhere to sit, or did not wish to join the vast ring which had already formed around the boundary, clambered up trees in search of a vantage point, or scaled the roof of the press box, which, at one point during the afternoon, was in "imminent danger of collapse", according to one reporter. Others mounted a raid on the unoccupied chairs in the reserved sections and special enclosures, which they carried off like looters and then proceeded to stand on, much to the fury of those behind them. "The unwashed crowds were gazed at in awe and horror," *Lillywhite's Companion* wrote, "not only by its members and ordinary frequenters, but by the officials ..." Many visitors who had paid half a crown, or five shillings for a reserved seat, left the ground without seeing a ball bowled, after being told by police that there was nothing they could do for fear of causing a riot. For the second time in a matter of days a London cricket ground was in a state of siege. "The experience of the Oval had apparently had little effect on the management at Prince's, as the arrangements in every way were as bad as they could possibly have been," *The Sportsman* reported. *Bell's Life* was even more vociferous: "Visitors to Prince's must have been truly astonished and disgusted. Advertisements had been issued stating that every arrangement would be made for the accommodation of the thousands that were expected ... and had the numbers anticipated put in an appearance, goodness knows what would have been the result."

It is more than likely that those numbers would have been realised, but for the start of Ascot week. The only measures taken by management in case of such an eventuality were to construct a temporary grandstand, capable of holding a few hundred people, and to curtail the playing area to a margin of 65 yards from either wicket, which, as it had done at The Oval, obscured the view of hundreds of spectators and exacerbated the overcrowding.

London was still abuzz with talk of the Australian cricketers, and the public's fascination for them had reached "fever heat", as one newspaper put it. The Eleven would be struck during the match by the amount of spectators who knew them by sight or reputation; "they were as familiar with our details as if we were members of the Marylebone or Surrey clubs". When they arrived at 11.30, the ground was creaking under the weight of a crowd of at least 8,000, and the scenes were nothing short of bedlam. There was already a compact ring of spectators, Horan noted, and by four o'clock they were standing 20 deep all around. The tell-tale would register that 14,000 paid a shilling a head or more to watch the first day's play. Another thousand members were also present, holding their tea parties beneath an avenue of leafy elms and umbrella tents by the club walls, where they took little notice of the cricket. "But apart from that avenue, the rest of the audience at Prince's is of the very rowdiest description," Horan recorded.

The Sloane Square club was opened by James and George Prince in 1850 and had a reputation for attracting high society and select exclusivity. Among its many amusements, other than a cricket pitch, were a croquet lawn, racquet courts, a fashionable skating rink, which was open all year round, a bandstand and even a Turkish bath. Although Middlesex played there for five years before moving to Lord's in 1876, and the ground hosted occasional matches between the North and the South, and the Gentlemen and the Players, cricket was deemed a "secondary notion, annexed to rackets and rinking". The Princes were happy to accommodate cricket but had no great love or understanding of it. The "excellent bands" played without let-up during matches, and "when a ball was hit into the bandstand, one of the brothers went out and asked the batsman to be more careful in future".

The Australians felt uncomfortable in this "idle fashion lounge" and considered it entirely out of keeping for a fixture of such importance; with the possible exception of MCC, they would meet few stronger batting sides on tour. "All true cricket spirit as we understand it is absent from the ground. There is no pavilion, which is normally the centre of cricketing activity, and cricket seems to be an excuse for congregations," Horan wrote disapprovingly. "The ladies come to sip coffee, eat fruit, engage in flirting and conversation and languidly patronize cricket." Horan may have found runs hard to come by in this match (he was not the only Australian to suffer in that regard), his batting instincts blunted by tiredness and travel, but his pen had surely never been sharper: Prince's "would sooner welcome a duchess than the finest cricketer who ever hit a sixer to leg … But it does not provide the hospitality of a pavilion and compels cricketers to force their way through silks and satins and over a net dividing the sanctity of the aristocracy from the unhallowed truck of the outer world."

Gregory won the toss on another cold, damp day and elected to bat first on a wicket which, despite having been protected overnight by a tarpaulin, was "dead and wet". W. G. Grace, with his brisk round-arm, and the 19-year-old all-rounder

A. G. Steel, who was in his first year at Cambridge University, opened the bowling for the Gentlemen. The Australians had heard much about Steel, who bowled leg-breaks and scored his runs in rapid style, and were intrigued to see whether he lived up to his reputation as the most brilliant young cricketer in England. It has been said of Steel that, even before he left Marlborough, where he played for four years for the school's first XI, he was worth his place in an England XI. He included an off-break among his box of tricks and a cleverly disguised quicker ball – leg-break bowling was considered something of a phenomenon at that time – and as an all-rounder would soon be ranked second only to Grace. Steel was in such a molten streak of form that by the end of the season he would top the national bowling averages with 164 wickets at 9.43 apiece.

It was Grace, though, who made the early incisions. First, he cunningly baited a trap for Midwinter, which involved his elder brother E. M. Grace (there was no better fielder at point in England), stealing a few yards on the batsman as W. G. delivered. Midwinter was pinned on to his stumps and forced to play back and E. M. threw himself full length to pluck the ball inches from the turf. W. G. then clean-bowled Horan, bringing one back sharply from leg, with the score on 32. However, Steel did not have to wait long before making his mark on the Australians, sending back Murdoch, Alec Bannerman, whom he caught and bowled, and Allan in the space of two overs. Only Charles Bannerman batted with any authority, once cutting Grace so hard to the boundary that the ball rattled against the skating rink. It took a stunning one-handed catch by the Surrey captain, George Strachan, off the devious underarm lobs of E. M. Grace to remove him. Australian wickets tumbled with the same alarming regularity as they had at Longsight, and by four o'clock, in between frequent stoppages for showers, they were all out for 75. Grace collected four for 25 – in the opinion of *The Sportsman*, he had "never bowled better"– and Steel four for 37.

Grace and Spofforth renewed their rivalry at the start of the Gentlemen's innings, but there was to be no reprise of Lord's where 'the Champion' lasted only four balls. As expected, though, it was an exchange to set the pulses racing. The *Argus* reported that he was missed at the wickets off a "rather easy chance", and was repeatedly knocked about his legs and body by Spofforth, before finding his range. After on-driving Spofforth for a couple to get the telegraph moving, Grace then cracked the fast bowler fiercely through square leg to the boundary, before off-driving him for four more to a volley of thunderous applause. Spofforth, struggling with his line and length, had not bowled so poorly since Nottingham, although the wicket was clearly not to his liking. "He kept pounding the ball into so much black pudding," the *Telegraph* wrote, "but the turf took the 'demon' out of the bowler." Grace and Gilbert had taken their opening partnership to 43 when Boyle, having replaced Spofforth, bowled the former for 25 with a rank full toss, which he attempted to heave through square leg. It was a disappointing end to an innings in which he had shown flashes of his old self.

Boyle captured the next five wickets and completed a hat-trick of Graces in doing so: Fred Grace, whom the Australians considered the luckiest batsman in England after his exploits at Longsight, was caught by Spofforth at mid-on for 11, while E. M. – still a formidable opponent at the age of 36 – edged a ball into Blackham's gloves, having just got off the mark. To complete the full house, Boyle also despatched their cousin, Gilbert, for 20, with the aid of another catch by Blackham. At 85 for six at stumps, the Australians were back in the game. Spofforth, refreshed after a night's sleep, whipped out Steel's leg stump for eight with a yorker shortly after play resumed on the second day, beating the young Lancastrian for speed. But a late flurry of runs from the last-wicket pair, Strachan and the Gloucestershire wicketkeeper Arthur Bush, enabled the Gentlemen to reach a total of 139. This was not the first time the Australians had stumbled in their efforts to take the last wicket, and more often than not it was a case of their opponents exploiting their tiredness. However, in claiming seven for 48 from 35 overs, Boyle registered his fifth haul of five wickets or more for the tour.

Gregory reshuffled the batting order in the second innings, promoting Horan to open with Midwinter, and shoring up the middle order with Alec and Charles Bannerman. But they were soon in trouble, and after Steel had bamboozled both Horan and Charles Bannerman, and Alec Bannerman was foolishly run out with the telegraph showing only 14 runs, the innings swiftly unravelled. Only Midwinter, with a top score of 26, batted with any degree of certainty against Steel before he fell to Grace for the second time in the match, magnificently caught by A. N. Hornby at long-on. So mesmerising was Steel that he picked up the last four wickets at a cost of only one run in three overs, bowling the Australians out for a miserable 63. The leg-spinner claimed seven for 35 and match figures of 11 for 72. The Gentlemen were victorious by an innings and one run and, at a quarter past four with a day to spare, Grace had his revenge. No doubt, he would have taken particular delight in winning his personal duel with Spofforth, whom he also dismissed in both innings.

The Australians were not sorry to leave Prince's and its "uncongenial atmosphere" behind. Successive defeats and the sudden spike in form – even their fielding at times deserted them – were of far more pressing concern. To their credit they did not attempt to make excuses, particularly for their batting, or to disguise the inadequacy of their all-round performance. In fact, they were their own worst critics. Their cricket, Horan admitted, was a "fiasco … eleven novices could scarcely shape worse … it is our fault that the match was over in two days"; nor was it the fault of the conditions or the "dull light" as "we ought to have been pretty used to it by this time …" Several of the newspapers were quick to revise their opinions of them, although one reporter did at least sound a sympathetic note: "Ever since the Australians arrived in this country the seasons have mysteriously changed. When our cricketers went over to Australia they managed matters so carefully that they gained two summers instead of one, but now that the Australians have come to England we are playing cricket instead of football …"

However, the reason for their setback at Prince's was not hard to fathom; as *The Sportsman* had commented before the start of the match, "The team gave the impression, even at this early point of their tour, of wanting a little rest." Perhaps the return to Lord's for their next match, against Middlesex, would revive them.

Nine
19–23 June 1878

"You haven't the ghost of a show against Middlesex"

London crackled with thunderstorms the day after the Australians' defeat to the Gentlemen at Prince's. It was the morning of Billy Midwinter's 27th birthday, and the air was heavy and oppressive; for the first time that summer the mercury started to rise. Within days temperatures of 32°C or more in the shade would be recorded in the metropolis, with the newspapers running stories under headlines such as 'The Tropical Heat'. It was too hot to go to the theatre in London; Gilbert and Sullivan's *HMS Pinafore*, which had opened to five encores at the Opera Comique on 25 May, played to half-empty houses. In Leeds, the rails buckled. It would be a summer of extremes. Nearly 700 miles away at the Congress of Berlin, the flamboyant Benjamin Disraeli was going in to bat for British interests in Europe and to avert the threat of all-out war with Russia. Within weeks he would be the toast of London, his brilliant brinkmanship beneath the gilded ceilings of the Reich Chancellery delivering what he hailed on his return as "peace with honour".

The Australians, meanwhile, had some politics of their own to negotiate before the start of their ninth match of the tour the following morning. Midwinter, an increasingly influential and prominent member of the team, had just made clear his intention to remain with the Eleven for the duration of the tour. His decision would effectively sunder his ties with Gloucestershire, and almost certainly bring the wrath of W. G. Grace down upon him. As he imparted his news to Conway and Gregory, he might have wondered whether the ominous rumble and boom overhead was not a portent of things to come.

On the morning of Thursday, 20 June, W. E. Midwinter's name appeared on two separate team-sheets: he was selected by Gloucestershire to meet Surrey in their opening County Championship match at The Oval (Gloucestershire were the reigning champions), and in the Australian XI to play Middlesex. For all his powers of reinvention, Midwinter had not yet managed the trick of being in two places at the same time. However, having pledged his loyalty to the tourists, he had no desire to travel to The Oval and attempt to brazen it out with Grace in person. Instead, Conway – accompanied by Boyle and Gregory, riding shotgun – set off in a cab from Lord's to "acquaint W. G. with Mid's decision".

A furious exchange between Grace and Conway ensued during which the simmering resentment and mistrust both men felt for each other quickly boiled over. Horan, writing in *The Australasian*, described it as a "very unpleasant affair". At no stage did it reach the point where both men threatened to remove their coats and roll up their sleeves, but it would not have been a surprise had they done so. Neither was capable of taking a backward step, nor reluctant to throw their weight around should the need arise. Conway could be belligerent and forceful and was reputed to have heaved a spectator over the pickets at Lord's for asking him, in particularly derogatory terms, whether he spoke English. "Yes, and we *act* English too, you jackass," Conway had growled. As "strong as a horse", with a 43in chest, the Australian manager was not a man with whom to take liberties. Grace, at 6ft 2in, was an equally intimidating opponent. His anger when roused could reach storm-force proportions – all thunderclaps and lightning – and he was not averse, as he had already demonstrated in his career, to resorting to his fists to settle a row.[1] Grace was "mightily riled", Horan reported, "and he openly told Conway that the Australians were a lot of sneaks to try to entice Midwinter away. High words, of course, followed on both sides." Conway strongly reiterated the Australian case: that no attempts had been made to coerce Midwinter or to put any pressure on him, and that his decision was of his own making. The

Australians, having delivered their message, returned to north London.

Grace, however, was not prepared to let the matter rest there and, summoning the burly Gloucestershire wicketkeeper and England rugby forward Arthur Bush, he hailed a cab and followed the gunpowder trail back to Lord's. In the words of *Bell's Life*, Grace had one aim in mind: "to recover the truant". On his arrival at Lord's he marched straight into the Australian changing room – an incendiary gesture if ever there was one – where Midwinter was padded up and waiting to open the batting with Charles Bannerman. "After about a quarter of an hour's pressing", which included a "good deal of talking and promising" from the Gloucestershire pair, Midwinter picked up his bag and, flanked by Grace and Bush, walked slowly away. As they did so, Grace was unable to resist a parting shot and, rounding on the Australians, told them, "You haven't the ghost of a show against Middlesex." Still in his pads, Midwinter was bundled into a cab and driven to The Oval, where E. M. Grace, in the absence of W. G., had won the toss and put Surrey in to bat. The match there would eventually get under way 55 minutes late.

Frank Allan, who later wrote an account of the tour for a Melbourne newspaper, claimed that Conway, Gregory and Boyle leapt into a cab and gave chase in a last-ditch effort to snatch Midwinter back. Another seething exchange then took place outside The Oval gates, in front of bemused bystanders, before the Australian posse returned "empty-handed". Neither Horan nor Grace made any reference to such an incident, although Grace's take on events is suitably spartan, stating only that Midwinter's departure from Lord's came about "after some persuasion". However, it seems unlikely that both would have neglected to mention it. Horan is extremely clear about the sequence of events and how they unfolded – his detailed reports in *The Australasian* appeared within hours of them happening – and are equally unequivocal about where to lay the blame. "That Grace lost his temper and sadly forgot himself there can be no doubt," he wrote, adding that nothing can excuse "his passion and language, nor his conduct in coming to Lord's and almost forcibly leading away the captive Middy, when the latter was ready to go in ... to commence batting for the Australians." The only constant in this drama was the indecision of Midwinter, "who did not seem to know his own mind for two minutes together". His vacillating behaviour, Horan continued, "cannot be too strongly deprecated"; he let himself be talked around and browbeaten by Grace, and "left us in the lurch without a moment's notice ... to play for Gloucestershire against Surrey at Kennington Oval".

Not for the first time since starting out on their adventure, the Australians felt badly betrayed by Midwinter.

———

David Gregory could not have picked a better time or place to play a captain's innings and to rediscover some form. Not unexpectedly, in the event of Midwinter's defection, Australian wickets tumbled after they were surprisingly sent in to bat by Middlesex under a cloudless blue sky and in conditions as perfect for batting as they had seen all summer. Their minds appeared to be on anything but the cricket: at 46 for six, their frontline batsmen – both of the Bannermans, Horan and Murdoch – were already back in the pavilion, raising the spectre of a third consecutive defeat. A more disquieting return to the scene of their greatest triumph would have been hard to imagine. Once again, it seemed, their credibility was on the line.

Gregory's contribution with the bat had been beggarly, just 27 runs from 12 innings in England before this match, but his decision to push himself up the order to No. 4 (he had batted as low as No. 10 against the Gentlemen) was to prove an inspirational one. Horan confessed that he had never seen him play better cricket in top-scoring with 42. "We were all heartily pleased to see our captain display his best form before an English company," he wrote. "He did not give a shadow of a chance." Gregory may not have been a stylist, in the mould of Murdoch, but he had a sturdy defence and was capable of giving the ball a fearsome thump when well set; with his flowing black beard and imposing physical frame, his similarity to a certain English cricketer would not have gone unnoticed in a crowd of almost 10,000. First with Garrett (19) and then the wristy Tasmanian George Bailey (39) – with whom he added 78 for the seventh wicket – Gregory put the innings firmly back on track before he was caught in the slips with the score on 125.

Garrett, Bailey and Allan – the latter who at the last minute took Midwinter's place in the Eleven – also announced themselves to an English audience during this encounter; in the case of Garrett and Allan, it was delivered with a fanfare. Bailey, who had played in fewer matches than any of the other Australians in England thus far, scored freely and elegantly on both sides of the wicket during his partnership with Gregory, eclipsing his best score of 16 against Elland. However, as befitted an all-amateur XI, Middlesex's bowling was not exactly menacing and, with no professionals to perform the more arduous chores, Blackham and Allan picked off some easy runs before the Australians were dismissed for a respectable, under the circumstances, 165.

Garrett and Allan then went to work with the ball after Spofforth and Boyle, on the surface where they had carried all before them against MCC, allowed Middlesex to get off to the most rapid of starts. "Spofforth came in for severe punishment," Horan wrote. Remarkably, Spofforth and Boyle would take only one wicket between them in this match: the same combination had pillaged 19 on this pitch a little under a month ago. It was the only time during his tour of England (he played in 34 matches in all, an astonishing achievement in itself for a fast bowler) when Spofforth went wicketless. Such was the fierce sense of purpose and unity between the tourists, however, that when an individual flagged or dropped off in form, as they inevitably would under such an exacting schedule, another invariably stepped into the breach. The Middlesex openers, A. J. Webbe and I. D. Walker, had put on 46 when Garrett, having relieved Spofforth, forced the latter to spoon a gentle catch into the hands of Charles Bannerman at short leg. It was to be the start of a devastating spell of fast bowling by the young New South Welshman, who took seven for 38 and surprised all the batsmen with his pace and lift. Five of his victims were clean-bowled and, from a position of some strength at 107 for three, Middlesex lost their next seven wickets for only 15 runs. Jack Blackham worked his own alchemy behind the stumps during this collapse, his glovework so fast that, according to Horan, it "frequently brought the house down". Allan also chipped in with wickets, including that of Webbe for 50, whose stumps he rearranged with a swinging delivery; the left-armer, however, would bowl even better in Middlesex's second innings.

The Australians started poorly again, in reply, losing the two Bannermans and Horan early on the second day, but Gregory – who matched his first innings score of 42 – and Garrett (34) and Bailey (32) all weighed in with valuable runs. Bailey demonstrated once more what a deft timer of the ball he was, scoring 24 of his runs in boundaries. The wicket was playing true and fast by this time, and with the sun shining gloriously and the ground teeming, the "old battlefield", as *Wisden* referred to Lord's, looked in pristine condition, a tribute to the "care, skill and labour that had been lavished" on it by the groundsman, Peter Pearce. "The spectators formed a ring round the ground, and were in many places four or five deep," the *Daily News* observed. Runs flowed quickly and none came quicker than from the bat of Spofforth. Irrepressible cricketer that he was, Spofforth could not be kept out of a game for long, and driving with considerable power and punishing anything loose, he struck five boundaries before he was caught at the wicket for a highly-charged 56. In surpassing the 50 made by Horan at Batley, Spofforth became only the second Australian batsman to record a half-century in England, and the first to do so in a first-class match. "He was greatly and deservedly cheered," the *Daily News* added. The Australian score had reached 240 when the last wicket fell shortly before five o'clock, with Blackham unbeaten on 21.

Needing 284 to win, Middlesex were quickly reduced to 13 for five in what *Wisden* called a "lamentable" batting display. Once again Garrett and Allan inflicted the damage, with the latter finally doing justice to his somewhat fanciful sobriquet "the bowler of the century". Allan was not the most resilient of tourists – to his team-mates he was "a martyr to sciatica", who was "plagued by illness" – and he struggled with English cricket's often adverse weather and wet conditions, spending most of his time bundled up in a thick woollen boating sweater. However, when fit and in form and with the sun on his back, his "high, easy action" was much admired, and his ability to swerve the ball in the air at pace confounded many a batsman. At stumps Middlesex were 79 for six, with only the Hon. Edward Lyttelton, 37 not out, standing between the Australians and an overwhelming victory. The Australians were convinced, though, that the Cambridge University batsman should have been given out leg-before to Allan, on not just one but numerous occasions by the umpire, H. Nixon.

Nixon proved only too trigger-happy, in the opinion of the Australians, when they batted and his decision to uphold an appeal for a run-out against Boyle in their first innings had particularly incensed them. Lyttelton was repeatedly rapped on his pads by Allan, often while "standing right in front", according to Horan, and, "though Allan was bowling over the wicket with scarcely any break", the verdict was always in favour of the batsman. The umpire's refusal to give Lyttelton out was rewarded each time with an approving bark of "Quite right, Nixon, quite right" from the batsman, although "from his position he could not possibly tell whether the decision was right or not", Horan pointed out. To compound the felony, Lyttelton would go on to score the one century conceded by the tourists during the 14 months they played as a team, from November 1877 to January 1879, and the first by an Englishman against the Australians at Lord's. The only other batsman to come remotely close to emulating the feat was the Philadelphian Robert Newhall, whose clean hitting was likened by many of Gregory's men to that of W. G. Grace or their own Charles Bannerman.

Lyttelton gave an indication of what was to come at the start of the third day when he cracked ten runs off the opening over from Allan. A stylist, who cut both late and square and drove with a flourish, Lyttelton set a scorching tempo on an afternoon that was so hot, *Wisden* recorded, the "glass stood at 105 [40.5°C] in the sun". At times the 22-year-old right-hander did just as he pleased with the bowling in an exhibition of "power and rapidity rarely equalled", one reporter wrote. Spofforth disappeared three times to the boundary in his first over after replacing Allan – a hit to leg and a couple of reverberant square cuts – and no sooner had Gregory plugged one gap than the batsman found another. One hundred runs were added in only 65 minutes. Astute and fearless captain that he was, Gregory seemed at a loss to know how to stem the onslaught, although his failure to post a deep third man for much of Lyttelton's innings gave the batsman licence to indulge his favourite cut shot. Writing more than 30 years later, Pelham Warner would cite Gregory's lapse in judgment, particularly to Spofforth's bowling, as a prime example of what he termed "the disastrous effects of bad captaincy": "Ball after ball was neatly cut on the hard true ground to the boundary, past the spot where third man ought to have been but was not. Fancy a fast bowler bowling on a hard ground, while a batsman made a hundred, without a third man; then think that this batsman was one of the finest cutters of his day, and you will wonder what had become of the management of the side!"

In the end it required an equally brilliant piece of cricket to dismiss him. He had scored 113 out of 185, in a blaze of 14 boundaries, when he aimed another drive at Allan and was caught off a flying edge, low down in his left hand by Gregory at short slip. Horan would later recall that it was as good a catch as he had witnessed. *Wisden* had no hesitation in declaring Lyttelton's century "the very finest hitting display of 1878" and noted that the 76 runs he scored that day were made in only 74 minutes, before he was last man out. Even the Australians were won over, admitting that they had never seen faster scoring; Spofforth, who had endured more than most at his hands, presented him with his walking stick. Allan, having dropped him in the deep earlier in the day, returned six for 76 from 43.1 overs, while Garrett collected match figures of ten for 82.

The Australian victory, by 98 runs, was undoubtedly one of the pinnacles of the tour, coming as it did hard on the heels of Midwinter's abduction – an act that left them in obvious disarray – and against a county that would not lose another first-class match all season. Their recovery, and subsequently restored confidence, did them much credit. *Wisden* accords the match a "special place in the history of the game", notably for the batting of Lyttelton and the broiling controversy involving Midwinter, although I. D. Walker's unusual decision, for those times, of putting the Australians in to bat in perfect conditions also attracted much comment. The victory, as one Australian player put it, "rather upset the opinions of certain 'gentlemen' cricketers who thought that we could not win without the help of Midwinter". It made nonsense, too, of Grace's dire prediction that the Australians would not stand "the ghost of a show against Middlesex". "Doubtless the result of the match has surprised him," Horan added. "The Champion"'s conduct towards the Australians would also come back to haunt him.

Midwinter's re-emergence in Gloucestershire colours at The Oval did not meet with success, either: clearly under some duress, he was dismissed for nought and four and gave an undistinguished performance with the ball in a match which Surrey won by 16 runs, inflicting the first defeat on the county champions for two years. "The misunderstanding which resulted in Midwinter's retirement from the eleven was unfortunate, in that it robbed the colonials of perhaps their best all-round player," *The Sportsman*, commented, although it had no doubts where its loyalties lay in the matter: "By virtue of birthright, in strict justice England had the first claim on his services."

The Australians would not see the renegade Midwinter again
– at least not on this tour. Once more they were Eleven.

———

On 22 June, with the dust barely settled on the Australians'
victory over Middlesex at Lord's, Jack Conway fired off a strongly
worded letter of complaint to the Gloucestershire club. The
missive, despatched from the Horse Shoe Hotel, stated in no
uncertain terms that "unless Mr. W. G. Grace apologises for his
insulting behaviour ... we shall be compelled to erase the
Gloucestershire fixture from our programme". The teams were
scheduled to meet at the Clifton ground in Bristol on 5–7
September in what promised to be a captivating – and highly
lucrative – denouement to the season.

The row would rumble on for another month, with claim
and counter-claim batted back and forth, in correspondence of
"increasing acidity", between the two camps. The Gloucestershire
committee, in reply to Conway's letter, expressed their regret at
such a possible course of action by the Australians, but added that
"Mr. W. G. Grace did not for a moment intend his remarks to
apply to Mr. Conway and Mr. Boyle". This elicited a stinging
response from David Gregory, in which he again reiterated their
determination not to play at Bristol, while pointing out that "he
[W. G.] publicly insulted the whole of the Australian Eleven in
most unmistakable language". Gregory made no attempt, either,
to disguise the contempt in which Midwinter was now held by his
former team-mates: "Moreover we are averse to meeting Midwinter,
whose defection from us we regard as a breach of faith."

The Australians felt their terms for Midwinter could not have
been fairer: he had been promised benefit matches in Melbourne
and Sydney on his return with them to the colonies – an act
which suggests that the Australians may not have been the
innocent party they liked to pretend – and offered a "liberal sum"
for each match he played on tour. Midwinter's prize for staying
with Gloucestershire was £8 for every county game he appeared

in that summer – a figure that was unlikely to match the amount the Australians were prepared to pay him. He was, however, almost certainly included in the expenses "scam" which the Graces ran at away matches, and where the host club footed the bill; this would have enabled him to augment his income by anything up to £10 a game. The county also awarded him a benefit match at the end of the 1879 season, against Lancashire. It was, in fact, rained off but Gloucestershire still offered him £100 by way of compensation. Typically, Midwinter would later claim that he made the wrong decision and should have stuck with the colonials all along.

In a forthright riposte to Gregory's letter, Gloucestershire justified Grace's conduct by accusing the Australians of attempting to bribe Midwinter in a bid to retain his services: "With the knowledge of Midwinter's engagement staring you in the face you attempted to induce him to break his promise, desert his County, and play for you by offering him a larger sum than we could afford to pay him. Such proceedings are to say the least uncommon and go far … to palliate Mr. Grace's stormy language at the Oval." The committee kept the cauldron bubbling by reminding the Australians that Midwinter was a "Gloucestershire man" who, upon returning to England in 1877, had played in all of the county's matches since his arrival. He had appeared for the county colts at Bedminster already this summer and "had promised Mr. Grace to play in all our County matches". His engagement was "well known all over England and can hardly fail to have been known to you".

The paper trail did not end there, and the Australians, sticking steadfastly to their guns, still refused to bring their team to Bristol unless Grace made a formal apology. They were, however, prepared to cede some ground over Midwinter, being "willing to overlook" his defection, although they still clearly believed that they had first claim on him. "Before he came to England he asked Mr. Conway to keep a place for him in the team," Gregory explained, "and we started from Australia relying upon his joining us."

After much beard tugging no doubt, Grace eventually relented and, in a letter addressed to Gregory on 21 July (it seemed he could not bring himself to write to Conway), he offered a full and dignified apology to Conway and the Australian team. He wished to "let bygones be bygones" and professed his deep regret that "in the excitement of the moment I should have made use of unparliamentary language to Mr. Conway". Grace assured the Australians that they would "meet a hearty welcome and a good ground at Clifton". At the end of a month's intense wrangling it seemed both sides were only too glad to put the matter to rest, to put down their pens and pick up their bats. The Australians accepted the apology and the fixture went ahead; although, of course, no amount of contrition could disguise the fact that it would be anything other than a grudge match.

There is no doubt, also, that Grace's reputation suffered in the poisonous aftermath of the Midwinter affair, and several newspapers were not above taking issue with him over it. "It is a pity that the strangers should have been discourteously used within our gates," ventured one reporter, before adding, "It is a pity too, that Mr. Grace should have so far forgotten the exact position in which he stands as a cricketer. He is practically a paid servant of the Marylebone Club, just as much as the ground bowlers or umpires. He has, as a matter of fact, been guilty of insulting his master's guests within his master's house." Grace's travails during the summer of 1878 would not end there, however, and before the season was out another newspaper would ask the leading question, "What has come over W. G.?" The answer was nothing that a thunderous century against the Australians at Clifton would not put right.

Ten
23 June–6 July 1878

"A rougher looking assemblage could scarcely be imagined"

The Eleven were back on their travels, leaving London on the five o'clock train from Euston to Birmingham on the evening of Sunday, 23 June. For the next three months their threadbare resources would be stretched to the seams and their mettle tested to the full. They may have emerged from the slough of consecutive defeats with their victory over Middlesex, but, as Horan put it, "The loss of Midwinter now means that we have no spare man. Thus we shall all have to travel and play all of the time and have no rest." There were three matches against the odds and a tough return fixture with Yorkshire – in the bear-pit of Bramall Lane – to negotiate before they returned to London on 7 July; and then it started all over again. The harsh reality was that many would have to play through injury and illness in support of the cause. Proud colonialists that they were, though, they would not be prepared to accept offers from opposition teams to make up the numbers. Perhaps, Horan wrote, "we shall uncover some fellow Australian cricketers on our travels and they may be able to come to our assistance". The hope was not as far-fetched as it sounded.

The tenth match of the tour, against a twenty-two of Birmingham and District at Bournbrook Park, started in soaring temperatures and ended in a torrential downpour. The Australians were much encouraged by the return to form of Spofforth, who bowled with his old fire and fury to take 11 for 60 from 40 overs. One of his victims was the Surrey professional Harry Jupp, who had been added to the Birmingham line-up along with his county team-mate Ted Barratt. Allan continued his revival with six for

17 to help bowl the locals out for 123 in reply to Australia's first innings score of 105. Despite the wicket being dry and fast, the Australian batsmen had struggled to make an impression; the one exception was opener Alec Bannerman, who carried his bat for 31. Horan described his five-hour vigil as a "masterly display of defensive batting", although his stonewalling severely tested the patience of even the most ardent cricket enthusiasts among a crowd of 8,000.

The standout performance by an Australian, however, came from Jack Blackham. He completed a stumping, off Allan, to the first ball of the Birmingham innings, and not for the first time on tour his artistry with the gloves drew repeated roars of appreciation from the crowd. Unlike modern wicketkeepers, Blackham, who stood at just over 5ft 9in, did not squat on his haunches while awaiting the bowler; instead, it was said, "he bent forward, rather like a man peeping through a key hole". Old photographs show him with his feet splayed out and his hands held slightly apart in front of his pads. Although he could be an urgent pacer in the dressing-room – he found it impossible to sit still for long periods – he shed his nervous energy the minute he stepped on to the pitch. He was always immaculately turned out: his black beard neatly trimmed, a narrow-peaked cap perched on the back of his head, his shirtsleeves buttoned down; in fact, the essence of calm. He was never one for exhibitionism or for ostentatious gestures behind the stumps, and his manner of appealing has been simply described as "quiet"; "sometimes he merely raised his hand questioningly" towards the umpire. The story goes that in a match in Victoria he once pulled off a leg-side stumping of such breathtaking speed that in response to his almost hushed "How's that?" the square-leg umpire is reputed to have answered, "Wonderful". Not even a nasty cut to his forefinger, sustained when catching a thunderbolt from Spofforth midway through the Birmingham innings, could detract from his virtuosity.

When the Australians batted again, Charles Bannerman was particularly severe on the bowling, hitting 31 out of the first 35 runs in partnership with his brother, before he was stumped by

Jupp off the slow left-arm of Barratt. The biggest hit of the match, though, was made by Tom Garrett. The all-rounder, whose reputation seemed to grow with every game he played, sent a ball from Barratt clean over the heads of the spectators and straight into a large fish pond in the grounds of the park. It appeared that no one had thought to bring another ball with them and, after several abortive attempts were made to retrieve it, a boat was fetched from an artificial lake nearby. The ball was eventually fished out of the water, amidst scenes of much amusement, after a delay in all of some 20 minutes. The Australians had moved their score on to 116 for six soon after, when a sudden rainstorm sent the players running for cover. Within minutes the ground was flooded and, shortly after two o'clock on the third day, with the rain showing no sign of easing off, the game was abandoned as a draw.

That evening the Australians caught a train to Leeds, where they would play eighteen of Hunslet and District, arriving at the four-square, red-brick Great Northern Railway Station Hotel three hours later. Hunslet was not known as the "Workshop of Leeds" for nothing, and on the drive to the Woodhouse Hill ground the following morning, they found themselves pitched into a world that could not have been more brutally transformed from the sylvan setting of Bournbrook Park. The throb and roar of iron foundries, steelworks and blast furnaces filled the air, while row upon row of grimy back-to-backs, divided by dark, narrow alleys, stretched for as far as the eye could see in every direction. There were in excess of 30 industrial mills and factories in Hunslet at the time and the Australians considered the three-mile journey by drag to the ground each day a "most depressing affair". In fact, so thick were the smoke and noxious fumes that they were forced to hold their handkerchiefs to their faces, a sight that was regularly greeted with hoots of derision and laughter by the locals.

The cricket was no less hostile. The Australians were faced for the third time on tour by the Gloucestershire amateur W. R. Gilbert, who would captain the eighteen. There was the usual recruitment of professional muscle, too, provided on this occasion by Yorkshire's Allen Hill, Louis Hall and Billy Bates, the latter, a talented all-rounder, arriving fresh from a century against Nottinghamshire. There were no such luxuries for the tourists. They were forced to press Jack Conway into service for Blackham, whose damaged forefinger had deteriorated overnight to the extent that he could barely grip the ball. The last thing they needed now was to pick up another injury.

They came perilously close to one, however. After Gregory won the toss and elected to bat on a "beautifully fast wicket", Horan was removed by a ball of ferocious pace from Arthur Motley, a 20-year-old fast bowler, which struck him full on the chest before cannoning back on to his stumps via his bat. What made the dismissal even more unedifying was that Motley was a chucker, and not just any chucker either. In the opinion of the Eleven, he was the most blatant thrower of a cricket ball they had seen. Indeed, he almost appeared to revel in his own flagrant disregard for the rules, openly admitting that he threw every ball he bowled. More startling, from the Australian point of view, was the fact that Motley's bowling (he would go on to play two first-class matches for Yorkshire) had "hitherto been allowed to pass unquestioned by English umpires". Gregory, who came to the wicket after the loss of Horan, refused to bat against him and informed Gilbert that, as the umpires seemed unable to apply the law, the Australians would abandon the match unless he was taken off. Gregory was also clearly concerned about the safety of his players, and, after what was reported as a "slight altercation", Gilbert backed down and Motley was not seen again during the innings.[1]

The captain was in equally authoritative mood with the bat, putting on 67 for the third wicket with Charles Bannerman, who registered his first half-century in England. Unquestionably Australia's outstanding batsman, it had nevertheless taken Bannerman longer than he might have expected – 11 matches in all – to reach the landmark, Horan and Spofforth, of course, having got there before him. The slow, muddy pitches had not helped his natural free-scoring game, but he could also be an impetuous batsman and, frustratingly, he often contributed to his own downfall. On this occasion, though, he fell to a smart slip catch after top-scoring with 52 out of a total of 205. Gregory struck the ball well for his 31 runs before he was caught and bowled by Hill, while Allan entertained a crowd of 4,000 in his own inimitable fashion, hitting an unbeaten 38.

Spofforth, with eight for 77, and Allan, six for 56, matched each other almost wicket for wicket when Hunslet batted, although a chanceless 79 from Louis Hall – a defensive batsman by instinct, who was not noted for his grace or elegance – enabled the eighteen to muster a 23-run advantage. A lay preacher from Batley, who was rumoured to hold the singular distinction of being the first teetotaller to play for Yorkshire, Hall appeared to draw his inspiration from facing the very "Demon" himself. His innings, which included one enormous six, was so good that the Australians rated it as one of the finest played against them all tour. *Wisden*, hardly given to flights of fancy or exaggeration, described it as a "genuine sensation".[2]

Murdoch just missed out on a half-century when the Australians batted for a second time, falling to Gilbert's teasing, slow round-arm for 49. However, Garrett, with 48, reinforced his reputation as a big hitter by striking a magnificent straight six off the medium-paced Bates, which carried into the neighbouring Hunslet cemetery. There was even a reappearance, as a bowler, by Motley, this time in the guise of a slow over-arm trundle. On only one occasion, however, did he fail to keep his arm straight and was promptly no-balled for it. With his sting safely removed, he got through eight overs for a cost of 15 runs and no wickets before the Australians were dismissed for 180. In reply Hunslet managed to cling on for a draw, in front of a crowd of 5,000, after Spofforth and Allan, reprising their form from the first innings and bowling unchanged for 31 overs, reduced them to 28 for nine.

However, there were accusations afterwards that the Australians had purposely spun out the match to increase the gate money. The suspicions were fanned in the minds of some spectators by the ease with which Spofforth and Allan had been able to knock over the Hunslet batsmen on the final afternoon, in marked contrast to the first innings. They would not be the last team – indeed, they were not even the first – to find themselves the subject of such rumours. Horan recalled that the heavy defeat of W. G. Grace's England team of 1873–4 by eighteen of Victoria (they lost by an innings and 21 runs) provoked a similar storm of protests: "All non-cricketers said that the Eleven could have beaten the Victorians easily." Although on a more prescient note, Grace's drubbing had prompted *Bell's Life* to predict that it would not be long before an Australian XI was "doing battle at Lord's".[3]

It was hardly surprising if at times the Australians felt that they could do no right, no matter what. At the start of their tour, it was said, they were so weak that the opposition had only to roll out of bed to beat them; now they were being suspected of toying with teams for their own personal gain. "Everyone in Leeds said that we allowed the Hunslet men to get the runs in the first innings and that Spofforth and Allan could have bowled them out whenever they chose!" Horan wrote. Needless to say he had no truck with the gossip-mongers: "All cricketers, naturally enough, laugh at the absurdity of this imputation, which nevertheless manages to spread."

Aggrieved as the Australians undoubtedly were by such allegations of sharp practice, they did not always help themselves with their actions. Additional rumours that they had instructed James Lillywhite to ask the Yorkshire committee to double the entrance fee for their rematch with the county at Bramall Lane were also doing the rounds, and may have been responsible for some of the trouble in the wake of the Hunslet game. As it was, the local authorities rejected the proposal out of hand and, it was reported, had even threatened to abandon the match unless the colonials climbed down.

"We topped a rise and there in a valley ahead of us hung a pall of mist. 'Sheffield,' laconically said the driver, and in another ten minutes we were in another world." The words were written by

Jack Fingleton, the Australian opening batsman and journalist of whom it can be said – as it was of Tom Horan – that his pen was "possessed of a silver nib". What Fingleton had mistaken for a mist was, he soon discovered, "the oppressive sky of modern industry, a sky belched forth by chimneys as numerous as stakes in a tomato patch". Don Bradman's 1938 tourists – the 19th Australian team to visit England – were about to do battle with the mighty Yorkshire at Bramall Lane. "The looks of the grim spectators ... the postures and gestures of the eleven robust Yorkshiremen ... the battle of fresh air and sun against the smoke fumes" imprinted themselves for ever on Fingleton's retina. Sheffield, he asserted, was the "survival of the fittest, whether steel, cutlery, business or cricket". Perhaps he even spared a thought that day for Gregory's pioneers of 1878.

If the first Australian touring XI thought that they had seen it all since landing in England on 14 May, Sheffield would make them think again. They had arrived in town at 10.30am on Monday, 1 July, travelling the 35 miles from Leeds by rail before driving straight to Bramall Lane for the commencement of their rematch with Yorkshire. Before their game in Sheffield, Bradman's men had passed an idyllic day in the Derbyshire hills, swimming "Huckleberry Finn style" in a stream, tickling trout and feasting on the "biggest strawberries in the whole of England"; Gregory's team, in stark contrast, had spent the day cooped up in their hotel, attempting to ignore the jibes that they were intent only on lining their own pockets. They arrived at Bramall Lane, through streets that were "smoky and unclean", Horan noted, to find a huge crowd of 10,000 awaiting them. By the close of play that attendance would have almost doubled.

Established in 1855 as the home of Yorkshire cricket from land leased by the Duke of Norfolk – on the provision "that matches be conducted in a respectable manner" – Bramall Lane had much to recommend it. In the opinion of the Australians it was one of the largest grounds they had seen in England and had accommodation superior to any they had played at with the exception of Lord's. "The pavilion is not much to look at,"

Horan observed, "but it is comfortable and roomy enough for anyone, while opposite it is a stand capable of seating about 1,000 persons." The ground also had the advantage of a terrace and a sloping embankment, although the latter "only extends a short distance on one side of the ground". Ironically, the site for Bramall Lane had been chosen because of its proclivity for natural light and clean air, but such was the growth of Sheffield as a hub of industry (the population was close to 300,000 by 1878) that the surrounding pastures soon disappeared beneath rows of houses and a forest of factory turrets and chimney stacks. In the words of the Yorkshire cricket writer J. M. Kilburn, the ground became "treeless, enclosed, begrimed".

Begrimed it may have been but Bramall Lane not only became a Test match venue – England took on Australia there in 1902 and lost overwhelmingly by 143 runs – it earned itself a place in history when it staged the world's first floodlit football match on 14 October 1878, before a crowd of 20,000. "It is somewhat remarkable that the first great triumph of the electric light should have been gained in the field of sport," the *Sporting Gazette* trumpeted. The newspaper likened the lofty electric structures at each corner of the ground to "huge inverted coal scuttles, covered with a tarpaulin", but hailed the experiment "of turning night into day" as an "extremely successful" one. "Indeed we are told that the moon was nowhere – quite paled her ineffectual fires, in fact, before this new rival." An achievement, it added, that came at a cost of electricity of only "threepence apiece per hour".[4] The newspaper also wondered whether the experiment might ever be used one day for cricket. "How nice it would be to field a hot return apparently coming from the 'light's eye' to the fieldsmen," it mused.

A case no doubt could have been made for the use of floodlights during the Australians' game with Yorkshire. The smoke from the factories frequently smothered the ground and was often so heavy "that the more remote onlookers could scarcely be seen from the pavilion," Horan remarked. The smut, he added, daubed their clothing – "our faces were almost black with it" –

making them look like a troop of chimney sweeps by the time they walked off the pitch. "I must say that we were glad to get back to the Wharncliffe [their hotel] and indulge in the luxury of a bath. One can't feel clean in Sheffield." At least the Australians did not have to face the lively left-arm swing of Tom Emmett in this match. The White Rose captain had been forced to withdraw after straining his side while playing for the North against the South at Trent Bridge. George Pinder, the accomplished wicketkeeper, was another injury victim, but their old adversaries George Ulyett, Allen Hill, Andrew Greenwood and Tom Armitage were all present and correct, and champing at the bit to exact revenge for their defeat by the colonials at Huddersfield. The Eleven were strengthened by the return of Jack Blackham, whose forefinger had healed sufficiently to enable him to take his place behind the stumps.

However, after winning the toss and taking what they hoped would be advantage of a fast wicket, the Australians found themselves in all sorts of trouble against the fast round-arm of George "Happy Jack" Ulyett. Sheffield through and through – he once plied his trade in the town's rolling mills – the all-rounder clean-bowled Alec Bannerman and Horan in a fiery opening spell during which the Bramall Lane crowd wasted no time in making their considerable presence felt, roaring their approval at the dismissal of each Australian batsman. Sheffield audiences were famed as much for their caustic wit and volubility as they were for their native pride, which burned as fiercely as their factory furnaces. Bramall Lane could also be a forbidding place for visiting teams to play and was certainly not for the faint-hearted. In 1861, William Caffyn's Surrey XI were making their way to the railway station after their game with Yorkshire had been abandoned because of rain, when they were apprehended by what was described as a group of ruffians and promptly ordered back to the ground to finish the match. "We've paid threepence to watch cricket and we want cricket for our money," the ringleader gruffly told the Surrey players. They duly did so, completing the game with water lapping over their boots.

As the Australians would discover, Bramall Lane – or t'Lane as it was more regularly referred to – had lost none of its reputation for menace. "A rougher looking assemblage could scarcely be imagined," the *Argus* wrote. "Their applause was very one-sided and very rough language was used when the Australians met with any success." Which was not very often: Garrett and Murdoch were soon making their way back to the pavilion after the dismissal of Horan, as 37 for two swiftly became 48 for six. Gregory and Bailey temporarily stopped the rot, adding 32 for the seventh wicket before the Australian captain had his off stump plucked out of the ground by Hill, and Bailey was caught at the wicket off Bates for a top score of 23. When Allan was last man out, caught at third man, attempting one of his more improbable strokes shortly after two o'clock, the Australians had only 88 runs on the board, Ulyett finishing with four for 14 from 13 overs.

Yorkshire's batsmen made an equally indifferent start and at one stage were 31 for four in reply, before the crowd decided to lend them a helping hand. There were no boundary chains or ropes, and by encroaching at regular intervals on to the pitch they ensured that the "slightest tap", as Horan put it, "counted for four", with the ball disappearing among the spectators before any of the fieldsmen could retrieve it. The runs quickly mounted and not for the first time, in the opinion of the Australians, the few policemen on duty proved "entirely ineffective in their efforts to keep the people back". As a consequence the fielding side was frequently inconvenienced and had no choice but to run through the crowd in pursuit of the ball. In doing so they were subjected to some particularly ripe language. "They had a nickname for each of our Eleven before the day was over, and these were not the choicest of selections," Horan recorded, before adding a little over-optimistically: "Indeed, I think that the spectators at a cricket match in Australia would be considerably astonished if such names emanated from their midst as the Sheffielders showered upon us."

Yorkshire were dismissed for 167 just before stumps – a handy lead of 79 – though some of the Australians felt that by not persevering with Boyle, who bowled himself back into form with three for 11 from 12 overs, Gregory had missed a trick. Armitage, with 45, and Hill (27) had been particularly rough on the bowling, even without the assistance of the spectators, during an entertaining late stand of 59 before Boyle, appropriately, returned to have the former caught and bowled. However, another rank batting display saw the Australians skittled out for 104 on the second day, with only Alec Bannerman and Allan, who both made 33, putting up any resistance; the homespun Ulyett (four for 27) turning in another match-winning performance with the ball. Needing 26 for victory, Yorkshire lost Ulyett cheaply to Boyle, before Ephraim Lockwood and Greenwood brought them home in front of a crowd of 9,000, who cheered every run with a gusto that might have been heard on the factory floors.

The *Argus* reported that the Australians felt the performance of the crowd had contributed substantially to their defeat but, as Horan explained, it went deeper than that: "I cannot really make out what is coming over our batting. We do not seem to play up to our Australian form." Too often it appeared to be a case of one step forward for the tourists and two steps back: an exceptional performance (Middlesex) followed by a miserable one (Yorkshire). The fact that the conditions might have been tailor-made for them – certainly no blame could be attached to the wicket, which played excellently throughout, while Yorkshire were missing their most dangerous bowler – only amplified their disappointment. But there was always another match, and on Thursday, 4 July – leaving the "smoke and grime of Sheffield in our wake" – the Australians once more crossed the Pennines into Lancashire, where they would play their next game, against an eighteen of Stockport and District.

The match would be remembered for Blackham's wicketkeeping – he disposed of ten batsmen in all (seven in the first innings and three in the second), and six of them stumped – although Spofforth and Allan, who maintained their good form, and Horan, who rediscovered his, also added handsomely to an Australian victory by 149 runs. If the Stockport ground was the smallest on which they had played since their arrival in England – "a hit to the ropes counted but three and the batsman had to clear the fence to be rewarded with four" – the wicket was also one of the most dangerous, making Blackham's dexterity all the more remarkable.

The Australians had needed their wits about them after they were asked to bat first, particularly against Martin McIntyre, the round-arm fast bowler who toured with W. G. Grace's team to Australia in 1873–4; the former Nottinghamshire professional had lost none of his potency and left more than a couple of batsmen wringing their hands and rubbing their ribs. At one point they were 59 for six but recovered to score 163, thanks to 34 from George Bailey and an unbeaten 33 by Blackham. Allan then collected ten for 50, including the wicket of the peripatetic W. R. Gilbert, who was stumped in "spectacular fashion" for a duck. The wicket, however, proved so unpredictable that a fresh one was used for the second innings and Horan, in particular, reaped the benefit, hitting 70 – the highest score by an Australian in England at that point. It enabled the colonials to reach a total of 225, leaving the eighteen the somewhat improbable task of scoring 284 to win. They never got close and were bowled out for 134 just before six o'clock on the third day, with Spofforth taking eight for 30 and Horan, who completed a memorable all-round performance, capturing five for 35 with his fast round-arm. Within minutes of their victory, though, the Australians were dusting themselves off and heading back to the station. As ever, they had a train to catch.

Eleven

8–21 July 1878

"A truly English hospitality"

For two days at least time stood still for the Australians. The 14th fixture of their tour, against the Orleans Club on the banks of the Thames in Twickenham, was intended to be nothing more than a delightful diversion from their travels – a chance to relax and catch their breath, and indulge in some none too strenuous cricket. As such, it was quite unlike any other first-class match that they played in England; even the result, for once, was secondary. Here, they could stop the clock for a brief moment, collect their thoughts and recover their senses, away from the prying eyes of the crowds, the incessant rattle of train wheels and the shriek of a midnight whistle. It was a "pleasant little social game," Horan wrote, a "pretty and happy holiday" – before they were thrust back into the tumult.

The idea for the match was dreamed up by the celebrated amateur hitter and former Cambridge University batsman C. I. Thornton, who "put it to the Orleans committee that at its beautiful Twickenham ground, the Eleven would find a domestic welcome, a truly English hospitality", a haven from the "round of monotonous toil and wide publicity". The estate was purchased in 1877 by Sir John Astley, a former soldier and enthusiastic sports benefactor, who had subsequently converted it into a luxurious country retreat and social club. The Australians travelled to Twickenham on the morning of 8 July from the club's town house in St James's for the start of the two-day game; the road between Richmond and Twickenham was, they agreed, the "most charming of any out of London". Nothing, though, could have prepared them for the beauty of Orleans House or its sumptuous surroundings. The rectangular Palladian villa dated from the early eighteenth century, when it had been built for James Johnson, the then Secretary of State for Scotland, although its most famous inhabitant was Louis Philippe, duc d'Orléans, who lived there in exile before later becoming King of France, and from whom the house derived its name. An enchanted garden stretched "halfway to the Thames" while "to the right and left of the lawn, we could see grottos and neatly-fixed up summerhouses," Horan waxed. "In the evening there is an aura of supreme quiet about the Orleans Club, save for the click of billiard balls, a piano playing and singing in the distance and the cry of a peacock on the terrace." However, an incident during the match would remind the Australians, had they allowed themselves to be lulled into a false sense of security, that not everything in the garden was beautiful.[1]

Their opponents, handpicked by Thornton, presented a felicitous mix of amateurs and professionals. The former included I. D. Walker, D. Q. Steel, a middle-order batsman and brother of the brilliant A. G. Steel, and William Yardley, the first man to score a century in the Varsity match, who doubled as an actor, playwright and theatre critic. Among the professionals were the Leicestershire fast bowler Arnold Rylott, who, in keeping with the literary bent, was a published poet, and Ted Barratt, the Surrey slow left-armer; and then there was the captain himself. Few men in the history of the game have ever struck a ball harder or further than Charles Inglis Thornton. A batting phenomenon, Thornton scorned the use of pads and rarely wore batting gloves. Such impedimenta, he believed, restricted the freedom of his movement down the wicket and the mighty arc of his bat; the only concession he made to the dangers of a cricket ball were a pair of shin pads – or his "oak guards" as he referred to them – tucked inside his flannels. Two years earlier, practising in front of the pavilion at Hove, he had hit a ball over the entrance gates of the ground into Western Road – an extraordinary carry of more than 160 yards – which landed with an unexpected thud among a row of idling cabs.

The Australians, meanwhile, were deprived of the services of Blackham, who had received another blow to his damaged forefinger during his heroic exploits with the gloves at Stockport; Spofforth was once again the offending bowler. On this occasion, however, Blackham's place was filled by a player from outside the Eleven: H. N. Tennant, described by the *Daily Telegraph* as "well known in the athletic world", was a native of Australia, residing in London, and "delighted to play for her". He was also the only non-member of the original touring party to appear for them in a first-class match in England. Unfortunately, his contribution with the bat (he made a single in the first innings and two in the second) was not much to write home about.[2]

There was the usual flurry of wickets after the Australians won the toss and batted first in glorious sunshine and a setting that could not have been further removed from the hostile environs of Bramall Lane. Among the many distractions at the Orleans Club was the band of the Eighth Hussars, who struck up at regular intervals during the day. The ground, ringed by a belt of deep green chestnuts, was small, too, and the fieldsmen soon discovered that unless the ball was hit straight at them they had little chance of cutting it off. "The frequent visits of the ball to the shrubbery," *Lillywhite's Companion* remarked, "remind one of cricket practice in our youth in the parental back garden." As was often the case with the Australian batsmen, however, an early clatter of wickets was followed by a doughty rearguard action, and an eighth-wicket partnership of 46 between Alec Bannerman – who carried his bat for 71 – and George Bailey enabled them to reach a total of 171. Invaluable though Bannerman's knock was, it can be succinctly summed up by the fact that he failed to score a single boundary during his three-hour occupation of the crease, despite the pocket-sized pitch. The Orleans Club made an even worse start, collapsing to 80 for eight before F. E. R Fryer and W. N. Powys took a leaf out of the Australians' book with a ninth-wicket stand of 44. They were trailing by 39 when Horan bowled Fryer off his pads for 61 shortly before six o'clock to terminate the innings.

Later that evening, after the crowds had gone home, the Australians delighted in having the gardens to themselves. It was, they agreed, "the most enjoyable part of the day". Some tried their hand at lawn tennis – a sport which they felt sure would soon catch on in Australia – while others wandered down to the river or dozed in the hammocks under the trees. They were like men making the most of their last few precious hours of freedom. Although if the more light-footed among them felt drawn to the ballroom after dinner, when the sounds of waltzes and quadrilles filled the house, one look from Jack Conway was enough to deter them. "Inside the ballroom may be the prettiest girls in all England: the sweetest voices, the most seductive ways," Horan mused, but no matter how captivating the prospect, the cricketers were not prepared to risk the wrath of their formidable manager. The sobriety of the Australians was testament not only to their discipline and commitment to the cause (and to the iron hand of Conway) but was also quite unique among touring teams of that time; the consumption of champagne by James Lillywhite's professionals in Australia had been legendary and was often reflected in their play. That is not to say the Australians did not like a drink – men such as Charles Bannerman were hardly abstainers – but they later admitted that they could not have carried out their huge workload had they not stuck so unswervingly to their regime. The following morning, Horan wrote, "we came out as fresh as paint and played even better cricket than the day before". And none more so than Horan himself.

No doubt it was a night spent in a comfortable bed and "lavender-scented sheets", for Horan, driven to distraction by his inability to sleep on trains, batted like a new man. He top-scored with 64 out of a total of 172, playing his favourite cut shot to telling effect and hitting the ball freely to all parts of the ground. In his own estimation he had not batted better all tour, before he was bowled attempting to pull a short ball from Barratt through square leg. The dismissal of the last man, Tennant, at four o'clock, meant that the Orleans Club had to score 212 to win in two hours, a tall order even for a batsman of such destructive capabilities as Thornton. However, he was not to be daunted and in no time the runs were rattling off his bat at a "furious rate". Gregory was soon forced into a double bowling change, replacing Spofforth and Allan, who had both been hit out of the ground, with Boyle and Horan. The move appeared to have had the desired effect as Thornton skipped down the track to Horan's second ball, missed it by some distance and was easily stumped by Murdoch. He was so far down the wicket, the bowler wrote, that the Australians did not feel the need to appeal, "presuming that Mr Thornton would retire". Much to their astonishment, though, the batsman appealed to the umpire, who promptly gave him not out "on his own appeal". It was hardly the model behaviour of a sporting amateur (or a glowing example of "truly English hospitality"), and whatever Horan thought of it he kept his views to himself, directing his displeasure instead at the umpire, who was typical of those who "have the happy knack of giving decisions invariably in favour of our opponents". Nevertheless, the spell was broken.

To rub it in, Thornton then hit Boyle way over the chestnuts into the blue yonder, a strike the Australians reckoned to be in the region of 130 yards. *Lillywhite's Companion*, however, stated that the blow was all of 152 yards, adding that "the hit was measured with a chain". One newspaper reported that the ball was discovered in a nearby hotel. "The force of his hitting will be better understood when it is remembered that a four had to be hit *over* the chains, under the chains scoring three," *The Australasian* pointed out. Horan was next to receive the treatment, recording that the ball soared into the ether beyond the tall trees, never to be seen again: "As our captain remarked, it probably travelled on to the next county." The secret of Thornton's success as a hitter was, Horan elaborated, "a good reach – every man of 6ft has that – a hawk-like eye, an intuitive knowledge of timing the ball and bringing the bat on to it at the right place, a belief that when a hit is attempted there shall be no finicky half measures about it, and a natural delight in feeling the ball sail skyward

The 1878 Australians. *Back (l-r):* Fred Spofforth, Jack Conway, Frank Allan. *Middle:* George Bailey, Tom Horan, Tom Garrett, David Gregory, Alec Bannerman, Harry Boyle. *Front:* Charles Bannerman, Billy Murdoch, Jack Blackham.

Lord's Ground.

M.C.C. AND GROUND v. AUSTRALIANS.

MONDAY, MAY 27, 1878.

M. C. C.	First Innings.		Second Innings.	
W. G. Grace, Esq.	c Midwinter, b Allan	4	b Spofforth	0
A. N. Hornby, Esq.	b Spofforth	19	b Boyle	1
C. Booth, Esq.	b Boyle	0	b Boyle	0
A. W. Ridley, Esq.	c A. Bannerman, b Boyle	7	b Boyle	0
A. J. Webbe, Esq.	b Spofforth	1	b Spofforth	0
Wild	b Boyle	0	b Spofforth	5
Flowers	c and b Spofforth	0	b Boyle	11
G. G. Hearne	b Spofforth	0	b Spofforth	0
Shaw	st Murdoch, b Spofforth	0	not out	2
G. F. Vernon, Esq.	st Murdoch, b Spofforth	0	b Spofforth	0
Morley	not out	1	c Horan, b Boyle	0
	B , l-b 1, w , n-b ,	1	B , l-b , w , n-b ,	
	Total	33	Total	19

AUSTRALIANS.	First Innings.		Second Innings.	
C. Bannerman	c Hearne, b Morley	0	b Shaw	1
W. Midwinter	c Wild, b Shaw	10	not out	4
T. Horan, Esq.	c Grace, b Morley	4	not out	7
A. Bannerman	c Booth, b Morley	0		
T. W. Garrett, Esq.	c Ridley, b Morley	6		
F. E. Spofforth, Esq.	b Shaw	1		
D. W. Gregory, Esq.	b Shaw	0		
H. F. Boyle, Esq.	c Wild, b Morley	2		
W. L. Murdoch, Esq.	b Shaw	9		
F. E. Allan, Esq.	c and b Shaw	6		
G. H. Bailey, Esq.	not out	3	B , l-b , w , n-b ,	
	B , l-b , w , n-b ,			
	Total	41	Total	12

Umpires—Rylott and Sherwin.   Scorers—W. Hearn and McCanlis.

BOWLING ANALYSIS.

M.C.C.—First Innings.				Second Innings.			
	O.	M.	R.	W.	O.	M.	R.	W.
Boyle	14	7	14	3	8.1	6	3	5
Spofforth	5.3	3	4	6	9	2	16	5
Allan	9	4	14	1				

Australians—First Innings.				Second Innings.			
Shaw	33.2	25	10	5	8	6	4	1
Morley	33	19	31	5	8	4	8	0

The day cricket changed for ever. The scorecard of the Eleven's victory over MCC at Lord's in a single afternoon's play, when Fred Spofforth claimed the first hat-trick by an Australian on English soil and spectators swarmed across the pitch. The scorecard erroneously gives Spofforth's second-innings figures as 9-2-16-5; he took four for 16. Boyle's second-innings figures should read 8.1-6-3-6, while Allan bowled the first over in MCC's first innings.

The Horse Shoe Hotel, on Tottenham Court Road, a home from home for the Eleven in London. Opened in 1875, the building was demolished in 2004.

The beautiful Orleans House, on the banks of the Thames in Twickenham, provided, in the words of Tom Horan, "one of the best treasured recollections of the whole tour".

The impressive Cambridge University XI who beat the tourists by an innings and 72 runs, with Edward Lyttelton (*middle row, second from right*) the scorer of the only century against the Australians (for Middlesex), and the gifted all-rounder A. G. Steel (*front row, right*).

Lord's Ground.

AUSTRALIANS *v* CAMBRIDGE UNIVERSITY.

MONDAY and TUESDAY, JULY 22, 23, 1878.

CAMBRIDGE.	First Innings.		Second Innings.
1 Hon. A. LYTTELTON	... b Murdoch	72	
2 H. WHITFELD, Esq.	b Spofforth	15	
3 Hon. E. LYTTELTON	run out	15	
4 A. G. STEEL, Esq.	run out	59	
5 D. Q. STEEL, Esq.	c and b Spofforth	13	
6 L. K. JARVIS, Esq.	b Murdoch	28	
7 Hon. IVO-BLIGH	c C. Bannerman, b Boyle	21	
8 P. H. MORTON, Esq.	c C. Bannerman, b Boyle	11	
9 C. PIGG, Esq.	b Boyle	11	
10 A. F. J. FORD, Esq.	not out	22	
11 H. WOOD, Esq.	b Spofforth	2	
	B 12, l-b 4, w , n-b ,	16	B , l-b , w , n-b ,
	Total	285	Total

AUSTRALIANS.	First Innings.		Second Innings.
1 C. BANNERMAN	b Morton	13	
2 W. L. MURDOCH, Esq.	b Morton	47	
3 T. HORAN, Esq.	b Morton	0	
4 D. W. GREGORY, Esq.	c A Lyttelton b Morton	5	
5 T. W. GARRETT, Esq.	b Morton	13	
6 F. E. SPOFFORTH, Esq.	b A Steel	0	
7 G. H. BAILEY, Esq.	c A Lyttelton b A Steel	5	
8 J. M. BLACKHAM, Esq.	l b w, b Morton	0	
9 F. E. ALLAN, Esq.	not out	12	
10 H. F. BOYLE, Esq.	st A Lyttelton b Steele	9	
11 A. BANNERMAN	b Morton	1	
	B 2, l-b 5, w , n-b	7	B 1, l-b , w , n-b ,
	Total	111	Total

Umpires—Price and Clayton.   Scorers—West and T. Mycroft.

*** The Telegraph Office is near the centre of the Grand Stand.

The match scorecard showing the Australians on the brink of their fourth first-class defeat of the tour, and their first at Lord's.

An illustration of the Eleven published in the Melbourne *Leader* on
30 November 1878, after their triumphant return to Australia.

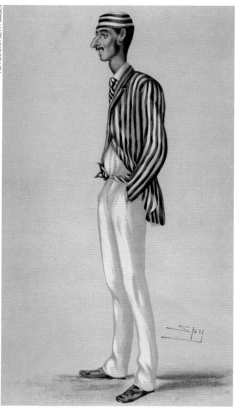

The "Demon Bowler" Fred Spofforth, sketched by the renowned cartoonist "Spy" in *Vanity Fair*, 13 July 1878. Spofforth was only the second cricketer after W. G. Grace to be so honoured by the society magazine.

Sussex's James Lillywhite *(above)* captained the fourth England team to tour Australia, in 1876-7, and acted as agent for the Eleven during their four-month tour of Britain.

Jack Conway, the tough, assertive manager of the 1878 Australians and the "presiding genius of the concept".

Sydney's Charles Bannerman (*right*), a relentless aggressor with a bat in his hands and Test cricket's first centurion.

"Kidnapped" by W. G. Grace before the start of the Eleven's match against Middlesex at Lord's, the Gloucestershire-born Billy Midwinter (*above*) deserted the tourists after playing in the opening eight matches of the tour.

W. G. Grace, who had numerous run-ins with the Eleven, pictured with the obdurate Surrey opening bat, Harry Jupp

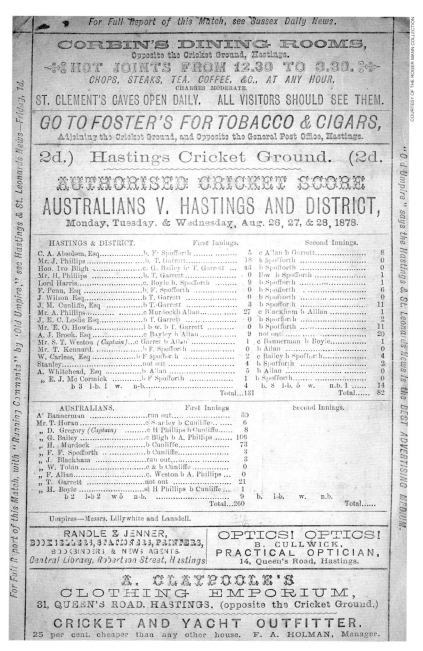

Tasmania's George Bailey hit the second century by an Australian in England (Charles Bannerman scored the first against Leicestershire) during the match versus an eighteen of Hastings. The future England captains Lord Harris and the Hon. Ivo Bligh were among a host of amateurs recruited by the locals.

A natural leader, the imposing David Gregory won many plaudits for his captaincy and "invincible self-confidence".

PRICE TWOPENCE.

SURREY COUNTY CRICKET CLUB,

KENNINGTON OVAL

On MONDAY, SEPTEMBER 2nd, and two following days.

Australians v. Players of England.

AUSTRALIANS.	1st Innings.		2nd Innings.	
A. Bannerman	c McIntyre, b Barratt ..	4	c and b Barlow	25
C. Bannerman	c Barlow, b Barratt	51	b McIntyre	15
T. Horan, Esq	c Watson, b Barratt	0	b McIntyre	4
W. Murdoch, Esq.	st H. Phillips, b Barratt.	0	c Hearne, b McIntyre ..	0
F. E. Spofforth, Esq.	st H. Phillips, b Barratt.	14	b McIntyre	0
G. H. Bailey, Esq.	c Lillywhite, b Barratt..	0	b Barlow	12
D. Gregory, Esq.	c J. Phillips, b Barratt..	0	not out	9
J. Blackham, Esq.	st H. Phillips, b Barratt..	0	b Barlow...............	0
H. Boyle, Esq.	c J. Phillips, b Barratt..	8	c and b McIntyre	4
T. Garrett, Esq.	c Watson, b Barratt	0	c Hearne, b Barratt....	10
F. Allan, Esq.	not out	0	b McIntyre	4
	B , l-b , w , n-b		B 3, l-b 3, w , n-b	6
	Total	77	Total	89

PLAYERS.	1st Innings.		2nd Innings.	
Rigley	c and b Allan	18	b Allan	10
Barlow	st Murdoch, b Allan	16	b Spofforth	8
J. Phillips	not out	19	c and b Boyle	14
G. Hearne	b Spofforth...........	8	b Garrett	12
Charlwood	c Boyle, b Spofforth	0	b Spofforth	12
Wheeler	b Spofforth	0	b Spofforth	4
Watson	b Spofforth	0	b Spofforth	7
H. Phillips	c Boyle, b Spofforth	0	run out	2
Lillywhite	c Allan, b Boyle	0	b Garrett	2
Barratt	b Spofforth............	0	b Spofforth	0
McIntyre	c Murdoch, b Spofforth..	10	not out	3
	B 4, l-b 7, w , n-b	11	B 2, l-b , w , n-b	2
UMPIRES:				
Caffyn and Potter.	Total	82	Total	76

JOHN ... c ... Pr ... 3, P ... Street, ... Hill ...

The Eleven beat the Players by eight runs in a tense finish at The Oval. Ted Barratt, the Surrey left-arm spinner, captured ten Australian wickets for 43 runs in the first innings.

W. G. Grace and A. N. Hornby, regular opponents of the 1878 Australians, depicted on the cover of *The Mask*, a weekly satirical review.

The tortoise to brother Charles's hare, Alec Bannerman was dubbed the most famous of all Australian stonewalling batsmen. "His patience was inexhaustible," *Wisden* wrote.

The Irish-born Tom Horan, a sturdy middle-order batsman and highly respected journalist.

Tom Garrett, the youngest member of the Eleven, celebrated his 20th birthday on tour.

Punch paid tribute to the Australians in verse on more than one occasion during their tour, famously so after their victory against MCC at Lord's. This cartoon of the Eleven appeared on 10 August 1878.

The first wicketkeeper to dispense with a long-stop, Jack Blackham's artistry behind the stumps repeatedly drew roars of appreciation from the English crowds. He regularly stood up to the stumps to fast bowling, most notably to Fred Spofforth.

The Melbourne Cricket Ground, photographed in 1878, staged the first three Test matches between England and Australia. Its palatial £4,700 grandstand, built in 1876, could accommodate as many as 2,000 spectators.

Fred Spofforth in full cry (*above, left and right*). Captured by the pioneering sports photographer George Beldam in 1904 at Hampstead Cricket Club, the fast bowler was still a fearsome prospect, even at the age of 51.

One of the first exponents of swing bowling, the left-armer Frank Allan was plagued on tour by illness and niggling injury.

The Australians opened the American leg of their tour with a match against an eighteen of New York at the St George's Ground at Hoboken, New Jersey. The sketch appeared in *Frank Leslie's Illustrated Newspaper* on 19 October 1878.

Harry Boyle, the inventor of silly mid-on and a match-winning medium-pacer who, in partnership with Fred Spofforth, formed Australia's "first great firm" of bowlers.

The Philadelphian XI, with Robert Newhall (*far right*) whose 84 against the Australians has been described as the greatest innings ever played by an American. He was one of four brothers to turn out against the Eleven, including Charles Newhall (*third from left*), a highly regarded fast bowler.

CRICKET MATCH Played at Germantown Between

FIRST INNINGS.

THE BATSMAN'S NAME	FIGURES AS SCORED	HOW OUT	NAME OF BOWLER	RUNS
Mr. Hargreaves	13132	ct Spofforth	Spofforth	10
F. Brewster	12322121	ct Murdoch	Allan	15
C. A. Newhall	3	b	Allan	3
R.S. Newhall	22333112313233323211112313 / 1222333313314	b	Allan	44
G. M. Newhall	233123	ct Spofforth	Hogan	13
R. N. Caldwell	112111332123	st Blackham	Boyle	23
E. Hopkinson		ct Gregory	Bailey	0
D. S. Newhall	113232113116131	not out		31
T. Hargreaves	1	b	Allan	1
E. Comfort	12	b	Allan	3
Meade		b	Allan	0
Byes	233			8
Leg Byes	2121			6
Wide Balls				
No Balls				

Mr. Hargreaves, Brewster, C.A. Newhall, G. Newhall, Caldwell, Hopkinson, R. Newhall, T. Hargreaves. Total 196

Number of Runs at the fall of each wicket: 1 for 28, 2 28, 3 33, 4 73, 5 110, 6 119, 7 178, 8 188, 9 196, 10 196 — 196

The scorebook showing Philadelphia's first innings score of 196 against the tourists at Germantown.

The Australians pose with spectators at Germantown. They were later hissed at by the crowd after David Gregory marched his team off the field in protest at a series of decisions made by the Philadelphian umpire.

The Eleven take in the sights at Niagara Falls. The spray, blown over on the breeze, left them soaked from head to foot and probably accounts for their grim expressions.

The genial Billy Murdoch, Blackham's fellow gloveman and a future captain of Australia, served his batting apprenticeship with the Eleven. He later led Sussex from 1893 to 1899. (*Below*) the wicketkeeping gloves worn by Murdoch on tour in 1878. Their owner, the cricket collector Roger Mann, likens the flimsy gauntlets to "a pair of slim kid gloves which a city gent might wear – no thicker than that".

George Bailey suffered the only serious injury to befall the Eleven during 14 months of non-stop cricket, when he broke his arm playing against New South Wales.

from the bat into the fields beyond". Above all he hit straight, with a perfect follow-through and no discernible trace of a slog.

The manner of his dismissal, therefore, was tame to put it mildly. Thornton had scored 40 out of 67 when a defensive push, of all things, lobbed gently into the hands of Charles Bannerman at point, off the effective but underused fast round-arm of Bailey, and the fireworks display was over. There was one more success for the Australians when Spofforth claimed his 100th wicket in England – a feat he accomplished in just 13 matches – sending back Yardley for 12; but Walker demonstrated why he was so highly regarded as one of England's foremost amateur batsmen, hitting a high-class, unbeaten 60. When stumps were drawn punctually at six o'clock – to enable the Australians to effect another swift departure for the station, although not before casting a last lingering look over their shoulder at the surroundings – the Orleans Club were 75 runs shy of their target.

"Our days in Twickenham will remain one of the best treasured recollections of the whole tour," Horan added. So much so, in fact, that they were content to forfeit their share of the gate receipts, the club having opened the ground to the public for an entrance fee of half a crown. More than 20 years later C. I. Thornton, recalling the match in A. W. Pullin's *Talks With Old English Cricketers*, told the author that the club netted £500, "which it was badly in need of", and of which the Australians did not help themselves to a single shilling.

———

Thereafter the matches came thick and fast and with no let-up. After leaving Twickenham, the Eleven endured a seven-hour journey from Paddington to Swansea for a contest with the Gentlemen of Wales on 10 July. They arrived in the principality at 4.30am, had something to eat, attempted to catch some sleep and were woken at nine to start the game at half past eleven. This was followed by another seven-hour ordeal by rail, to the north of England, to take on an eighteen of Werneth and Oldham on the 12th and 13th. By the time the show rolled into Leicestershire for a three-day game with the county side on the morning of the 15th, they had clocked up nearly 400 miles since their departure from London. If at times they batted as if they had a train to catch, it was because they probably had. According to the *Argus*, the non-stop travel, cricket and lack of sleep had taken its diminishing toll, and all of the Eleven were simply "out on their feet". After the match in Oldham, one of the team wrote home to his family in Australia, "You will laugh when I tell you that I was too tired to go to sleep!" The "bright summer holidays under the chestnut trees at the Orleans Club" – as one reporter wistfully put it – must have seemed like a dream.

Nevertheless, they still managed to dispose of the Gentlemen of Wales inside two days, winning by an innings and 27 runs. The Australians were surprised to discover that the St Helens ground had been fashioned from a reclaimed sandbank five years earlier, and were impressed by its "spacious oval, 560 yards in circumference", and its "neat and commodious pavilion". They were also surprised by the pace and accuracy of the former Cambridge University fast bowler F. C. Cobden, who had lit up the Varsity match of 1870 – a game *Wisden* dubbed "the Charge of the Light Brigade". Oxford had required four runs to win with three wickets in hand when Cobden, in a momentous last over, claimed a hat-trick to bowl Cambridge to victory by two runs. Proving he was still a force to be reckoned with, the fast bowler took five for 41 to help dismiss the Australians for 219, but the local eighteen were no match for Spofforth and Boyle. The pair bowled unchanged through both innings, routing the Welshmen for 94 and 88, with Spofforth capturing 17 wickets and Boyle 15.

However, there was no respite for the Australians. Having attended a mayoral banquet that night, they were roused at 2.30am to catch a train for Oldham, which had been specially laid on for them, stopping en route for breakfast in Shrewsbury. The endless round of banqueting and speeches, the *Sporting Gazette* suggested, was proving every bit as tiresome as the unremitting travel and cricket: "They have no objection to playing cricket all day, but as regards ... the compulsory attendance at banquets ... though they do their duty like men, they are terribly tired of accepting hospitality which they cannot with good grace decline." On their arrival in Oldham at half past ten, they were whisked straight to the ground, the match starting an hour later. "We did not even have time to go to our hotel," Horan wrote, "but sent our portmanteaux to our lodgings in charge of a railway porter." For the second time on the tour, they were forced to look outside the Eleven for an Australian (Allan having been given leave to visit relatives, while Alec Bannerman was nursing a bruised hand), calling on Conway and requisitioning H. H. Hyslop, a right-handed batsman and wicketkeeper who had played several first-class matches for Hampshire. Hyslop's inclusion in the Eleven is curious to say the least: it seems to be based on "the belief that he had been born in Australia"; in fact, he was born in Southampton in 1840, and his engagement would appear to have been made on the somewhat tenuous grounds that he once played for the Richmond and Melbourne clubs while staying in Victoria.[3]

As exhausted as they were, the Australians still managed to bowl out the eighteen (with the usual influx of professionals) for 138, with Spofforth taking six for 41 and Horan seven for 40. However, runs proved elusive for both teams and, after trailing by nine runs on first innings' scores, the Australians despatched the locals for 117 second time around to leave themselves with the task of scoring 130 to win in two and a half hours. They finished just 18 runs short with three wickets remaining, having been 53 without loss at one point, when stumps were drawn at half past six in front of a rapt crowd of 7,000. "I suppose we should have been happy to come out of the match with honours even," Horan confessed. "We were exceedingly jaded after our journey." But for the performances of Gregory – he scored 42 in the first innings and was undefeated on 37 at stumps – and Spofforth, who made light of his excessive workload to return figures of 14 for 97 from 57.2 overs, they might not have been so fortunate.

As well as making news on the pitch, Spofforth was much in demand off it. On 13 July a caricature of "the Demon" fast bowler, sketched by the renowned cartoonist "Spy", appeared in the weekly society magazine *Vanity Fair*. Selection for a *Vanity Fair* cartoon, which had become a national institution, conferred a stamp of importance on its subject, and Spofforth found himself rubbing shoulders with some particularly exalted company: Benjamin Disraeli, or the Earl of Beaconsfield as he was then (he was no stranger to these pages), and James Whistler, the American-born artist, had already been portrayed in the magazine that year. Significantly, Spofforth was only the second cricketer to be so honoured. The first was W. G. Grace, who appeared in the issue of 9 June 1877. Depicted in his blue and white striped blazer with matching pillbox cap, belt, and brown brogues, his hands thrust into the pockets of his white flannels, there is an almost jaunty air about Spofforth; the heavy drooping moustache and sweeping sideburns had yet to become part of the warpaint. The caricature accentuates his imposing height – all "wire and whipcord" as "Banjo" Paterson, the bush poet and balladeer, once described him – and the great beak of a nose.

However, the somewhat condescending tone of the caption which accompanied the illustration – "Mr Spofforth is Australian by origin and breeding, yet like all the better kind of Australians, he is not distinguishable from an English gentleman" – would not go unnoticed or, indeed, uncommented upon in Australia. One newspaper retorted that, although the intention of the magazine was "doubtless to be complimentary to him and to Australians in general", the "left-handed sort of way" in which it had carried it out was more than a little amusing. "Clearly the writer laboured under doubt as to how far it would be safe to commit *Vanity Fair* in regard to Australians," it added. The magazine also praised Spofforth's "quick eye, true hand, and good judgment as a bowler. He is withal of excellent manners, modest and diffident, and has become a favourite with all who have known him in England." The last bit was certainly true, but as many a batsman who had been on the receiving end of his glower, or had his stumps unceremoniously scattered, would testify, there was nothing remotely diffident about "the Demon".

———

Leicestershire were among the first counties to agree to a match with the Australians all those months ago, and the only side to offer to pay a lump sum for the privilege of playing against them. It was also at Leicester that Charles Bannerman – the natural hitter who had struck a glorious 165 against the All-England XI at Melbourne and was rated by James Lillywhite as the best professional batsman in the world – properly introduced himself to an English audience.

Perhaps it was the grand scale of the ground, it certainly had the look of an Australian arena, which made Bannerman feel so at home. The Leicestershire club had staged its first match at the new Grace Road ground only three months earlier, having turned 16 acres into a gleaming new cricket pitch with an athletics track and hotel. Horan went so far as to describe the ground as "perhaps the largest cricket enclosure in the world". The playing portion, he pointed out, was more than half a mile round: "Hits to the rink counted for four, but the ground being so large, five runs were often scored before the ball reached it." However, despite having made the five-hour trip to Leicester from the north the day before – a scenic journey through the Derbyshire dales and the fox-hunting country of Leicestershire – and arriving at the ground reasonably well rested for once, the Eleven did not make an auspicious start.

The Leicestershire openers put on 113 before the Australians had their first success, but a rush of wickets later in the day, triggered by Spofforth, saw them bowled out for 193 on a pitch that played as well as it looked. Another listless batting display by the tourists in which they were disposed of for 130 then handed the initiative back to Leicestershire, who closed the second day on 129 for four. It was on the third day, however, that the game finally came to life. Victory was probably the last thing the

Australians had on their minds when they walked out on to the field that morning, but another dramatic collapse by Leicestershire – their last six wickets went down for the addition of only 16 runs to Spofforth and Garrett – left them needing 209 to win in four hours. According to one newspaper, the swell of opinion among a huge crowd of almost 13,000 (as many as 35,000 were reported to have thronged through the turnstiles during the three days) was that the task would prove beyond them.

Bannerman immediately accepted the challenge and, providing the crowd with an inkling of the plunder that was to follow later in the game, cracked the left-arm Rylott for three successive boundaries in the first over. At lunch he had made 58 out of 78. He lost Murdoch soon after for 24, but Horan, timing the ball sweetly from the first, kept him company and the runs continued to flow at a rapid rate. So discontented had the crowd become by this stage, though, that when Bannerman reached his century – the first Australian batsman to do so on English soil – it was greeted by a wall of silence. It was the same when Australia passed 150, while the hoisting of the 200 was met by what one reporter dryly described as "the gaze of the public". Only when Bannerman was finally adjudged run out for a chanceless 133 – and most unfairly, too, in the opinion of the Eleven – did the crowd find their voice again, cheering loudly, but the match was already over by then. Moments later Gregory made the winning hit, leaving Horan unbeaten on 40. In all, Bannerman struck a five and 23 fours during his two and a half hours at the wicket, scoring 97 of his runs in boundaries and only nine in singles. This was the return of the batsman who shaped the destiny of matches, rather than specialising in the cameo performances which had become his stock in trade since arriving in England. "His hitting all round was splendid and his innings altogether was quite equal to his great performance on the Melbourne ground," Horan declared. "It showed that when a score was needed, Bannerman could hit with the daring and success which astonished and defeated the last England Eleven that visited Australia." *Lillywhite's Cricketers' Annual* was equally beguiled, describing it as an innings which was "absolutely without fault and one which for fine, clean, well-timed hitting has never been surpassed".

That evening the Australians started the long trek back north, for a three-day match against Hull, with their spirits visibly lifted. The original intention had been to play against a local eighteen, but as the team was composed almost entirely of professionals from Yorkshire, Derbyshire and Nottinghamshire, it was agreed to recast the match as an 11-a-side contest and to rename them the United North of England. In the end, it did not matter much what they were called as the Australians completed victory by the emphatic margin of ten wickets. They also passed 300 for the first time in England, with Allan top-scoring with 78 and Horan and Blackham both making half-centuries; the latter's batting was said to be similar to that of a pinch-hitter in baseball and proved particularly effective on this occasion. There was even a muscular 46 from Jack Conway, batting as low as No. 10, before Boyle, with eight for 30, dispersed the mercenaries for 68 in their second innings. After that it was back to London and the familiar surroundings of the Horse Shoe Hotel, where they arrived in the small hours of Sunday, 21 July, 12 days since leaving Twickenham. Disraeli had already made his triumphal return from the Congress of Berlin, and the heatwave, which had burned on and off for almost a month, was all but over.

Twelve
22 July–25 August 1878

"The last great match of the season at Old Trafford"

The third and final appearance by the 1878 Australians at Lord's on 22–24 July should have been against MCC. It was to be an opportunity for the club to exact what the *London Daily News* described as "sweet revenge" for its humiliation on 27 May. However, in failing to raise a good enough team, in its own words, to challenge the Australians (or, as the *Argus* suggested, "not caring to risk another defeat"), MCC decided, with reluctance, to pull out of the rematch. The chance to return matters to the old order having therefore been passed up, the Australians found themselves pitted instead against Cambridge University, "the form team of the season" and an altogether more formidable proposition.

The 1870s were a golden era for Varsity cricket, and the Light Blue XI of 1878 has often been described as the greatest University team of all time. Certainly, with the likes of A. G. Steel – it is doubtful whether there has been a more gifted University all-rounder – Edward and Alfred Lyttelton, Ivo Bligh, A. P. Lucas and P. H. Morton in their ranks, they were the envy of any team in the land. They were also unbeaten, having won all seven matches they had played that summer: victories against MCC (twice), the Gentlemen of England, Surrey, Yorkshire and an England XI (including W. G. Grace, Billy Midwinter and C. I. Thornton) had been surpassed only by the 238-run annihilation of Oxford, in which Steel, with match figures of 13 for 73, despatched the Dark Blues for 32 – a total which remains to this day the lowest ever recorded in the Varsity match. As Steel (for his sorcery with the ball for the Gentlemen of England at Prince's) and Edward Lyttelton (with his imperious century for Middlesex) had also left their imprint on the Australians, producing the two outstanding individual performances against them on tour to date, interest in the match was naturally running high. The Australians had unfailingly risen to the occasion on their previous visits to Lord's, and although Cambridge were installed as 2/1 favourites, there was more than enough evidence to suggest that the University would not have it all their own way, even against a team in such dire need of a break. Tired though they were, the "presence of the welcome strangers", *The Spectator* remarked, had "vastly increased the popularity of cricket as a spectacle … [and] we may expect to see a gathering at Lord's which will equal the greatest that has ever met there".

An estimated crowd of 10,000 – it would grow to some 15,000 before the close – had already assembled when Edward Lyttelton won the toss and decided to make first use of a lightning fast outfield. This time it was the turn of the younger Lyttelton brother, Alfred, to impose himself on the Australians after they made what was by now their customary sluggish start. An outstanding all-round athlete like his brother – he was the best amateur tennis player in the country and would become the first man to represent England at both cricket and football – he was quickly into his stride, setting a tempo that never slackened throughout the Cambridge innings. The Australians enjoyed a slice of fortune when Edward Lyttelton, looking in ominously good form, needlessly ran himself out for 15, after hitting three boundaries in his brief stay; but it was when Steel joined Alfred Lyttelton that the game started to get away from the tourists.

The hundred went up in just 75 minutes, and such was the dominance of the batsmen that it was not until the 30th over that Boyle finally completed the first maiden of the game. The Cambridge score had reached 169 for two when Steel, all dash and daring and hitting the ball "wonderfully hard", in the words of the *Daily News*, took one liberty too many with the fielders and was run out by Alec Bannerman, at mid-off, for 59. Only six more runs were added to the total before Lyttelton followed the

Marlborough freshman back to the pavilion for 75, and after an enterprising 21 from Bligh the Cambridge innings finished on 285. There were three wickets apiece for Spofforth and Boyle who were once again unstinting in their efforts, bowling almost 70 overs between them, even though both men had had to drag themselves back into battle before the start of play.

Steel, though, was straight back into the action, bowling the first over from the nursery end to Charles Bannerman when the Australians began their reply shortly after 4.30, although it was his fellow opening bowler, Morton, who would prove the sensation this time. With a disconcerting ability to generate explosive pace off an ambling run-up of no more than two or three paces – some of his deliveries were positively "Spofforthian" in the opinion of Horan, one of seven first-innings victims for the right-armer – the Australians were bundled out for 111 in the space of an hour and a half. Even a batsman of Charles Bannerman's class, who was one of nine men in the match to have his timbers rattled by Morton, was hopelessly deceived and beaten for pace. The Australians were even more astonished to learn that Morton's form was so erratic going into the Varsity match he had been in danger of losing his place in the eleven. For a bowler who could not deliver a "well-pitched ball to save his life" only a few weeks earlier, his performance was nothing short of startling. Not to be completely outdone, Steel nipped in with three wickets to maintain his glittering success rate against the colonials, who, 174 runs in arrears, were promptly invited to follow on by Edward Lyttelton. They would have to attempt to stave off defeat with only ten men, too. Alec Bannerman's hand injury, sustained against the Gentlemen of Wales almost two weeks earlier, was showing no signs of improvement, and, despite batting at No. 11 in the first innings, the "incorruptible stonewaller" had been in such discomfort he could barely hold the bat. His mood cannot have been improved either by having his stumps summarily rearranged by Morton.

Not surprisingly, perhaps, the Australians were soon staring defeat in the eye. Morton struck twice early on the second day while Murdoch, who had played a lone hand in the first innings with a measured 47, was trapped by Steel for a duck. Charles Bannerman, well supported by Horan, briefly threatened to make it a more even contest until he was run out by a whipcord return from the athletic Bligh, fielding at cover, for 26. However, he did at least play the shot of the match – a blow, off Morton, of such unbridled power that it would still be talked about years later. Pelham Warner, in *Lord's 1787–1945*, records that "the ball pitched short of the ring, bounded over the low stand on the left of the pavilion, and cleared Lord Londesborough's drag, striking the wall behind with a lovely thud". It was the one bright spot for the Australians before Cambridge cantered to victory by an innings and 72 runs. The verdict of the *Sporting Gazette* was that the Australians had been roundly "beaten at all points" in bowling, batting and even fielding, before concluding, "'Advance Australia' is an excellent motto, but when it is a question of advancing against a superior force it becomes rather difficult to act up to it." In bagging a further five wickets in the Australian second innings, Morton finished with match figures of 12 for 90.

"There is no doubting that we were severely defeated," Horan admitted. "Good batsmen have seldom collapsed as we did in each innings and I can assign no reason for it except that we are stale through overwork." And none more so than Spofforth: his designation may have been "the Demon" but he was after all only mortal and badly in need of a rest. The fast bowler, it was reported, had asked to be stood down from the matches with Leicestershire and Hull in order to keep himself fresh for the contest with Cambridge University. The Australians would have been more than happy to comply with his wishes, too, but for the worrying injury to Alec Bannerman's hand. At the conclusion of the game with Cambridge, Spofforth had worked his way through a mammoth 836 overs in 18 matches, missing only one since the start of the tour at Trent Bridge. The meteor of the summer was in danger of burning himself out.

The defeat (not to mention the loss of their unblemished record at Lord's) would remain a sore point throughout the rest of the tour for the Eleven, who believed that, had they not been so overworked, they would at the very least have given their opponents a run for their money. As the *Sydney Morning Herald* put it, they were "half-beaten" before the match even started: "In the field the Australians seemed jaded and fagged, and the bowlers complained of want of rest." The *South Australian Chronicle* took a similar line: "In bowling and fielding, where freshness and vigour are the main agents of success, they were overdone." But as the Australians set off once more for the station the following day and their next destination – Crewe, a five-hour journey on the London and North Western Railway – rest was not an option.

———

The Australians would not play another match on even terms until taking on Lancashire at Old Trafford on 15 August, by which time they would have completed seven more games in 22 days during their latest whistle-stop tour of the north and the midlands. They were, according to one newspaper, "starring the provinces" and no doubt there would be the occasional fluffed line or missed cue along the way as they struggled to keep pace with the frantic and ever-burgeoning schedule.

They started with an easy 99-run victory over twenty-two of Crewe inside two days on a pitch that was so rough it was described as being "full of hills and hollows" and regularly sent fielders sprawling on their faces in pursuit of the ball. The miserable weather returned, too, but not before Spofforth and Boyle, harvesting 39 wickets between them on a rapidly deteriorating surface, had bowled out the opposition for 54 and 79. During their stay the Australians were shown round the London and North Western Railway Company locomotive and steelworks, as if they needed any reminding of the hundreds of miles and endless, unravelling track that still lay ahead of them. The sheds "stretched in a line for more than a mile", Horan recorded, "and inside we saw iron and steel treated like so much dough. In less than five minutes a block of steel three feet long was forced into a rail over 20 feet in length, much to our astonishment." Then, naturally enough, it was back on the rail and an 84-mile journey to the Yorkshire Dales to play an eighteen of Keighley.

There, a young middle-order batsman by the name of William Tobin caught their eye. Scoring his runs stylishly and effectively after coming in at No. 5, Tobin was only one run away from a thoroughly deserved half-century when he was dismissed by a Spofforth "cannon shot"; not only that, he was an Australian. The tourists were delighted to discover, in the words of Horan, a "native-born Australian" in the wilds of Yorkshire, and one who so obviously knew how to handle a bat: "We are all quite pleased to think that one of our countrymen should be the heaviest scorer against us in this contest."[1] Formerly of St Patrick's College, Melbourne, and now a pupil at Stonyhurst College in Lancashire, the 19-year-old Tobin did not repeat his success in Keighley's second innings, falling to a catch behind off Boyle for seven, but he had done enough to convince the Australians that they had unearthed a gem. It was no surprise, therefore, when he appeared for them two weeks later against an eighteen of Dudley and District and was recruited to play in a further six games before the end of the tour. There was another piece of good news: Alec Bannerman's injured hand had cleared up sufficiently to enable him to return to his rightful spot at the top of the order where he scored a typically watchful 55, putting on an opening stand of 97 with his brother and laying the foundations for a seven-wicket victory.

However, the Australians were fortunate to come away with a draw in their next match, against a Rochdale eighteen, and even more fortunate to escape without a serious injury on what they branded as the "most treacherous pitch we have encountered on the whole of the tour": more perilous, Horan wrote, than the "bare chocolate surface of the Toowoomba racecourse and the Oamuru potato paddock!" Several of the Australian batsmen received blows to their bodies, while George Bailey, whose 38 was the highest score in the match, was even given out caught off his arm. One Rochdale man took a ball full in the face from Spofforth, only to be run out for his pains by Charles Bannerman as he reeled away in a dazed state from his crease. Tom Garrett, with his ability to make the ball rise alarmingly off the wicket, cut a particularly "terrifying prospect for the batsmen", regularly bumping the ball over the wicketkeeper's head (Murdoch having drawn the short straw on this occasion) straight into long-stop's hands. The match was eventually abandoned after a torrential downpour flooded the ground, leaving Rochdale 58 short of victory with 11 wickets still intact.

At this point the Eleven were to have travelled to Trent Bridge for a rematch with Nottinghamshire over the Bank Holiday on 5–7 August, but the county had been forced to postpone, citing the same reason as MCC. Matches with a twenty-two of Buxton and an eighteen of Burnley, who had no trouble raising teams, were hastily arranged in its stead. After arriving at Buxton (already world-famous for its mineral springs), the Australians found that for once they were not the only strangers in town. "There are evidently a great many believers in the efficacy of these baths," Horan noted. "In our hotel, *The George*, we had representatives of nearly all nations ... and the confusion of tongues around the dinner table was worthy of Babel." If Sheffield and Rochdale were the smokiest places they had visited, Buxton was undoubtedly the prettiest and cleanest. Although the pitch, according to Horan, was one of the more eccentric they would play on, "The pavilion, which consists of two small rooms, stands on the top of a hill so steep that the batsman in going to wicket has to travel at a sling trot, until he reaches the base. He is then in a valley, for the rest of the journey to the wickets is up a gentle sloping hill." In fact, it was uphill work for all the batsmen, with the exception of Alec Bannerman who was in his element on a soft, sticky wicket, compiling 42 – the highest score on either side – in another low-scoring, rain-affected draw.

No sooner had stumps been drawn than the Australians were leaving the Peak District of Derbyshire behind and journeying the

55 miles to the cotton town of Burnley. The fixture, which took place on 7 August, owed everything to the resourcefulness and persistence of its club secretary, who had made it his business to shadow the tourists, bombarding them with requests for a match; flatly refusing to take no for an answer, he even promised to throw in all the gate receipts and expenses if they complied. It either proved too good an offer to refuse, or it was the only way to get shot of him, but the Australians (despite giving up a precious day off) finally agreed to make a detour on their way to Liverpool, where they were scheduled to play eighteen of the Stanley Club.

They received a spectacular reception on their arrival at Burnley and were all but mobbed at the station, evoking memories of their welcome in Nottingham almost three months earlier. On the morning of the match the whole town closed down, the factory hands were given the afternoon off, the mills stood idle and a crowd of some 6,000 crammed into the club's Turf Moor ground. "Had the weather been at all favourable the muster on the ground would have been over ten thousand," Horan ventured. In fact, the rain did not let up all day, and it is claimed that the ubiquitous secretary, fearful there would be a riot if play was abandoned, instructed both teams to take the field and see out the game. The conditions were so woeful that the Australians "did not even bother to change" after arriving at the ground, fully expecting the game to be called off.

Burnley batted first and were soon reduced to 20 for ten by Spofforth and Boyle, but a powerfully struck 39 by W. Burrows, a former Lancashire batsman, hoisted the total to 102. Alec Bannerman, keeping wicket so that Blackham (who umpired in this match) and Murdoch could rest their bruised hands, proved so expert that he not only stood up to Spofforth, Boyle and Garrett, but pulled off two stumpings. By the time the Bannermans started the Australian reply at half past three, it was to the accompaniment of thunder and lightning, as well as rain.

Wickets fell steadily. Charles Bannerman, Horan, Murdoch and Allan all departed cheaply, and Gregory and Alec Bannerman – the only Australians to reach double figures – both succumbed with the score on 35: Bannerman was bowled by a ball he barely saw, and Gregory holed out at long-on. Spofforth and Boyle quickly perished amidst the atmospherics, and when Bailey was the ninth batsman out, caught at third man for the addition of only five runs, the Australians were slipping towards an excruciating defeat. There were still ten minutes left to survive when the last man, Garrett, walked out to the middle to join Hyslop, the recruit from Hampshire. The bowlers hustled through their overs and the tension proved unbearable, particularly for the Australian players, some of whom could hardly bring themselves to watch. However, so successfully did the last-wicket pair batten down the hatches that the clock ticked round to 6.30 without any further alarms. The steely-eyed Garrett played out the final over on 47 for nine, eschewing all risks – he even ignored an inviting full-toss outside the off-stump – and the Australians escaped with a draw. The crowd, who had cheered every wicket and every run with equal gusto from beneath their umbrellas, mobbed both batsmen at the end although, as Hyslop recalled, "the victory was really that of the eighteen".[2]

Before their departure to Liverpool that evening, over a well-earned glass of wine, the Australians were handed £130 in takings (the club having charged a fourpenny entrance fee). The Eleven, however, considered that £100 was a "fine recompense" and returned £30 to the secretary for his troubles. They boarded the train for Liverpool and were safely ensconced in their "comfortable quarters" at the Union Hotel some two and a half hours later.

Their next match, the following day, took place in the magnificent hundred-acre setting of Stanley Park – or the People's Park as it was known – which in a year would become the home of Everton FC and the "birthplace of Liverpool football". The generosity of the Australians was again much to the fore, when, after defeating the local eighteen by an innings and 71 runs in a day and a half with Gregory (70) and Boyle (58) recording their highest scores of the tour, they were persuaded to fill the time by playing an exhibition game. This was no ordinary request, however. It came from an old man who dolefully informed the Australians that he had travelled 40 miles and "paid his shilling solely to see Spofforth bowl" but the match had ended before he got the chance to do so. His disposition had not improved any on learning that "the Demon" had finished with a haul of 20 wickets. So, as Horan explained, "We felt that it would have been most inconsistent of us if we had not put our wares on display once more … and done something to entertain the cricket enthusiasts of the great Lancashire port." It did not, of course, do any harm to the Australian coffers either.

The crowds at Dudley two days later were not so fortunate, though: they did not get to see "the Demon" trundle. Having sat out only one game, against Batley back in early June, Spofforth was finally granted his wish and rested for the three-day encounter in the midlands. However, William Tobin, the promising school-boy batsman, debuted for the Australians, who were in an unassailable position, having reduced the eighteen to 40 for seven in their second innings – still 116 in arrears – when rain intervened to force a draw. The tourists had earlier recovered from being bowled out for 59 on a "spiteful surface" when, for the first time on tour, both Bannermans failed to score in an innings. Among their opponents was the Derbyshire professional John Platts, who had propelled the ball that felled Nottinghamshire's George Summers on that fateful day at Lord's eight years earlier. Platts bowled 30 overs at Dudley, taking just the one wicket, that of Tobin, whom he bowled for six. His fires, however, had long been extinguished and the former terror of Lord's was now no more than a purveyor of gentle medium-pace.

At seven o'clock on the evening of 14 August, the Australians were back on the London and North Western Railway, returning to Manchester and the start of their 27th match of the tour, against Lancashire at Old Trafford, the following day.

————

Three weeks earlier Old Trafford had played host to a volcanic County Championship game between Lancashire and Gloucestershire over 25–27 July in what was the first meeting between the two clubs at the Manchester ground. The contest, which pitted the Graces against the likes of A. N. Hornby, A. G. Steel and Dick Barlow, and was widely expected to have a bearing on the destiny of the county title, attracted a massive audience: 16,000 were in attendance on the Saturday when a record £400 for the ground was taken in gate money. In all, 28,000 spectators witnessed the game during the three days it was in progress, contributing towards receipts of some £750.[3] The match between Lancashire and the Australians, despite being blighted by the return of the cold and wet weather, would fall fractionally short of that figure, netting in excess of £700.

Predictably, with so much at stake – Gloucester would finish second in the table, one place above Lancashire at the end of the season – the encounter between these two titans was not without incident; and, just as predictably, W. G. Grace provided the flashpoint. It was during Lancashire's second innings (after a rousing century from Hornby) that W. Patterson drove the ball hard to the ring, where the spectators immediately shouted "four". The ball was then retrieved by a member of the crowd and returned to a Gloucestershire fieldsman. Patterson and Steel had stopped running, in the belief that four runs had been scored when it was thrown in and the stumps were broken at Steel's end. An appeal for a run-out by Grace was upheld, provoking a furious exchange between the Gloucestershire captain and Hornby, during which play was held up for several minutes. Eventually Grace was persuaded by the forceful Hornby to consult the crowd, who assured him in no uncertain terms that the ball had crossed the boundary, and Steel was recalled to the crease. There was further trouble later in the match when, as was often the case, spectators spilled on to the field of play, causing disturbances and delays. Many were protesting at the inadequate arrangements, in which wagons and drays doubled as grandstands; "a ruffian mob even took to tearing up the ground and throwing sods at players and spectators, and arrests had to be made". To ensure there was no repetition of these scenes during the game with the Australians, the committee had temporary grandstands constructed and employed a mounted policeman to patrol the boundary.

The game between Lancashire and Gloucestershire ended in a draw, with honours evenly distributed. When the bails were finally lifted, Gloucestershire, requiring 111 to win, had five wickets in hand with Grace, in rumbustious form and with a point to prove, unbeaten on 58. A certain Billy Midwinter, now firmly back under lock and key with the county, was not without influence either; batting at No. 3 he scored 22 and 25. Perhaps more significantly, the game was immortalised years later by the Lancashire-born poet Francis Thompson. It is a nostalgic paean to the match he watched as a young man, and although misleadingly entitled 'At Lord's' (the verses were written after he received an invitation to watch Lancashire play at Lord's, an offer "he could not bring himself to accept"), it is generally considered to be the greatest of cricket's idyllic poems: [4]

> … For the field is full of shades as I near the shadowy coast,
> And a ghostly batsman plays to the bowling of a ghost,
> And I look through my tears at a soundless-clapping host
> As the run-stealers flicker to and fro,
> To and fro:–
> O my Hornby and my Barlow long ago!

There was, however, nothing particularly poetic about the start of Lancashire's innings against the Australians on the morning of the 15th, in weather "more suitable to football than cricket". Once again, however, the crowds came in their thousands for what the *Manchester Evening News* promoted as the "last great match of the season at Old Trafford". They had barely time to settle into their seats before Hornby departed to the second ball of the match, a low full toss from a recharged Spofforth which struck him squarely on the pads as he shuffled across his stumps. It was so plumb, Horan commented, that the Lancashire umpire raised his finger without a flicker of hesitation.

Barlow followed shortly after – another victim for Spofforth – to a ball that fairly sizzled off the turf and took the outside edge of his bat for Gregory to complete the catch at slip. Hornby's fellow "run-stealer" had made only two. Wickets continued to fall, and at 16 for six, Lancashire were in disarray. Alec Watson fired off a few boundaries to give the score a semblance of respectability, but deprived of the services of Steel (the Australians' chief tormentor had gone grouse shooting in Scotland) the county were despatched for 97. Spofforth returned the remarkable figures of nine for 53 from 36 overs.

The impressive dimensions of Old Trafford were soon ringing to the crack of Charles Bannerman's bat; he hit with exceptional power when the Australian reply started shortly before four o'clock. Indeed, Hornby and Barlow would both remark that they had never seen the ball struck harder. Bannerman passed fifty for the fifth time in England, putting on 62 with Horan (33), but the dismissal of the sturdily built opener with the score on 110 prompted a sudden collapse, and the Australians were bowled out for 140 on the stroke of lunch on the second day. The left-arm Barlow, whose trademark was his unwavering accuracy, picked up five wickets with his medium-pace.

It was Barlow who held the Lancashire second innings together after Hornby, suffering the ignominy of a pair, was bowled by Spofforth, attempting to pull a ball through square leg. Hornby and his "good henchman" could not have been more different in style or temperament: Barlow, the dour, thrifty professional, was a pioneer of forward-defensive play who sold his wicket dearly; Hornby, as befitted the son of a cotton mill proprietor, batted like a millionaire. "He runs you out," Barlow claimed, "and then gives you a sovereign." He was also quite unable to lay a bat on Spofforth. Barlow was the fifth wicket to fall, having scored 40 out of 99 when he was deceived in the flight by Boyle and caught and bowled. The Lancashire crowds were as partisan as their great Yorkshire rivals, but they had also become accustomed to seeing their side win and "sat glumly" through the dismissal of each batsman. "The silence was profound," Horan noted. Spofforth, Boyle and Garrett met with little resistance after Barlow's departure and Lancashire were all out for 160 before lunch on the third day, leaving the Australians with 73 to win.

Charles Bannerman blazed away again, scoring 39 out of an opening stand of 47 with his brother, and was in a hurry to get the job done. But the weather was against them and the frequent showers, which had caused delays during the first two days of the match, turned to heavy rain by the afternoon. As Horan put it, "in a very short space of time the Old Trafford Ground resembled the banks of the Yarra at Richmond in flood time", depriving the Australians of their sixth first-class victory.

More worryingly, Charles Bannerman had strained a thigh muscle during his second-innings onslaught and, according to one report, "could scarcely walk" after the game. The injury was serious enough to prevent him from playing in the next match with Yeadon on 19 August and the two after that. He would not reappear until the end of the month when the Australians travelled to Hove to play against James Lillywhite's Sussex. The injury could not have come at a more untimely moment for the opener, who was hitting the ball better than at any stage on tour.

The Australians had already intended that Gregory, in need of a rest from the continual grind of cricket and travel, would miss the next couple of games. He had not only captained the Eleven with authority and purpose, winning the utmost praise for his generalship and uncomplicated approach, but played in all 27 matches in Britain so far without a break and with little or no diminution in his performance. However, Spofforth's failure to catch the train with the rest of the Eleven on the first morning of the match against Yeadon, and his subsequent late arrival at the ground, was not part of the plan. Unaccountably absent when the team mustered at the station, "the Demon" – his timing for once all awry – missed the train and had to make his way there under his own steam. "We were," Horan recorded of the game, "at sixes at sevens." Matters were not improved by the fact that the team journeyed to Yeadon each day by the most circuitous of routes, involving a train from Leeds to Apperley Bridge (situated four miles outside Bradford), followed by a two-mile ride by drag – all uphill – to the White Swan ground. Tobin replaced Charles Bannerman, while Charles Butler, a 23-year-old who had accompanied the Eleven on their journey to England, took Gregory's place, becoming the 16th player to represent the Australians on tour. A right-handed middle-order batsman from Hobart, Tasmania, Butler had been invited to replace Midwinter following his desertion to Gloucestershire, but, having played in a couple of non-first-class matches with W. G. Grace earlier in the season and been injured as a consequence, he had declined the offer. Grace had stayed with Charles Butler's family during his tour of Australia in 1873–4, and it was during this time in Hobart that the two struck up what was to prove an enduring friendship: Grace would later pay him the great honour of naming his fourth child after him. Boyle assumed the captaincy in the absence of Gregory, but it was not an occasion he or the Eleven would remember with any great fondness.

The match attracted an enormous turnout and as many as 10,000 poured in from Leeds, Bradford and the neighbouring villages to see the first day's play. All forms of transport, from "wagonettes, gigs, carts and even wheelbarrows", were used to ferry people to and from the ground. Among the 17 professionals hired by Yeadon were Lancashire's Barlow and the future England slow left-armer Ted Peate, who would not make his first-class Yorkshire debut for another year when no less a judge than W. G. Grace remarked that he had "taken rank with the very best bowlers" in the game. Boyle's first decision upon winning the toss was to put the eighteen in to bat on a decidedly sticky wicket. Allan (eight for 33) made the early inroads – including the wicket of Barlow whom he bowled for two – before Spofforth finally appeared like the US Cavalry over the brow of the hill to take six for 18 and round up the innings for 91. However, Barlow and Peate found the conditions particularly receptive, taking nine first-innings wickets between them to dismiss the Australians for a paltry 54 – a score that would have been even more embarrassing but for Alec Bannerman, who carried his bat for 27. They fared little better in their second innings when, chasing 109 to win on the third day, they folded for 84 (Bannerman top-scoring again with 24), losing their last six wickets for only 29. It was their first defeat by an eighteen since falling to Longsight in June.

However, as they so often did, they rebounded with a victory in their next match, beating a Scarborough eighteen (captained by the formidable former Yorkshire fast bowler George Freeman) by an innings and 46 runs, even though the game began in far from propitious circumstances. They had arrived in town the night before to discover (not for the first time on tour) that there was no room at the hotel where they were booked. The Eleven were left with no choice but to "forage for digs for ourselves". With the hotels and boarding houses full of holiday-makers – it was the height of the season – the only lodgings available were of such "inferior quality" that they lacked even the basic requirements of a mirror or a bar of soap. At least the pitch, for once, was a good one. Spofforth top-scored with 64 – no doubt he felt he owed the team some runs after his no-show on the first morning at Yeadon – while Blackham, in his best pinch-hitting style, struck 55 out of a commanding 295. Freeman, whom W. G. Grace rated as highly as any bowler he faced, showed that at 35 years old he had lost none of his stamina or appetite for the fray, recording the extraordinary figures of 79-46-72-2. He may no longer have been the scourge of every batsman in the land but he was, in the eyes of Horan, "still very fast" with "an easy, graceful delivery which makes the ball get up very quickly from the pitch". Spofforth, meanwhile, continued in irresistible form, picking up seven wickets in the first innings when the eighteen were forced to follow on and a further six in the second to help bowl them out for 125. In the process he more than wiped the slate clean.

At seven o'clock that evening, having chalked up their 13th victory, the Australians were back on the rail, embarking on the longest haul of the tour so far. Their next match was at Hastings, almost 310 miles away. They would not, however, attempt to complete the journey in one fell swoop. Instead, they would spend Sunday night at the Horse Shoe Hotel – arriving "tired and utterly played out" some eight hours later – before continuing on to their final destination from Charing Cross the next day. They booked into the palatial Queen's Hotel on Hastings' esplanade at ten that evening and flopped wearily into their beds. However, the end was now in sight: by the time they started their 30th match, against an eighteen of Hastings and District, on Monday, 26 August, the tour had little more than three weeks left to run.

Thirteen
26 August–7 September 1878

"Surely all concerned cannot be telling lies ..."

Lord Harris and Ivo Bligh were among the hired hands this time, although a more aristocratic pair of mercenaries would have been hard to find. In all, Hastings had enlisted six players from Kent, three from Sussex and one from Surrey, sparing no effort in their determination to beat the Australians. The itinerant nature of many of the eighteens did not go uncriticised by the press, but in the case of Hastings, the *Sporting Gazette* commented, the mercenaries at least belonged to the district, or "had some connection with that part of England". Among the Kent intake were the accomplished middle-order batsman Frank Penn and the former Cambridge University all-rounder Charles Absolom, an effective if somewhat eccentric hitter who "trained on beer and haymaking", but was highly regarded by his county captain, Lord Harris. Sussex provided the Phillips brothers: the batsmen, James and Albert, and the county's wicketkeeper, Harry. David Gregory, looking "fresh after his week's sabbatical", returned to the head of the team for the tourists, while William Tobin stood in for the still-hamstrung Charles Bannerman.

When the Eleven arrived at the Central Recreation Ground on a grey, overcast morning, it was to be informed by some of the crowd – emboldened by the gathering of such a luminous cast – that they would do well to avoid an innings defeat. It was nothing that the Australians had not heard before and, as they had already shown, they were never more dangerous than when they were written off or disparaged.

Those spectators were soon made aware of their folly when Spofforth bowled the impressively bearded Absolom with a ripsnorter, sending his middle stump flying for five. Absolom's method – he gripped his bat at the top of the handle as though it were a sledgehammer (not for nothing was he known as "the Cambridge Navvy") – may have served him well against lesser bowlers, but was ruthlessly exposed on this occasion by Spofforth. James Phillips and Bligh, who drove elegantly for his 43, then put on 55 to restore the confidence of the crowd, but when the Sussex man was bowled by Garrett for 18 and Spofforth removed Lord Harris and Penn in succession, the rot quickly set in. The wicket was so much to the liking of the Australian bowlers that Spofforth later remarked he would have been happy to carry it around with him on his travels. The Central Recreation Ground was not without its charms, either: overlooked by Hastings Castle and enclosed by grand four-storey villas and cheek-by-jowl boarding houses and hotels, it was an atmospheric setting in which to play cricket. The proximity of the tightly packed houses was such, the Australians observed, that it allowed the inhabitants a better view of the game than the paying spectators. From their vantage point they might have seen Garrett crown an exceptional spell of fast-medium bowling by removing Charles Cunliffe and J. Leslie in the space of two balls before pinning E. Howis in front of his stumps with the next to become the third Australian to accomplish a hat-trick in England. The eighteen – 64 for two at one stage – subsided to 131 all out, with Garrett taking seven for 35 and Spofforth six for 51.

George Bailey would also have good cause to remember Hastings. All too often left to languish down the order, the Tasmanian was promoted to bat at No. 4, where he seized the opportunity to leave his mark on the tour and freshen up the batting in the process. First, he put on 61 with Alec Bannerman (30) and then a blistering 119 with Murdoch (73), in a shade over an hour, during which he completed the second century by an Australian in England. The wristiest of batsmen, he did not need to rely on raw power but placed the ball into the gaps with what appeared to be the minimum of effort and fuss. Indeed, so well did he bat that he might have benefited from a move up the order earlier in the tour. He had struck 11 boundaries, mainly with crisply executed cuts and drives, when he was well caught in the deep by Bligh for 106 out of a total of 260. "It was," wrote Horan, "an inspired innings."

Spofforth, with Allan as his foil this time, continued his inspired form. He collected 12 for 39 from 33 overs – including his second hat-trick of the tour, bowling all three of his victims, Cunliffe, James Phillips and James Wilson – to dismiss the eighteen for 82 in two hours. The blue bloods, Lord Harris and Bligh, also had their stumps spectacularly rearranged by Spofforth, managing only one run between them, as the Australians galloped to victory by an innings and 47 runs. Allan, making the ball swerve prodigiously in the sea air, picked up four for 25. Spofforth always maintained that Allan swung the ball more than any other bowler he had ever seen: a trick, he said, that was achieved by the bowler bending his knees in delivery and releasing the ball a yard or two before he reached the crease.

The Australians left behind a thoroughly chastened crowd and set off on the 36-mile trip along the coast to Brighton at nine that evening, putting up at the Old Ship Hotel two hours later. They would be most taken with England's foremost seaside resort, as they were with their venerable Georgian hotel on the seafront. Charles Dickens had been a regular guest there on his many tours, where he gave impassioned readings in the establishment's Regency Room. From their rooms the Australians could see the rows of bathing machines lined up along the beach. Brighton "is a splendidly built town, and, so far as I can observe, puts Hastings and Scarborough completely in the shade," Horan noted shortly after their arrival. But despite their good humour, trouble, as ever, was not far away.

———

A fixture between the Australians and the professionals of All England, scheduled for 2–4 September at The Oval had been thrown into doubt after an unseemly squabble involving appearance fees. Some newspapers had even reported as early as 25 August (while the Australians were travelling to Hastings) that the match was "definitely off". Significantly, the contest had been billed as a follow-up to the combination matches played in Melbourne the previous winter, and as such was widely expected to attract huge crowds and a handsome profit.[1] However, the professionals, including seven of the powerful Nottinghamshire team, had demanded an appearance fee of £20 per man – a figure the Australians "deemed excessive". The *Sporting Gazette* disclosed that the Australians had originally offered the professionals £6, which they then increased to £8. Jack Conway, with the support of the Surrey committee, upped the amount to £10 – the standard figure for a representative match – but insisted that that was his final offer. Matters finally came to a head when a letter signed by nine of the professionals (seven from Nottinghamshire and two from Surrey), stating that they would boycott the match as a consequence, appeared in *Sporting Life*:

> *Sir, – having observed at the Oval that we are announced to play the Australians there … we wish, through your columns, to inform the public, so that they may not be misled, that we are not engaged at all in the match and do not intend to play. We also beg to inform the public that it is not the intention of any of the recognised Yorkshire players to take part in the match. If, sir, any letters may be addressed to you on the subject of our remuneration, we beg to inform the public that we only asked for what we paid the Australians in our benefit match in the Antipodes.[2]*

The signatories were Shaw, Shrewsbury, Selby, Morley, Oscroft, Barnes and Flowers of Nottinghamshire, and Jupp and Pooley of Surrey. However, the last point of the letter was strenuously rebutted by Conway, who wrote to the editor of *The Sportsman* explaining that only one Australian had been paid for his services. "C. Bannerman did ask and receive £20 for the benefit match alluded to," he confirmed, "but it must be remembered that in order to play in that match he had to travel 600 miles from his home, and incur a loss of two weeks' time." Conway declared that Spofforth, Murdoch, Allan, Blackham, Boyle, Gregory, Garrett and Horan had repeatedly played against the English tourists in 1876–7, "never expecting even a single penny". In addition, he pointed out, two of the Nottinghamshire professionals, Barnes and Flowers, had originally agreed to play at The Oval for £10, only to suddenly and inexplicably withdraw their names. Both camps stuck rigidly to their side of the story following the publication of the respective letters, as the *Sporting Gazette* noted, "In justice to both sides … whatever has been advanced by one party, has been definitely and fully contradicted by the other". Although it could not resist adding, "Surely all concerned cannot be telling lies…"

James Lillywhite's failure to keep any accounts or records in Australia, apart from a crumpled piece of paper upon which he kept a list in pencil of some of the more substantial expenses, meant that the wrangle amounted to little more than the word of the professionals against that of Conway and the Australians.[3]

The root of the problem, though, went far deeper. It was abundantly clear by this stage of the tour that the Australians had made a considerable return on their profit-sharing venture, and it was more likely that the professionals, in making their stand, were reacting to this rather than the £20 referred to in their letter. Some newspapers were even speculating just how much of a windfall the Australians might take home with them; all agreed it would run into thousands. "We have heard it calculated that each man will net £1,500," *The Spectator* whispered. Indeed, the rapacity with which they had gone about their business had not only caused much resentment and discontent among the majority of professionals, but refocused public attention on the running sore of English cricket – the remuneration of amateurs. The *Sporting Gazette* was unquestionably speaking for many when it suggested that the controversy could easily have been nipped in the bud by the colonials, saving themselves much ill will and bad publicity, had they been prepared to show a little more generosity towards their opponents:

After all, would it not have been just as well if the Australians had paid £20 per man for the Players' match? It would have been a fine advertisement for them, and would have raised them much in the estimation of those who do not admire their money-hunting. The opinion would have been that although they took plenty of money, they knew how to lay it out to advantage; and their payment on a liberal scale in one match would have been quoted as covering a multitude of sins.

In a further twist, Horan revealed that the Australians suspected the hand of W. G. Grace in all of this. The prompt change of heart by Barnes and Flowers "without explanation", after they had initially agreed to play for £10, "smelled of collusion", he wrote. "At that time, it was commonly rumoured that W. G. Grace, having split with us over the Midwinter affair, and being considerably nettled by our winning so many games, had induced the professionals to make exorbitant demands on our purse." There was no doubt in the minds of the Australians that Grace set out to make mischief and to undermine them at every turn, but Horan's claim, in this case, seems more fanciful than evidential. In truth, Grace was no more likely to interfere in the matters of the professionals than they would have been eager to enlist his support. Arthur Shrewsbury and Alfred Shaw, who played a prominent role in the dispute, were both shrewd and spirited individuals who knew their own minds. Shrewsbury, in particular, did not lack in conviction or political motivation, and although he was described as "looking less like a cricketer than a churchwarden", his appearance belied a quiet determination and a stubborn, independent streak. He was not afraid to challenge the feudal system or to take a stand against authority. Three years later he and Shaw were the ringleaders of a strike by seven Nottinghamshire professionals in which they sought – un-successfully as it transpired – to improve the terms of their contracts, the right to organise their own matches and to be awarded benefits after ten years' service. If Shrewsbury, then, was merely cutting his political teeth on the Australians, there is no doubt that he also envied them the capacity to be masters of their own destiny.

The nine professionals having made their decision to down tools at The Oval, Lillywhite was immediately instructed by Conway to recruit a replacement eleven. It did not take him long. Most professionals knew only too well which side their bread was buttered, and for each one who considered the appearance fee of £10 "insulting", there were any number prepared to break rank and to jump at the chance of playing in such a high-profile game. Some may not have been in the same class as the men whose boots they were about to fill, but within no time at all Lillywhite had his team, and the match was back on.

———

Lillywhite also had his work cut out on the field, after Sussex, having won the toss on the morning of Thursday, 29 August, were bowled out for 80 before lunch by Spofforth and Boyle at Hove. Sussex may not have been at the forefront of county teams in terms of playing strength, but, like Leicestershire, they possessed a ground "as good as any" the Australians had played on. "The playing area is about 500 yards round," Horan noted, "and boundary hits counted for four [there would be precious few of those in what would prove a particularly low-scoring encounter] clean outside the ground, six." There were also two pavilions – one for the amateurs and another for the professionals – with "capital accommodation in each of them". The scoring box reminded the Victorians of the one at their beloved Melbourne ground, while adjoining it was a "spacious room for representatives of the press", which, as usual for a match involving the tourists, was filled to capacity.

Hove was also, of course, Lillywhite's patch, and he was soon wheeling away to good effect, delivering his "twisters" on a probing length, in front of a crowd of some 5,000 when the Australians replied at three o'clock. One of his victims was Charles Bannerman, who was bowled by an "absolute beauty" for 15 in his first appearance since injuring his thigh muscle against Lancashire at Old Trafford. Bailey, Gregory, Garrett and Allan all perished to the left-armer and, at a derisory 29 for eight, Australia were in serious danger of being bundled out for under 50. But a last-wicket stand of 37 between Blackham and Boyle restored a fragment of pride before the latter was dismissed for 18 with the total on 75. The Australians' agent – more an agent of destruction in this instance – was in his element on a wicket "admirably suited to his mode of delivery" and returned five for 25 from 36 overs, 22 of which were maidens.

After another spectacular collapse, with Spofforth claiming three wickets in five balls, Sussex were reduced to 41 for nine at stumps. However, a ferocious storm during the night appeared to have washed out any prospect of play on the second day. The town had taken a battering, and broken glass, tiles and rubble were strewn around the streets. It was still thundering when the Australians arrived at the ground, while the "wind was so severe as to lift the roof off one building" and pick up a marquee "as if it was a feather". Miraculously, though, Horan wrote, "the dark clouds dispersed, the sun came out and by one o'clock the ground was fit for the resumption of play". Lillywhite, who was five not out, attempted to fork some lightning of his own, striking Spofforth's first ball for four and his second for two, before the third – a yorker – did for him. Spofforth finished with six for 31 and Boyle four for 15, leaving the Australians to score 53 for victory. A crowd of 3,000 had their hopes raised by the loss of three early wickets, after Lillywhite accounted for both Bannermans, but Bailey and Murdoch, coming together at 30 for three, batted with increasing confidence to knock off the remaining runs. The congenial surroundings of Hove would later become familiar territory for Murdoch, who captained the county from 1893 to 1899, overseeing in the process a marked revival in their fortunes.

With the match having finished at four o'clock, the Australians agreed to play an exhibition game against eighteen Gentlemen of Sussex, braving some dismally wet and cold weather to entertain an enthusiastic crowd of 2,000 on the final day. They departed Brighton "with a great deal of reluctance", Horan noted in his diary, on Sunday, 1 September. "We liked Brighton well, and our only regret was that we had so short a time to pass in such a handsome and fashionable town." The beach, as at Scarborough and Hastings, may not have compared with those back home, but the "splendid piers" of the English resorts offered, in Horan's view, compensatory pleasures and delights, as did the spas, aquariums and elaborate theatre halls.

As they travelled back to London for their game against the professionals the following day, they would have been intrigued, though hardly surprised, to learn that W. G. Grace had been up to his old tricks again, playing fast and loose with the rules, during Gloucestershire's county match with Surrey at Clifton. 'The Champion' had run three when a throw-in from the outfield lodged in his voluminous shirt. Never slow to turn a situation on the pitch to his or his team's advantage, he promptly ran three more before he was finally "collared by the fieldsmen". He had refused to return it to the fielders, so he claimed, for fear of being given out "handling the ball".

After the monetary shenanigans, which had threatened the abandonment of the match at The Oval, the Australians were doubly keen to ensure that it passed off without incident of any kind, on or off the pitch. In fact, it would turn out to be the "best contested and most exciting match" they played in England, doing much to restore their image in the eyes of the public. The estimable Lillywhite – who would captain the professionals – had recruited well, and among the replacements were the Lancastrian Dick Barlow, Surrey's Ted Barratt and the promising Kent all-rounder G. G. Hearne, who had represented MCC against the tourists at Lord's in May. Undeterred by the withdrawal of some of the most revered names in English cricket, the crowds had flocked to The Oval and there were in excess of 10,000 at the ground when Lillywhite won the toss and inserted the Australians.

The conditions dictated that the match would be dominated by bowlers, and two in particular, Barratt and Spofforth, delivered, in their contrasting ways, to devastating effect. In a remarkable spell in which he bowled unchanged for 29 overs, the Surrey slow left-armer claimed all ten wickets to dismiss the Australians for 77 in just under three hours, eclipsing the eight for 58 he had taken against them earlier in the tour. In the words of *Wisden*, Barratt was "a very fine slow bowler ... being able on certain wickets to get more work on the ball than almost any other cricketers of his generation". Although on this occasion the failure of the Australian batsmen to use their feet to him – "they shaped like tyros ... and fell blindly into the snares set for them" – contributed substantially to their downfall. The notable exception was Charles Bannerman, who struck a scintillating 51 and was the last wicket to fall. "One hit of his will not be forgotten by those who saw it," the *Sporting Gazette* marvelled. "He drove Watson to the on, right over the heads of the 'ring,' and the farther the ball went the faster it appeared to go." Without him Australia would have been in a sorry mess.

Once again Gregory threw the ball to Spofforth and the fast bowler responded superbly, taking seven for 37 in 34.2 overs – including his third hat-trick of the tour – to rout the professionals for 82. H. Charlwood was caught at mid-on by Boyle off the first ball in the sequence, the Leicestershire batsman J. Wheeler had his stumps scattered by the next, and Alec Watson was bowled off his chest by the third. At the termination of the innings, Horan recorded, "no fewer than 13 *duck's eggs* were inscribed in the register; seven to our men and six to the Players' side". Batting remained a forlorn task, however, and the Australians could manage only 89 in their second innings. Once more they were indebted to a Bannerman, Alec on this occasion, who scored a doughty 25 before becoming one of six wickets for the Lancashire fast bowler William McIntyre, leaving the professionals requiring 85 to win.

At 56 for three on the second day they appeared to be well on course for victory, but when Spofforth bowled Charlwood for 14, and Boyle caught and bowled Jim Phillips three balls later, the tension, in the words of one reporter, became "intense": 25

runs to win, five wickets to fall. Watson cracked Spofforth for four through square leg, but "the Demon" claimed revenge in his inimitable fashion, bowling the Lancastrian for seven. Harry Phillips scampered two quick singles but then ran himself out in pursuit of another, tilting the advantage back in favour of the Australians and the icy nerve of Spofforth, who swiftly castled Wheeler. Lillywhite was then yorked by Garrett for two, bringing Barratt, the last man, to the crease, with 12 still needed to win. McIntyre edged a couple of runs to deafening applause, but Barratt, looking extremely pale and nervous, was soon exposed to Spofforth, who needed only one ball to dispose of the No. 11. It was a "well-disguised slower one" which hit the top of his off stump to a resounding roar, and the Australians had scraped home by eight runs. Spofforth finished with 12 for 75 for the match.

As they had done at Lord's after the Australian victory over MCC, the crowd immediately converged on the pavilion, and "one after another the Colonials were called before the curtain" to take their bow. An estimated 24,000 watched the game during the two days it was in progress, and the *Sporting Gazette* calculated that, had the match been carried out as intended, it would have drawn the biggest attendance ever seen at a cricket ground. Amidst the cheers, Conway made a point of informing the crowd that the Australians would increase the professionals' rate from £10 to £20 per man, with a further £5 bonus to be awarded to Barratt for his ten-wicket haul. It was a gratifying gesture, and it certainly had the desired effect, although it did rather beg the question why it could not have been made in the first place.

Within hours, however, the pent-up excitement and drama of those last few overs had paled into insignificance in the wake of a horrific shipping accident on the Thames. Cricket would certainly have been the furthest thing from the minds of the Australians as they left Paddington Station at five o'clock the following afternoon, bound for the West Country and their eagerly anticipated showdown with W. G. Grace and Gloucestershire. As one reporter feverishly scribbled, "London is full of consternation. Every man you meet has the latest edition of a paper in his hands and may have stories to tell you relating to [the] accident, which have not yet found their way into the papers." The sinking of the paddle steamer *Princess Alice*, on the evening of Tuesday, 3 September, engulfed the city in a tide of shock and grief – a state which intensified with each passing day as the gruesome details of the tragedy unfolded. More than 600 people – mainly women and children – lost their lives in what remains to this day the worst death toll of any disaster on a British river.

The *Princess Alice* had been returning to Swan Pier, London Bridge, after a day excursion to Gravesend and Sheerness, when she was struck by the *Bywell Castle*, an iron-screw collier, steaming towards Newcastle from Millwall dry docks. The much heavier *Bywell Castle* carved straight through the wooden paddle steamer, splintering her almost in two. Equipped with only two lifeboats, the *Princess Alice* sank within four minutes. It was claimed that the bodies "floated like bees, making the water almost black with their heads and hats and clothes". This particular stretch of the Thames was also one of the most heavily polluted in England, and the sewage was so thick that it was graphically described as "hissing like soda water".

The sinking of the *Princess Alice* was not the only tragedy to blight the end of the summer. Just days earlier, on 21 August, the Ramsgate express, packed with holiday-makers on their way to London, ploughed into a freight train that was being shunted across a bend in the tracks near Sittingbourne station, killing eight passengers. The inquest into the rail collision was being heard on the same day that the *Princess Alice* suffered her terrible fate. A relief fund for the families of the victims of the Thames Calamity, as it became known, was swiftly set up and raised almost £40,000 in five weeks. The money was reported to have poured in at an astonishing £2,000 a day. Cricket would play its part, too, and the proceeds of the game between the North and the South at The Oval – an occasion graced by the likes of Lord Harris, Thornton, Shrewsbury, Shaw and Emmett – were donated to the fund. The Australians had originally been approached to play in the charity match, but declined the invitation, stating that they could not find the "vacant days" in their schecule. However, the Eleven also gave generously, contributing £100 (worth almost £9,000 today) from their own pockets – a sum that was matched by Queen Victoria herself.[4]

———

There was an unmistakable sense of unfinished business in the air at Clifton after Gregory won the toss from W. G. Grace and put Gloucestershire in to bat on the morning of Thursday, 5 September. The county eleven, with the notable exception of one Billy Midwinter, were at full strength. The all-rounder had not played since splitting his thumb against the All-England XI in mid-August, and, although his absence deprived the game of a fascinating subplot (the exchanges with his former team-mates would have been nothing if not lively), it at least allowed the Australians to concentrate their ire on Grace. For 'the Champion', the match offered a last chance to make runs against them before they departed for home. His failures at Lord's and Prince's – he had mustered only 29 runs in three innings – would have undoubtedly irked him and, typically, he promised to "make it hot" for the colonials on their first visit to Bristol.

The heat, though, came from the Australian bowlers. Spofforth swiftly disposed of their old adversary, W. R. Gilbert, and then proceeded to make life distinctly uncomfortable for Grace; but it was Boyle who picked up his wicket for 22, although not without assistance from Spofforth, who clung on to a smart catch at mid-on. The all-amateur Gloucestershire slumped to 83 for seven, and despite some lusty blows from E. M. Grace, who finished unbeaten on 23, were bowled out for 112 in a little over three hours. Spofforth added to his rich harvest of wickets by taking seven for 49 from 39.3 adrenalin-fuelled overs. The Australian batsmen were in no mood to squander their advantage, and after Charles Bannerman had given them a flying start with 33, Garrett and Spofforth set about the bowling of W. G. Grace. According to Horan, Garrett had informed the dressing-room before he went in that he would "slate W. G". So successful was he, in fact, that the bulk of his 43 runs came from "the Champion"'s arm. Spofforth, who went one run better than Garrett, also dished out some severe punishment to Grace, and the Gloucestershire captain – as unproductive with the ball as he had been with the bat – finished with one for 90 from 35 overs in an Australian total of 183.

Grace's decision to shuffle the batting order at the start of the Gloucestershire reply was also to no avail, and he was dismissed leg-before by Garrett for five after dropping himself down four places. The innings quickly subsided for 85. Spofforth plundered another five wickets in a bravura all-round display, and the wholehearted Garrett (three for 14) was not far behind. Left to score 15 for victory, Spofforth was sent in with Bailey to hit off the winning runs, and by half past four on the afternoon of the second day, in front of a crowd of 4,000, Gloucestershire had been soundly beaten by ten wickets. The third day was taken up with a "knock-up match", which ended with honours even, although the Australians would have considered that the hard work had already been done. However, Grace was spared no mercy by the avenging Spofforth, who clean-bowled him for a duck, just for good measure. There is no doubt that the Eleven derived as much personal satisfaction from their success rate against Grace – he had managed only 56 runs against them in three matches in England, and had had his bowling badly knocked about at Clifton – as they did from the very glow of victory itself. It was a record that Grace would more than atone for during the coming years, but for now the Australians had his measure, and Horan, in particular, could not resist one last dig:

No victory could be more popular in Australia than this, both on account of the personal offensiveness of W. G. Grace when in the colonies, and his unfriendly treatment of the Australians in England. To take the Cricketer Of All Time down a peg or two by beating his crack team on his own ground and convincing him that there are others beside himself and his immediate companions who understand something about cricket, will be gratifying to Australians, and a wholesome lesson to W. G. Grace himself, if he have only sense to read it aright.

For his part, Grace told the tourists during a banquet in their honour at the Clifton Downs Hotel – an occasion for "good fare, flattering toasts and some plain speaking" – that it had been the "great desire" of the county to beat them, but they had not been good enough to do so. It was hardly surprising if the words stuck in his throat: Gloucestershire had just lost a match at Clifton for the first time, and to the Australians of all people.

Fourteen
9–17 September 1878

"The Colonial players have not belied their great reputation"

By agreeing to a hastily arranged rematch with the Players of England at Prince's Ground on 11–12 September, the Australians lumbered themselves with a ferocious run-in to the end of the tour: between 9–17 September, they would complete their final four matches, covering 1,060 miles in all – including a titanic ten-hour train journey from London to Glasgow – without a single day's rest. The last of those four games, against an eighteen of Sunderland, was even tacked on to the itinerary at the eleventh hour, and would prove, for some of the Eleven at least, a step too far. As Horan reported on 12 September, the players did not even learn about it until a few days before it was due to be played.

The 34th fixture of the tour, against the Gentlemen of England at Scarborough on 9–10 September, was a sequel to the game which the Australians lost at Prince's in June. This time they got the better of a draw, although the contest was more notable for a controversial incident involving the Oxford University fast bowler A. H. Evans. Despite his capturing 12 wickets in the Varsity match, when he was said to have bowled with "indomitable fire and stamina", the Australians harboured grave concerns over the legitimacy of his action. Tempers flared when Charles Bannerman was felled by Evans after being struck a nasty blow on the forehead in the second innings. Gregory left the pavilion to confront his opposite number, Middlesex's W. H. Hadow, but was promptly ordered off the pitch in what the Australians described as a "very ungentlemanly manner". However, although Hadow vigorously defended his fast bowler, he limited him to only 15 of the 135 overs bowled during the tourists' second knock, which suggests that Evans may indeed have had a case to answer. The hard-as-nails Bannerman washed the blood off his face and returned to the crease to hit 54 – an innings which included two sixes and a fusillade of boundaries – in a total of 249 for eight. The Gentlemen, despite boasting strokemakers of the calibre of Alfred Lyttelton, Thornton, A. G. Steel and Hornby, had earlier been dismissed for 109, in reply to the Australians' first-innings score of 157, with the insatiable Spofforth picking up six for 44.

The return bout with the Players was also destined for a draw – played over two days, there was little likelihood of any other result. It appears to have been an attempt to purge the atmosphere of ill will which overshadowed the game at The Oval (the request for the fixture came from the professionals themselves), although the Australians were of the opinion that their opponents were more motivated by revenge than reconciliation. In returning to London from Scarborough on the overnight train to "accommodate the braggarts", as Horan referred to the professionals, the Australians had passed up the chance to attend the St Ledger at Doncaster racecourse: "Travel weary or not, [we] were ready next day at noon on the Prince's Ground to expose the boasting of the Players for what it was – mere boasting!" Clearly, reconciliation was not exactly top of the Australians' list of priorities either, and *Bell's Life* and *The Sportsman* both reported that the Eleven pocketed a provocative £36 a man for taking part in the rematch. Four of the Nottinghamshire professionals who played truant at The Oval – Shaw, Shrewsbury, Flowers and Selby – were included this time, as were the talented Yorkshiremen Ulyett and Lockwood. Despite the earlier furore and hard bargaining over payment, the *Sporting Gazette* claimed that the professionals were prepared to settle for a match fee of £7 a man. In the light of their refusal to play for anything less than £20 at The Oval, their mood in this instance appeared to be one of resignation rather than indignation. They would not, though, be the only ones feeling short-changed. "Wonderfully fine weather gave the proprietors of the ground some reason for expecting to get back the £400 paid to the Colonials and the Players' £7 per man," the *Sporting Gazette* commented, "but there was never any more than 6000 present during either day, and the margin of profit must have been small."

After winning the toss, the Australians scored 236 on a fast wicket against a potent cast of Shaw, Ulyett, Barratt and the Lancastrian William McIntyre. Charles Bannerman, hitting the ball with as much venom as he had against the Gentlemen, made 61, while Gregory compiled a watchful 57 in four hours to record his highest first-class score in England. Shaw, captaining the professionals, ploughed through a mammoth 75 overs – 52 of which were maidens – for two wickets and a cost of 47 runs. His efforts, though, did not prevent Horan from claiming that the "crack Notts trundler could get no work on, and was very easy to play". Ulyett – dropped at long-on by Bailey off Spofforth at the start of his innings – top-scored with 79 for the Players, who were bowled out for 160 by Garrett (seven for 41), with the last five wickets going down for only 17 runs.

Shortly after stumps at six o'clock on the second day, the Australians left London for the last time, bringing down the curtain on Prince's as they did so. The draw would be the 37th and final first-class fixture to be played at the elite Chelsea venue. With the capital in the throes of a building boom, the developers and speculators were moving in. The Prince brothers had already sold off various portions of the site, and throughout the match the ringing of builders' hammers and pickaxes vied with the echo of leather on willow and the rattle of bone china from the umbrella tents.[1] Within a few years the brothers had sold up completely and, by 1883, the ground where W. G. Grace once struck 261 for the South of England versus the North, and Oxford University ran up 612 against Middlesex,[2] would be lost for ever, buried beneath the concrete and scaffolding of what soon would become Lennox Gardens.

After enduring a journey of more than 400 miles on the overnight train from London to Glasgow, the Australians' adventure north of the border turned out to be short and sweet. The penultimate match of their tour, against twelve of the West of Scotland, was played at the leafy Hamilton Crescent ground in the suburb of Partick. It was tucked away behind impressive town houses and described by Horan as a "neat little cricket club ... no more than 400 yards around". In fact, it was much more than that. Eight years earlier it had staged the first official football international, played between Scotland and England in front of 4,000 spectators – a game which resulted in a 0-0 draw. Scottish cricket was not without its pretensions either, and a national team had been in existence since 1865 when it regularly competed against All-England XIs and MCC, often meeting with surprising success.

However, the Eleven considered the West of Scotland bowling to be the poorest they had faced all tour, and, despite playing through a mist of exhaustion (they had managed to snatch just an hour or two's rest at their hotel before the start of the match), they quickly rattled up a score of 268. It was just as well, then, Horan noted, that it was bowling they might have played in their sleep: "During our innings scarcely one good length ball was sent down. Long hops and full tosses were the order of the day, and, if some of our batsmen had not hit out recklessly ... our total might have reached fully 400 runs." Tellingly, perhaps, not one Australian batsman reached 50, although Spofforth, who hit a rollicking 48, would have done so had he not let his impetuosity get the better of him. The West of Scotland twelve could not compete with the hostility of Spofforth and Garrett and were soon beating a hasty retreat to the pavilion. They were bowled out for 99 and 85, losing by an innings and 85 runs. The popularity of the Australians was reflected in the gate – more than 10,000 watched the game during the two days it was in play – and the tourists took £289 from takings of £385, "the match being quite a good money maker". Not since W. G. Grace was lured to Scotland eight years earlier, for a substantial fee, to play matches in Edinburgh, and Holyrood Park, in Glasgow, had there been such excitement in cricketing circles north of the border. On Sunday, 15 September, to the skirl of the pipes and the cheers of a large gathering of well-wishers at the station, the Australians were on their way again, travelling the 165 miles to Sunderland, the last stop on the trail.

For Spofforth and Horan, the encounter in Glasgow was to be their final bow in Britain and neither took the field against the eighteen at the Chester Road ground – described as a "windswept spot in the shadow of the workhouse" – the following morning. Horan had taken the opportunity to nip across the Irish Sea and visit relatives in Cork; he would meet with the rest of the team when they docked in Queenstown. Spofforth's no-show, after bowling himself to a virtual standstill, was met with "unconcealed disappointment" by a big crowd, according to the *Sunderland Echo*. Bailey, who had not featured against the West of Scotland, was also conspicuous by his absence. W. C. Wilkinson, an Australian recruit who had filled in for the Tasmanian at Glasgow, once again came to their assistance. Their happy knack of drumming up fellow Antipodeans whenever they were a man or two down had served them well, but on this occasion they had no choice but to break their rule and replace Spofforth and Horan with two local players. They could not even call on the services of Conway, who had sailed in advance to New York to finalise arrangements for the American leg of the tour, where they planned to play six matches.

To make matters worse, Sunderland were reinforced by Tom Emmett, the Yorkshire fast bowler, and Surrey's Ted Barratt, who was chalking up his sixth appearance against the Australians. Yet Garrett, with 11 for 28, continued his outstanding all-round form to bowl out the locals for 59 in 90 minutes. Allan (ten for 42) also did his bit, restricting Sunderland to 147 in their second innings, thereby leaving the tourists with a target of 130 to win. But their tired minds and bodies were no match for Emmett and his deadly "sostenutor"; the Yorkshireman's "electrical zigzags" worked their destruction – he returned figures of 13 for 66 for the match – and they finished 71 runs short. The two local recruits, W. Abraham and M. Thompson, contributed only four runs between them. "The fall of the Australians for such a low figure [they were skittled out for 58 in their second innings] caused considerable surprise," the *Sunderland Echo* wrote. It would have been easy for the newspaper to gloat, but it resisted the urge and, in the interests of balanced reporting, concluded on a sympathetic note: "It must be remembered that although they are nominally playing Sunderland, they are really pitted against almost the best professional bowlers England can produce … Under those circumstances, and with eighteen fielders … against them, the Colonial players have not belied their great reputation."

Nonetheless, the tour ended much as it had begun in Nottingham four months earlier: in filthy weather and with an overwhelming defeat.

Fifteen
19–29 September 1878

"Englishmen in Australia are as good as Englishmen at home"

The Australians received a send-off to remember at Liverpool docks on Thursday, 19 September, amidst scenes that could not have contrasted more starkly with their arrival 128 days earlier. This time, as many as 2,000 well-wishers crowded the landing stage to catch a last glimpse of them before they sailed for New York on the evening tide. They were accompanied on board the SS *City of Richmond* by several cricketers, among them the ever-dependable James Lillywhite; glasses of champagne were raised and farewell toasts proposed. In a short speech Gregory made a special point of singling out the press, for "their splendid support", and the railway companies, "who did everything in their power to make our long night journeys as little irksome as possible". The Australians also received a telegram from the players taking part in the North versus the South game at The Oval, in aid of the *Princess Alice* relief fund, congratulating them on their great success in England and wishing them a safe journey home. Finally, at sunset, with the farewells all said and the speeches delivered, the *City of Richmond* steamed slowly out of the Mersey towards the Irish Sea. Three hearty cheers rang out from the landing stage, joined by a barrage of ships' sirens in a deafening salute. On the bridge the Australians took off their hats and waved them in the air in acknowledgment. For some, it was to be their last glimpse of England. The noise did not let up until the twin funnels and the three full-rigged masts of the 450ft *City of Richmond* had receded completely from view.

The following day, a letter penned by Jack Conway to coincide with the Australians' departure from Liverpool appeared in the national press:

> *Sir – On behalf of the Australian cricketers I take this opportunity of publicly expressing the gratitude they feel for the very kind and hospitable treatment extended towards them by the cricket-loving public of England during their four months' sojourn in this great country. From all shades of society their reception has been of the most cordial description. From the Marylebone Club – the Cricket Parliament of the World – to the cricket institutions in the manufacturing towns of England, open-handed liberality has been the order of the day, and the feeling entertained towards us has been of the most genuine kind. The enthusiasm evinced by the public in the doings of the Australians in every contest in which they have been engaged, and the thorough impartiality with which the onlookers have meted out their praise without regard as to whether the recipients thereof were Englishmen or Australians have created the liveliest feelings of gratification . . . I can assure all lovers of the noble game throughout Great Britain that the kindness we have received in our parent country will always be alluded to by us in terms of the warmest praise.*

There was to be no triumphalism and exultation. As Gregory regularly reminded audiences at countless dinners and banquets, the Australians had come not to "lick creation" but to match themselves against the very best England had to offer, and to give of their best. They did that and much more besides, of course, exceeding their own wildest expectations in the process. Whatever mistakes they made, and they were prone to a certain insensitivity and intransigence at times – their hard-headedness during the dispute with the professionals over match fees was undoubtedly a misjudgment, and left a lingering resentment – no one could have accused them of arrogance. The arrogance belonged to those who had branded their venture a presumptuous gamble and a fools' errand.

They docked briefly at Queenstown on the morning of 20 September, where Horan came aboard, before setting off again for New York at four o'clock that afternoon. For the next ten days there would be endless ocean and time aplenty to reflect (a rare luxury during the past four months) on an expedition in which, against seemingly insurmountable odds, and a legion of critics, the "fame of Australian cricket was established for all time".

———

In all, the Australians played 37 matches in Britain. Fifteen of those were first-class fixtures, of which they won seven, lost four and drew four. In 20 contests against the odds, they won nine, lost three and drew eight. The matches against Leicestershire and Hull, both of which the Australians won, were played against 11 men but not awarded first-class status. The statistics, though, only tell a fragment of the story. By defeating MCC in a day, they not only ensured the financial success of the tour at a stroke – "they could have easily filled up their list of engagements for a second season", they were so popular, *Sporting Life* suggested – but changed for ever the way in which England viewed Australian cricket, and indeed Australia itself. They "excited a greater curiosity about Australia than half a century of books and political ovations" had ever achieved. Their victory over MCC remains to this day one of the most astonishing upsets in sport, the catalyst for the modern game, and the point at which England's interest in international cricket was first piqued. "The cricket of huge crowds at Lord's, of the blazing headlines, of the hourly communiques about the state of the pitch, of the posters, cartoons and the signed articles by professional players … was born after the visit to England of the first Australian cricket team in 1878," the influential *Daily News* reflected. However, in the opinion of another reporter, to have inflicted a first defeat on Gloucestershire and the Graces on home soil – for so long the powerhouse of English cricket – was worthy alone of a "famous place in the annals of the wicket".

The legacies for the insular game in England – one newspaper had no hesitation in referring to the summer of 1878 as "the Australian season" – would be profound and far-reaching. "The Australian eleven is thought to have revitalised English cricket," Horan wrote shortly before their departure for New York. "Before our arrival, the principal matches in England had resolved themselves into contests between the Graces and the bowlers of the north. But the cricketing public say that we have changed all that." They changed it not only with their bowling, batting and brilliant fielding, but with the fierce commitment and efficiency of their teamwork, "of combining the individual skill of each other with the due subordination and co-operation of all", a dexterity which English teams, often riven by the deep divisions between amateurs and professionals, could only envy. It was this as much as their durability and resilience – "they have played almost every working day since May 20," *Sporting Life* pointed out – which enabled the Australians to wax stronger in each other's company, Victorian alongside New South Welshman and one Tasmanian, as the tour moved towards its conclusion. As Horan put it, "It is an immense advantage to field day after day in the same places with the same comrades." And to have so successfully buried the burning enmity that existed between the rival colonies.

For all their steely adherence to the principles of teamwork, however, three of the Eleven clearly stood out above the others. "The name from amongst all the others in the side, which will be remembered by the English public, is that of Spofforth," the *Daily News* insisted, "without whom the results of all Mr Conway's management and Mr Gregory's generalship would have fallen short of the actual achievement … Taking a long run, delivering the ball at the full extent of an unusually long reach, and so disguising his intentions that few men can tell whether the coming ball will be one of the famous fast yorkers or a slow back-break, Mr Spofforth is simply the most puzzling and destructive bowler this generation has seen." James Lillywhite, who in his capacity as agent, and sometimes umpire for the

Australians, was perhaps better placed than anyone to assess the merits of Spofforth, considered him "second to none in the world … A great many of the best batsmen in the country had a taste of his quality, and several thought he was the most difficult bowler they had ever played." The *Argus*, meanwhile, delighted in informing its readers that the first imperial sports celebrity, W. G. Grace, was no longer the master of all he surveyed, "and Spofforth is the hero of the cricket-field".

In 15 first-class matches Spofforth took 97 wickets from 658.1 overs at 11.01 each in England, and 352 all told. He bowled a Herculean 1,677.3 overs – 633 more than the next man, Boyle – and 630 maidens, capturing ten wickets 19 times, and five on 41 occasions. There was not a club in the land, it was said, where some aspiring fast bowler had not earned himself the nickname of "Spofforth". As English bowling was still predominantly round-arm, and depended almost primarily on accuracy for its wickets, "the Demon" would soon spawn an army of imitators across all levels of the game. To accommodate these new high actions, the standard of first-class pitches in England – unpredictable at best – would be subjected to rapid improvements over the coming years. Spofforth was also more than handy with the bat – his prowess as an all-rounder is often underestimated and overlooked – and he contributed 304 first-class runs, with a highest score of 56, the maiden first-class half-century by an Australian in England. Only his impulsiveness, and an unbridled desire to hit the ball out of the ground, precluded him from scoring more.

Unquestionably the best batsman in the Eleven was Charles Bannerman, and in the opinion of many sound judges, including Lillywhite, superior to any English professional at that time. By using his feet and refusing to stay rooted to the crease against the quicker bowlers, Bannerman was said to have successfully "challenged batting orthodoxy". "Until he became accustomed to the slow and treacherous English grounds, his impatience and rashness led him into misfortunes," the *Daily News* noted, "but for the past two months he has played as good cricket, and scored as consistently well, as any batsman in the country. His defence is strong and his driving and cutting extraordinarily hard and clean." He scored 566 runs in 15 first-class matches, with four half-centuries, at 20.96, and 1,276 in all; no other Australian batsman came close to matching him, in terms of quality or weight of runs. If English cricket had much to learn from Australia's bowlers, then the great strides soon to be made by colonial batsmen could be traced back to 1878.

The third titan was Jack Blackham, the newspaper added, who was without equal behind the stumps, bringing off 40 catches and 30 stumpings in total: "Mr Blackham will, after Spofforth and Bannerman, leave behind him the highest reputation. He stands up close to all the bowlers and takes on the leg-side with almost as much facility as on the off. All things considered, there has seldom been a better wicketkeeper."

Indeed, most newspapers could find little with which to quarrel and were unanimous in their praise for the Australians. In a leading article on 20 September, *The Times* congratulated them on the "complete success of their visit", and for sending over a team, which, it proclaimed, was as hard to beat as it was impossible to despise:

> *To the public of this country it was an event of striking significance that an eleven should come from Australia and should hold its own, always with credit and generally with triumph, against the best skill that could be pitted against it. It seemed much more natural, as well as more soothing to the national pride, that a picked professional eleven should go to Australia in order to show the colonists what English cricket was like. The tables have now been turned. If the Australians had been generally overmatched in their adventurous enterprise, we should have admired and applauded their courage without being much surprised at their defeat. But they have given us no opportunity of indulging this pleasing sense of compassionate supremacy. They have shown that, as far as cricket is concerned, Englishmen in Australia are as good as Englishmen at home.*

Even the Australians' most trenchant critic, the *Sporting Gazette*, composed an eloquent farewell, extolling them as much for their ability on the field of play as for their "thorough discipline and humility". "There never were eleven young men so *fêted*, petted, be-praised and hero-worshipped who were less spoilt or put on less side," it commented. However, it could not resist returning to a subject close to its heart – the "money-grabbing spirit" of the colonials – and proposed that the next Australian XI to tour England ("we should think that it is certain to come off") will not depart with their pockets so well-lined, as club secretaries "will want to make better terms than those which have allowed the visitors to walk off with so large a proportion of the gate-money". On the matter of a future tour, the *Daily News* had no doubts that a "hearty welcome would be accorded another Australian eleven" but warned that the "English public would expect to see the lessons of the present visit turned to good account by their own cricketers". In the interim, the newspaper ventured, "English cricketers will do well to look to their laurels".

The pick of some of those cricketers, in fact, would soon be busying themselves for the fifth tour of Australia by an English team. The twelve who sailed from Southampton on 17 October, under the banner of the Gentlemen of England, and the captaincy of Lord Harris, did so at the invitation of the Melbourne Cricket Club. Among those riding in the wake of the Australian Eleven were A. N. Hornby, A. P. Lucas, A. J. Webbe, George Ulyett and Tom Emmett. It had been intended that the twelve would be composed entirely of amateurs, but I. D. Walker, the Middlesex batsman and the original choice to lead the party, had, according to one of the Australians, informed them that "he would give up the idea of getting the team together … as he could not get one strong enough to meet the colonies". The Gentlemen were eventually forced to call on two professionals, Ulyett and Emmett, to shoulder the bowling for them; James Lillywhite and Nottinghamshire's Fred Morley had earlier turned down similar invitations. Paid £200, plus expenses for their services, the hard-bitten Yorkshiremen could expect to be treated little better than beasts of burden. They would travel second-class and stay in inferior accommodation – an arrangement with which they were perfectly happy, so the tour promoters claimed, as they had no desire to dress for dinner each night. Harris and Hornby were accompanied on the trip by their wives, while one of the twelve – Warwickshire's Henry Maul – had yet to make his first-class debut; another, the Irishman Leland Hone, had only just done so that summer. As for Walker's last-minute withdrawal, Horan concluded, "Probably he did not care to risk defeat, and expected it, after seeing what we can do at home."[1]

What the Eleven had achieved at home, as the representatives of one and a half million people, was to have "met the chosen players of thirty million at their national game, upon their own grounds, and under every condition of weather, and been almost uniformly successful". It was hardly surprising, therefore, that in bidding adieu to the departing Australians, *Punch* saw fit to rework its earlier tribute to them in verse (this time omitting all mention of W. G. Grace):

The Australians came down like a wolf on the fold,
In a trice the M.C.C. were caught, stumped or bowled.
Not a batsman 'gainst Spofforth "the Demon" could stay,
And the match, a rare marvel, was won in a day.

They have travelled since then, many cricket fields through,
From Swansea to Sheffield, from Cambridge to Crewe;
And though here and there scoring a casual "duck",
They have everywhere shown us good play and good pluck.

They have given us rare proof that the noblest of games,
May be learned near the Murray as well as the Thames;
That courage, good temper and patience abound,
Whether commons or "Lord's" be the cricketing ground.

So hearty God Speed on their homeward-bound way,
To the gallant eleven whose watchword is "play!"

With their comrades, we'll make ever free of our soil,
Captain Gregory, Bannerman, Blackham and Boyle.

———

Their homeward-bound way via America would prove anything but plain sailing, however. Five days out, the *City of Richmond* ran into a full-blown storm, forcing all 600 passengers to stay below decks. The waves rose high and swept over the vessel, reducing her speed from a purposeful 15 knots to 11. Then her mighty compound engines, capable of delivering 5,000 horsepower and fed by the steam from ten boilers and the heat of 30 furnaces, developed a fault. For six perilous hours, as the engines lay idle, the vessel remained at the mercy of the buffeting winds and waves while the crew worked frantically to restore full power. "During this time the vessel tossed about in such a manner as to quite alarm some of the passengers," Horan wrote. None more so than Alec Bannerman, it seemed, who sent several messages from his sick berth to the deck to ask when the lifeboats were being got out. Each time he received the cheery answer that the "boats were not being got out because it would be impossible for any boat to live in such a sea". Eventually, Horan recorded, the sea subsided, the engines were restarted and, much to the relief of all, the *City of Richmond* continued on her way: "The passengers appeared on deck once more and games of chess, draughts and cards were resumed, and went on as pleasantly as before."

The rest of the voyage passed off without further incident. The cricketers were the objects of much interest on board, according to the reporter for the *Argus*, and were regularly sought after for the "American mania" of autograph collecting. One young woman bagged all 11 after stumbling across the team playing cards in the saloon, and recalled how they happily passed the autograph book around. On the seventh day there was a concert in aid of the Yellow Fever Fund. The epidemic, which ravaged the sweltering towns and cities of the American South, would claim some 20,000 lives before the year was out, reducing Memphis to bankruptcy and laying waste to much of New Orleans, where one newspaper reported that the only sound was the tolling of funeral bells and the hum of mosquitoes. A sum of £40 was put into the hat by the passengers. Three days later, at four o'clock on the afternoon of Sunday, 29 September, the *City of Richmond* steamed serenely into the bay of New York. Within minutes of their arrival the Eleven were shaking hands again with Jack Conway, who had come aboard to greet them, accompanied as ever by several local cricketers. One look at the sturdy frame and implacable features of their manager was enough to remind them that there was still work to be done.

Sixteen

30 September–19 November 1878

"Local detectives are on the lookout, but there is no trace of the thief"

The first English cricketing expedition overseas was made by George Parr's pioneering professionals of 1859, who journeyed to Canada and the United States. It took more than two weeks to cross the Atlantic in those days. In a remarkable feat of trailblazing, Parr's intrepid twelve covered 7,500 miles between September and October, spreading the gospel and playing matches in Montreal, New Jersey, Philadelphia, Ontario and finally New York, where it was so cold they fielded in muffs and greatcoats. When Kent's Edgar Willsher returned with another all-professional team nine years later, it was to discover that the civil war, among the many other changes it wrought, had installed baseball beyond any doubt as the "national pastime" of the United States. As one American writer explained, "The difficulties of getting proper cricket equipment and of marking and maintaining pitches were too great during the four years of war; it was easy to throw down four bags to mark bases and to play baseball on any ground available." Others, such as Henry Chadwick, an English-born journalist and prime mover in the expansion and popularity of baseball, saw it rather differently: "Americans do not care to dawdle – what they do, they want to do in a hurry. In baseball, all is lightning. Thus the reason for American antipathy towards cricket can be readily understood."

In 1872, a third English team crossed the Atlantic when R. A. Fitzgerald brought over a star-studded all-amateur selection, including a 24-year-old W. G. Grace, who, on his first overseas tour, added considerably to his mountain of runs and celebrity status. Two years later the trend was reversed when 22 American baseball players landed in England on 27 July for the start of a month-long adventure. The players, divided equally between the two leading clubs, the Boston Red Stockings and the Philadelphia Athletes, played a series of exhibition games – interspersed with a little cricket – in an attempt to establish baseball as a credible rival to England's national sport. However, despite hiring such showpiece venues as Old Trafford, Lord's (where they drew 5,000 spectators), Prince's Ground, The Oval and Bramall Lane in which to promote their game, the crowds were left singularly underwhelmed. The cause of the Americans was certainly not improved by the timing of their arrival (in the height of the cricket season) or by the hostility of the English press, many of whom regarded baseball as nothing more than "a simple game of rounders". Albert Spalding, of the Boston Red Stockings and the outstanding pitcher in professional baseball at the time, admitted that "the game did not prove to be the strong rival of Cricket, which had been expected … [and] little was accomplished". The venture was also a financial failure, and the two clubs were reported to have suffered a combined loss of some $2,500.

By the time the Australians pitched up in New York, the National Baseball League had been in existence for two years. The sport was taking off to such an extent that railroad companies were even rescheduling their timetables to comply with game times. Nevertheless, Gregory's XI would break new ground, as they so often did, by competing with Philadelphia on even terms – the first time an American side had done so against an international touring team – and reawakening, however briefly, an enthusiasm for cricket. Their ability to make news wherever they went, and, indeed, to attract controversy, remained as highly attuned as ever, though.

———

The Australians went sightseeing before the start of the first of their six matches, against an eighteen of New York, on Tuesday,

1 October at Hoboken, New Jersey. A reporter from the *New York Herald* was assigned to pilot them through the city. They took in the marble mansions on Fifth Avenue, the shop-front displays of Broadway and gazed in wonder at the elevated railroad, where trains rattled and clattered on their sinuous journeys past hoardings and tenement windows "at a height of about twenty feet from the pavement". A report in the *New York Times* described the "horrible shriek and squeak of metal on metal, as if the cars were being dragged over the track with brakes down", but declared that, with the movement of the engine, it was noisier still inside the train, where the "sifting of dust and cinders [was] constant and disagreeable". The elevation was also so pronounced, it added, that "the sensation of the ride … is very far from one of pleasure or security. The train appears to be moving in mid-air upon nothing; the people in the streets below are reduced to pigmies, and the sound of moving vehicles is very faintly heard." Nevertheless, by 30 September 1878, it was calculated that in a year the railroad had transported as many as 14 million passengers across this vast metropolis and at a paltry cost, too. Horan, though, was in no doubt as to what the inhabitants of his beloved Melbourne would have made of the sight of a train rushing past "their second storey windows every five or ten minutes throughout each day in the year".

For their purposes the Australians rode a ferry across the Hudson to the Hoboken ground, although the short journey was not without its element of surprise. They drove from their hotel – the imposing brick and marble Grand Central on Broadway – straight on to the ferry in their coach and four. "It was a novelty for us to see a vehicle, with four horses attached, and its occupants, conveyed in this manner across a river," Horan recorded.

When Parr's "English champions" first played at the St George's Cricket Club's ground in Hoboken, they discovered a pitch that had been newly laid, and a crowd of some 5,000 awaiting them. Thirteen years later, Fitzgerald's team noted that the ground was "approached by unfinished streets and surrounded by 'carcasses' of houses in an advanced state of non-completion"; W. G. Grace, in particularly destructive form, twice hit the ball out of the ground into the half-built streets. Horan's description of Hoboken as a "large town" suggests that it had burgeoned in the intervening years, as had the ground: "There was a neat pavilion belonging to the cricket club and another to the baseballers, and the latter was set aside for our use. In each portion there were two capital shower baths, and these proved quite a luxury to us, after playing on so many grounds in England without seeing one." In addition, a temporary grandstand had been constructed, rows of seats ringed the ground and booths dispensed "lager beer to thirsty visitors". Despite the size of the enclosure – it was so small that a "decent hit from the centre would have sent the ball clean over the outside fence" – the pitch was in as good condition as any the Australians had seen on their travels.

Neither side, however, could take full advantage of it. Spofforth, with eight for 33, quickly despatched the New York batsmen for 63, many of whom had never seen – let alone faced – a bowler of such pace and penetration. Indeed, Horan ventured that they "appeared to be inspired by a dread of *the Demon*". The Australians, though, were no more convincing and batted as if they were still on the rolling decks of the SS *City of Richmond*. At one stage they were reduced to 32 for seven by William Brewster, a former English professional who bowled left-arm medium-pace, and the fast "dew-skimmers" of Ed Sprague, a retired pitcher for the New York Excelsiors, which were almost impossible to hit. Only a last-wicket stand of 34 between Boyle and Allan – even the American crowd found much merriment in the latter's eccentric batting style – enabled the tourists to save face and earn a first-innings lead of seven. If the spectators were disappointed by the failure of the Australian batsmen to live up to their sizeable reputations, Spofforth more than compensated with the ball, producing another prodigious burst of fast bowling to capture 12 for 31 and dismiss the eighteen for 98. Needing 92 to win, the Australians once again did not have things all their own way, and after Alec Bannerman, Horan and Boyle had all perished cheaply to Brewster, it was left to Gregory, with an unbeaten 23, to procure their first victory on American turf, by five wickets.

As an introduction to American cricket it could not have made a more favourable impression on the Australians. A crowd of some 3,000 visited the ground during the two days of the match and "appeared to appreciate and enjoy the display as heartily as the keenest lover of cricket could desire". While the batting and bowling of the New Yorkers may have fallen short of the standard the Australians had become accustomed to, the fielding, they noted, was exemplary, with "not a chance being thrown away, nor an overthrow made". The response of the American audience towards the Australians was equally effusive. Their arrival in New York had been eagerly anticipated and keenly reported in the press. The *American Cricketer* advanced the tour as "an unprecedented feat in the annals of athletic sports", and one that was unlikely "ever to be equalled": "It is estimated by Conway … that on their return home they will have travelled the enormous distance of 70,000 miles!" Remarkably, it added, "they have, so far, missed no connection, met with no accident, and nothing has occurred to mar the unity and good-fellowship of the members of the team towards their captain and towards each other". The journal went as far as to suggest that the locals would have to field 69 men, not 18, if they were to stand any chance of beating the men from a "land as remote as Mars". The *New York Times* had also held out little hope for the eighteen, but argued that the benefits of playing the Australians far outweighed the result: "What could be more manly than playing the game and if you have to lose, then losing to the best."

Many of the crowd at Hoboken were baseball players and aficionados, who were intrigued by the achievements of the Australian cricketers (the powerful resonance of the victory over MCC at Lord's had been felt as far away as the United States), and they would not be disappointed by what they saw. So much so that cricket clubs in New York even reported an upsurge in interest and, for a short but not insignificant span of time while the Australians exerted their influence, baseball ceased to be the only game in town.

———

There was just time for a "parting glass" with their New York opponents before the Australians were thrust back into their familiar routine: making their apologies and hurrying away to the station to catch a train for the start of their next match the following day. This time, their destination was the city of Philadelphia – the crucible of American cricket – 95 miles southwest of New York, where they arrived at 11pm. There, they were met by a deputation of local cricketers, who escorted them to their hotel, the handsome 400-room Colonnade, on the southwest corner of 15th and Chestnut streets. Philadelphia was most pleasing on the eye, Horan wrote, "Elegant houses meet the gaze in every avenue, some built of red brick and others of white marble, which has a beautifully fresh and clean appearance. Shady trees are planted in regular order in most thoroughfares and add greatly to the beauty of the place." There was another journey to the Germantown club ground to negotiate the next morning, which involved travelling in a tram for two miles and a train for another five, but once again the Australians were impressed by what they found: a luxurious pavilion, a grandstand capable of holding 800 spectators, and a pitch which was fast and true and a tribute to its Yorkshire caretaker. An aggregate of some 25,000 attended the match over the three days, "including a brilliant muster of ladies", and nowhere in America would the Australians encounter a more partisan or vociferous crowd. The local representatives, as Horan was eager to point out, were hardly rookies, either: "All members of the Philadelphian eleven are genuine Yankees, and they can play the game of cricket well. There are seven or eight good clubs and they play regularly Saturday after Saturday throughout the season, which lasts only four months. Baseball has to play second fiddle to cricket in this beautiful Quaker city."

Philadelphia's cricketers had earned their reputation six years earlier, when a twenty-two nearly pulled off a fanciful victory, against all the odds, over Fitzgerald's twelve amateurs at Germantown. Despite requiring only 33 runs to win – a seemingly innocuous task for the likes of Grace, Hornby and the future Lord Harris – the tourists collapsed in the face of some magnificently hostile fast bowling from Charles Newhall (a bowler whom Grace rated highly) and Spencer Meade. Accompanied by screams of excitement from the ladies in the grandstand, and an atmosphere not unlike a Wild West saloon, the amateurs eventually squeezed home with four wickets to spare in a contest which had severely tested the nerve of all the Englishmen. Seven of the Philadelphians who played that day, including three Newhall brothers – an American cricketing family to rival the Graces – and the left-arm opening bowler Meade, lined up against the Australians.

Gregory lost the toss for the second time in a row, and by lunch the Philadelphians had reached 107 for four, impressing the Eleven with the range and quality of their strokeplay. Although they were not so impressed, Horan remarked, by their custom of calling for ice water and lemons every two or three overs: "One of us suggested to them that a bucket of cold water and another of lemons should be placed near the umpire to prevent the delay caused by bringing them from the pavilion so constantly." The locals were dismissed for a more than respectable 196 on the stroke of five o'clock, with the mercurial Allan clattering the timbers on five occasions to take six for 27. The highlight of the innings, though, was provided by Robert Newhall, who scored 84 in two and a half hours. Batting well outside his crease – no mean feat against Spofforth – Newhall displayed hitting powers worthy of Grace or Charles Bannerman, in the estimation of the Australians, with "nearly every ball being driven hard and clean, and all along the carpet". There could, of course, be no higher praise. It was an innings to rank alongside Edward Lyttelton's 113 against them for Middlesex, or Louis Hall's 79 for Hunslet, and has been described as the greatest innings ever played by an American. Only the decision by the Philadelphian committee to limit a boundary hit to three runs prevented him from becoming the second batsman to take a century off the tourists. One reporter suggested that, had they not done so, Newhall would have actually scored 106 instead of 84. He gave only two chances, if they can be described as that. The first was struck back at the bowler, the granite Boyle, with such ferocity that all he could do was "to shield his face with his hands"; the ball "glanced off his head and flew past him". The other chance went to short leg, and was hit so powerfully that the fielder was "fortunate in escaping injury". He was finally undone by a leg-stump shooter from Allan, whereupon he was hoisted on to the shoulders of his colleagues and carried back to the pavilion in triumph. The applause, Horan recalled, was "tremendous – and he merited it all, for his innings was a genuine exhibition of scientific cricket".

However, the Australian batsmen were still all at sea despite the decorous behaviour of the pitch, and after losing both Bannermans, Spofforth, Gregory and Bailey in swift succession to Charles Newhall and Meade, it was left to Boyle, this time in partnership with Blackham, to reprise his New York rescue act. The tourists were 46 runs in arrears when Boyle was the last man out for 30. They had been prepared to turn a blind eye to Charles Newhall's no-balling during their reply – the fast bowler's front foot persistently landed well outside the crease – and the home umpire's habit, so Conway asserted, of unashamedly applauding his own team's runs: "When one of the brothers Newhall made a good hit off 'the demon' the umpire could not suppress his enthusiasm. He turned in the direction the ball was travelling, and clapped his hands in the most exuberant fashion, not noticing whether the batsmen were running 'short runs' or not." Predictably, though, matters took a turn for the worse at the start of the Philadelphians' second innings.

Trouble flared when Spofforth rapped the opening batsman John Hargrave on the pads with a particularly rapid delivery. Horan recounts that the ball then clipped the bat and flew to point, where it was caught by Charles Bannerman: "Bannerman, when he saw the batsman was not inclined to go, appealed to Mr Brown, the Philadelphian umpire. The words '*How is that?*' were barely out of Bannerman's mouth when the batsman turned to the umpire saying – '*The ball hit the ground first*' – and the fiat was '*not out!*'" This was a surprise to the Australians, Horan added, "as Bannerman had not even stooped to catch the ball". The reporter for the *San Francisco Weekly Post* claimed, however, that Spofforth had originally shouted for a leg-before against Hargrave, and Brown, in turning it down, "would not hear the appeal of C. Bannerman". Another 17 runs were added before Blackham proved too quick on the draw for Hargrave, stumping him off Spofforth. Horan records that the batsman returned to the pavilion "snarling at the decision", which was a "perfectly fair one", made by "a Mr Freeman, an Englishman, and an ardent lover of cricket, whom we had met on board the S.S. *City of Richmond*". From then on matters quickly unravelled, and when the Philadelphian umpire refused to give Dan Newhall out stumped off Allan soon after – the batsman was "fully two feet out of his ground" – Gregory did what he had threatened to do on at least one occasion in England, and marched his players off the pitch.

The Australians told their opponents that they would return to the field of play only if Brown was removed from his post. The Philadelphians refused and countered by claiming that they had no confidence in the "gentleman acting in the capacity for the Australians". In an atmosphere of mounting antagonism from the capacity crowd, and with the stalemate between the two teams growing staler by the minute, the Australians proposed, in the interests of fairness, that both umpires should stand down for the game to resume. Once again the Philadelphians backed their man to the hilt and would hear none of it. It was at this point, Conway wrote, that the Australians, "at my insistence, under great pressure, consented to continue the game under the same umpires, provided it was recorded that they still had no faith whatsoever in the ability of the Philadelphian gentleman for the post". However, there appeared to be a rather more persuasive reason behind the Australians' decision to return to the field, as William B. Morgan, who was reporting on the game and happened to be in the pavilion at the time, suggests: "It seemed that the committee in charge had that very morning given the Australians a cheque for $2,500, their share of the gate receipts … Captain Gregory was informed that the payment of that cheque had been stopped, and if he did not take his team back on the field, they would not receive any portion of the gate receipts." The Australians were also informed that an omnibus had been stationed on a private estate at the back of the ground, should they decide not to continue; and if they wanted to "escape injury from the spectators, they had better board it and slip away quietly".

After an hour's wrangling, in which both teams had eyed each other like a pair of gunfighters waiting for the other to blink, the Australians reluctantly emerged from the pavilion. Horan reported that they were loudly hissed at from all sides of the ground as they retook the field: "A manner of receiving strangers which we had thought until then was not a characteristic of Americans."

Spofforth (five for 24) immediately went on the warpath, and with Allan picking off the batsmen at the other end, the Philadelphians were knocked over for only 53. It was an archetypal response from the Australians, who required exactly 100 runs to win in an hour and 20 minutes. They fell short, however, despite the best efforts of Charles Bannerman and Bailey, and were 56 for four at stumps, both captains having agreed not to play on beyond five o'clock each day because of the fading light. In the end, Gregory's decision to take his men off the field, and the resultant loss of an hour's play, told against the Australians and determined that the "greatest match of American history terminated in a draw". Again they were angry that Charles Newhall – who removed both Bannerman and Bailey in a torrid 18-over spell – was allowed by Brown to continue bowling no-balls, often by "half a foot" or more. In one over alone, the fast bowler managed to hit Bannerman an agonising blow on both elbows, culminating in the "unusual spectacle of two umpires busily engaged in massaging one disabled batsman". Bannerman was in such pain that he was barely able to continue. Horan had no hesitation in describing the game as the "most unpleasant we have played in during the whole tour", while branding the crowd the most partial they had encountered, forgetting perhaps, in the heat of the moment, the open hostility of the mobs of Bramall Lane. "Love of fair play during the contest appeared to be as foreign to the onlookers as hissing is to English or Australian crowds," he claimed. They would not be the last words on the matter.

Conway made his feelings plain in a letter to a friend, written at Niagara Falls on 6 October, in which he succeeded only in further inflaming the situation. If trouble was making a habit of seeking out the Australians, their refusal to take a backward step exacerbated it. The cordial relations between the two teams at the start of the match – the Australians had been accompanied by some of the Philadelphia XI to the Chestnut Street Theatre to see Sheridan's *The School for Scandal* after the first day's play – made the subsequent fallout all the more regrettable. Conway described Brown as "not fitted for the post" and unreservedly defended Gregory's decision to take the team off the field. The Australians had never objected to an umpire before, he insisted, but had been compelled to do so in this instance: "There is nothing to prevent the finest team in the world from being defeated at the hands of one much inferior, if the umpires, by their ignorance of the game, give a few adverse decisions against them. The Australians think they were badly treated in having to submit to the adverse decision of an incompetent umpire; hence their action in leaving the field." He concluded with the words, "You can make whatever use you like of this letter."

The friend did – as no doubt Conway had intended – and after adding a few comments of his own, he signed the letter "A Sometime Australian" and passed it on to the *Philadelphia Evening Telegraph*, which printed it in full. Under the headline

"That Cricket Unpleasantness", the newspaper responded by berating the tourists for indulging in what they considered to be sharp practice: "The sum of it is that the Australians were determined to win or break; if they could not win they meant to make some difficulty which should place the reproach of their not being allowed to win upon the American side." The Philadelphia XI, it pointed out, had "equally good cause for complaining against Mr. Freeman, but they did not insult their guests by leaving the field on account of close decisions of which they failed to see the justice". With the ink barely dry on his first letter, Conway wrote another, this time to the Philadelphian committee and, in an abrupt change of tone, apologised on behalf of the team for their "hurried and apparently cold departure from the ground". He even dismissed the furore over the umpires as nothing more than a "little *contretemps*", declaring that the Australians "enjoyed the match very much, and were both pleased and surprised at the excellent quality of the cricket displayed by their courteous and gentlemanly antagonists".

However, the American newspapers now had the bit between their teeth, and were not prepared to let the matter drop. Amidst the mounting chorus of disapproval of the Australians, one newspaper even claimed that Philadelphia had won a momentous victory by an innings, and reported it as such. Among other things, the tourists were accused of attempting to intimidate the umpires and their opponents, with the usually placid Jack Blackham, so the Philadelphian committee asserted in a statement to the press, the worst offender: "He removed the bails almost every time that the ball passed the batsmen, and he again and again appealed for the umpire's decision when to appeal was to insult the umpire by practising on his credulity or timidity." When the decisions went against them, the committee added, the Australians walked off the field "with a promptitude that was very suggestive of pre-arrangement".

The affair was still smouldering a month later, when Conway expended more ink on a third letter. There had been some stern criticism of the tourists' conduct in the British newspapers, and he wrote to the editor of *Bell's Life*, ostensibly, to put the facts straight – "I have been induced, at the request of the Australian team, to state their case" – but also, it seems, to have some fun at the expense of the American press:

> *The papers teemed with the diatribes against us. The same columns which had ascribed to us the most gentlemanly and heroic attributes, "the champions of the world", etc., sorely taxed the extensive repertoire of Webster's unabridged for words sufficiently harsh to expose our villainy. Large capitals described how we were vanquished, "out-batted, out-bowled and out-fielded" … The ignorance of the writers on the subject of cricket is splendidly ridiculous, and there is not one of us "blasted Britishers" who did not feel much amused at their frothy outpourings.*

The words carried a sting in the tail, too: by the time they were reprinted in the *American Cricketer*, the Australians were already aboard the SS *City of New York* and on their homeward voyage to Sydney.

———

The insistence of the Philadelphian crowd on carrying Charles Newhall off the pitch at the conclusion of the match in Germantown – they celebrated the draw with all the gusto of victory – had expedited the Australians' swift getaway. They had not taken the threats made against them lightly. Indeed, William B. Morgan, in his report, wrote that, had the game not been resumed when it did, "the visitors from the Antipodes might be in danger of being mauled by the crowd on their way out". The Australians left nothing to chance. They slipped out the back way, boarded their coach and made straight for the station, where they caught a train for Niagara Falls, and the start of the Canadian leg of the tour. The next morning they rattled into Buffalo, on the eastern shores of Lake Erie, "having slept like tops" – even Horan – in the comfort of their Pullman. The Pullman sleepers, or "palace cars", were marketed as luxury travel for the middle classes, and described as "marvels of beauty". It had been George B. Pullman's notion to provide American railroad passengers with all the trappings and elegance of the river steamboats, and no expense or detail was spared: the lacquered walnut, plush carpets and French upholstery were a world away from the cramped conditions and sleepless nights the Australians had all too often endured on the rail in England.

On their arrival at Niagara they rumbled over the railway suspension bridge on to the Canadian side of the border, where they put up at the Prospect House hotel, "a stone's throw from the stupendous Horse Shoe Falls". Like the thousands of tourists who flocked to Niagara Falls, they were anxious to take in the sights. "We all went to look at the mighty mass of water roaring and tumbling into the abyss below," Horan wrote, "and the more we gazed at it, the greater its magnitude and attractiveness seemed to us." The fascination did not stop there. They rode in cars, hydraulically powered up and down the banks of the River Niagara, to view the irresistible power of the rapids up close, before crossing over to see the American side. There, they donned oilskins – "except two or three who funked it"– and followed a guide along a platform constructed between the rock face and the solid wall of water. Blinded by the spray – "we couldn't see anything at all" – and deafened by the incessant roar, Horan recounts that the intrepid explorers were only too glad "to get back and put our ordinary dress on again!"

Before leaving Niagara on 7 October for their next engagement, against a twenty-two of Ontario the following day, they posed for a photograph with the Falls thundering and roiling in the background. The team, dressed in their dark suits and Derby hats (Charles Bannerman was unaccountably absent), had to brave the spray that blew over on the wind while they waited for the shutter to open and the sulphur to flare. The frequent drenchings probably explain the grim expressions and the fact that Conway appears to be ignoring the camera altogether. They caught the 1pm train for Toronto pretty well soaked and, on arrival later that afternoon at Union Station, booked into the imposing Walker House hotel on Front and York streets. Toronto was booming and there was much to admire, from its broad, well-kept thoroughfares to its handsome houses, theatres and shop-front displays. Even the cricket ground was built on a grand scale, possessing a playing enclosure of almost a quarter of a mile around, and an ample grandstand. The local cricketers, however, proved no match for the Australians and were easily beaten by ten wickets inside two days. They were especially out of their depth against Spofforth, Garrett and Boyle, who between them captured 27 of the 42 wickets to fall. Once again the game was marred by controversy, although there could be no argument as to who the injured parties were on this occasion.

The Australians had returned to the pavilion at the close of play on the first day to discover that they had been robbed. Among the missing possessions were five gold watches, belonging to Conway, Gregory, Horan, Allan and Garrett, together with souvenirs, medals and a "considerable sum of money". In the case of Horan and Allan, the watches had been presented to them in recognition of their efforts in helping Victoria defeat Lillywhite's professionals at the Melbourne Cricket Ground in December 1876, and were irreplaceable. "The local detectives are on the lookout," Horan wrote in his diary, more in hope than expectation, "but so far there is no trace of the thief." Later that day the Australians attended a banquet at the Walker House hotel, where they were welcomed "not only as sportsmen, but also as fellow colonists" and roundly applauded "for showing the English people that their colonials were their equals in muscle and skill in their own manly game of cricket". The thief, however, was not seen for dust.[1]

At ten o'clock on the night of 9 October they left Toronto behind and headed 340 miles north-east on the Grand Trunk Railway to Montreal. They pulled in under the domes and spires of Bonaventure Station at nine in the morning and started their next game, against a local twenty-two, an hour and a half later. "There was only time for a bath and breakfast," Horan wrote. The Montreal ground made for a spectacular setting in which to play cricket, situated beneath the wooded slopes of Mount Royal and encircled by pretty terraces and villas, no more than three or four hundred yards from the centre of the city. It was here among the gold and orange of the chestnut and maple trees that the Australians ran up their highest score of the tour – 319 – eclipsing the 305 they made against Hull in July.

The innings was dominated by Charles Bannerman, who in hitting 125 became the first Australian batsman to register centuries in England, New Zealand and Canada. It was not, however, vintage Bannerman. According to Horan, he offered as many as 15 chances, "most of them easy ones, but the Montreal men were such butter-fingers that none of them could hold the ball. After the first half-dozen missed catches, Bannerman, when hitting a skier, would say rather slightingly: 'Come on, it's safer there than anywhere'." He made three or four good hits but not one out of the enclosure, Horan added, despite the excellence of the pitch and the ground being only 400 yards in circumference. The one notable hit was made by a Canadian, J. L. Hardman, who had the temerity to drive Spofforth back over his head and into a neighbouring garden for six. Hardman did not belie his name, bludgeoning 31 out of a total of 91 after Montreal had won the toss and batted first. The tourists were 228 runs in front and nine wickets down at stumps on the second day when the final game of their Canadian venture concluded in a draw.

From Montreal they steamed back down the line to Toronto, where they boarded a train bound for Detroit in the American Midwest, a journey of some 230 miles. The country was "very pleasant and well-cultivated, not unlike some portions of the Australian landscape", Horan recorded. On reaching the Detroit River, the train and all its occupants were ferried across the rapidly flowing water in a "huge and oddly constructed steamboat". The Australians took their last look at Canada and were soon back on American soil. In Detroit they quartered at the Biddle House, a magnificent brick edifice on the busy corner of Jefferson Avenue and Randolph Street, which advertised itself as "Strictly first class in all its appointments". It certainly lived up to its boast: Ulysses S. Grant, the Commander General of the US Army and the idol of the nation, had stayed at the hotel in 1865, four years before his inauguration as the 18th President of the United States. The following day the Australians were shown the sights by some of the local cricketers and, as with every city they had visited from New York to Montreal, they liked what they saw. The business district, the tall blocks and elegant residences, they agreed, "would do credit to any leading city in the world". It would become all that and more, of course, after Henry Ford designed and built his first automobile there in 1896 and Detroit became synonymous with the mass production of the motor car.

Australia's well-oiled machine of Spofforth (nine for 26) and Allan (nine for six), meanwhile, proved far too efficient for the local nineteen, who were steamrollered for only 34 having been put in to bat by Gregory. Needing 147 to avoid an innings defeat, Detroit collapsed again for 81 despite Gregory giving most of the weakest bowlers a run (the captain himself enjoyed a rare trundle to pick up seven for 26) and the Australians completed the easiest of wins. The victors were treated to an oyster supper at the Biddle House, and a few hours later they were back on the railroad, heading out to San Francisco, where they would play their final match in America.

―――

If Australia's sporting frontiersmen had so far been spared the hardships and dangers of travel in the West, they would receive a reminder of some of those grim realities during their long journey to California. They arrived in Chicago on 16 October, having travelled for several miles along the shores of Lake Michigan. There was an all too brief but tantalising glimpse of the Windy City, before they changed trains on to the Burlington and Quincy Railroad. On reaching Omaha a day later, they transferred to the Union Pacific Railway and continued on to Ogden in Utah, a distance of more than a thousand miles. The scenery, Horan observed, was not particularly interesting at first: "We crossed a vast stretch of undulating and sunburnt prairie, without a house, tree or other thing upon it to break the monotony of the short, waving grass." However, the monotony was broken when they clattered into the railroad town of Cheyenne, almost 500 miles down the track, and were met by a detail of US soldiers, who immediately boarded the train. "They were armed to the teeth," Horan wrote.

The passengers were informed that a rail, fixed with a wire so it could be removed at any moment, had been discovered along the line and the authorities feared an attempt might be made to derail the train. A Union Pacific train had been held up only a month earlier, they were told, and the railroad company was preparing "a warm reception for any train robbers". The shooting and killing of the outlaw Sam Bass by lawmen in Texas three months earlier was claimed as a significant victory by the authorities, but had done little to deter the spate of robberies. Passengers on stage coaches in bandit country between Cheyenne and the Black Hills also came under attack, they learned, and the attempts at bringing the perpetrators to justice often proved fruitless. As the Australians were among a mere handful of passengers who were not carrying guns, they were warned by the conductor to keep their heads down once the shooting started and "not to go runnin' about and picking up any bullets that might be flying around!" They were hardly travelling light, either. Their battered strong box was stashed to the brim with their winnings and would provide rich pickings for any train robber. The prospect of a gunfight had done nothing to impair their sense of humour, though, and they joked with Conway that as he was in sole charge of the money – he regularly travelled with the strong box padlocked to his arm – he would make a sitting target in the event of a shootout.

No one slept that night. The heat was stifling, itchy fingers sweated on triggers and the train made painfully slow progress. Each creak and rattle of its mighty iron frame, every hiss of steam and grinding motion of the carriage wheels was magnified many times over as it inched its way along. Eventually the darkness receded to reveal the vast, familiar prairie billowing for miles around them. The danger had passed. The soldiers, their gun belts still bulging with cartridges, alighted at a small, dusty station called Carter, and the train picked up speed again. The perils of the Wild West were behind them, and the rhythm of the rail took over once more.

During the journey the Australians also attracted the attention of one of their fellow travellers, an audaciously dressed, silver-haired raconteur who called himself "the Colonel". He quickly adopted the eleven as "my boys". But no matter how many tales he spun for their amusement or how many times he asked about their travels or feigned an interest in cricket he could not, they noticed, resist a furtive glance at the strong box. At one station, a railroad detective boarded the train and advised Conway that "the Colonel" was a notorious conman and swindler, and to keep their money safe. Having already rumbled him, the Australians decided to have some fun at his expense. They noted how he was always the first into the dining car at mealtime and the first to vacate his table, and they ensured that whenever he made his excuses and hurried back to the Pullman, he found two of the Eleven seated on the strong box, greeting him with a knowing smile. It came as no surprise when, at one of the many stations down the line, he suddenly upped and left without another word, crossed to the other side of the platform and threw his bags on to a New York-bound train. They were almost sorry to see the back of him.

In between their adventures they expended some energy by pelting each other with snowballs after the train ascended the slopes of the Rocky Mountains and stopped at Mount Sherman, more than 8,000ft above sea level, to take on more water. Later they passed beneath the towering peaks and spurs of the Wasatch Mountains on the approach to Ogden, where the train barrelled over culverts and swished its long tail around the sharp defiles and fantastical rock formations of the canyons. The scenery was "wild, rugged and majestic," Horan recorded. On arrival at Ogden, there was another change of trains, this time on to the cars of the Central Pacific Company, before setting off on the 900-mile journey to San Francisco. It was at one of several stops along the track, between Ogden and the Sierra Nevada Mountains, that they caught sight of their first American Indians. At one station, "a squaw came up to one of our fellows, begging for tobacco," Horan wrote. As soon as she was given some, one of the men – "two or three of them were intelligent-looking and of good physique" – snatched it off her. "They were all – men and women alike – wrapped in coarse blankets and looked like destitution personified." A more familiar sight was the contingent of Californian cricketers who joined the train at Sacramento. "They had come over one hundred miles to meet us," Horan enthused.

They pulled into San Francisco's Oakland terminus at sunset that day, Monday, 21 October, "heartily glad" that their long journey was finally over. Since leaving Chicago they had endured five days on the rail and travelled in excess of 2,000 miles. By the time they arrived at their hotel, the Baldwin, on the corner of Powell and Market streets, a considerable crowd had gathered to greet them. The Union Jack and the Star Spangled Banner flew side by side on the flagstaff and a brass band struck up 'See the Conquering Hero Comes!' and 'God Save the Queen'. They spent the next two days looking around the city before the start of their last match, against a twenty-two of California, on the 24th.

San Francisco had grown at an extraordinary rate since the California Gold Rush of 1848. By 1878 its population had soared to over 200,000, almost trebling since the mid-1850s. Often referred to as "the Paris of the West", the city was flourishing, awash with theatres, music halls, hotels, saloons and French restaurants. Its streets, the Australians found, were broad and airy; cable cars scaled its precipitous hills, where the railroad barons kept their mansions, and the breadth of its architecture – both brick and wood, private and public – was elegant and extensive. Indeed, the Baldwin, they agreed, was the pick of the hotels they had stayed at during their travels. Owned by Elias

Jackson "Lucky" Baldwin, a celebrated mining speculator who had struck it rich, the hotel was described as "the finest west of New York" and, adjoined by the purpose-built Baldwin Theatre, it occupied an entire block. "Lucky" Baldwin even lent the Australians his prize drag and four, replete with a harness mounted in gold (according to Horan it was worth at least £1,000), in which to ride around the city.

It was during their stay at the sumptuously furnished Baldwin that Conway was approached by another "Colonel". His name alone should have been enough to alert Conway's suspicions. It seemed that every conman in the West employed the title, no doubt expecting it to provide them with a patina of respectability. This particular character was every bit as slippery as the first, however, and he offered to make a "substantial donation to team funds" if the Australians contrived to finish behind the Californians on first-innings scores. His wager applied only to the first innings, he took pains to point out, and would have no bearing on the result of the game. As Conway was not averse to using his brute strength when the situation demanded, he simply picked the man up by the collar of his jacket and heaved him back on to the street from where he had come.

The Australian batsmen proved equally forthright against California's bowlers, scoring 302 after Gregory won the toss and batted first. They had arrived at the Occidental ground, no more than three miles from the Baldwin, to discover a reserve "about the size of the Melbourne Cricket Ground, surrounded by blue gum trees". Worryingly, though, there was barely a blade of grass to be seen on the outfield and what there was on the wicket appeared coarse and patchy. They expected the worst, but, as Horan recorded, "We were surprised by the first-rate way in which it played from start to finish." Charles Bannerman and Spofforth led the way with a carefree exhibition of clean hitting. Spofforth fell five short of his half-century, but Bannerman, batting with exhilarating power – he struck three huge sixes and regularly peppered the boundaries – made 78 before departing to an excellently judged catch in the deep. In reply the twenty-two were dismissed inside two hours for 63. Spofforth took seven for 14 to complete a haul of 69 wickets from six matches in America and Canada, and Allan, bowling with a zest he rarely displayed in England, 12 for 19. The pair were rewarded with a well-deserved rest when the Californians followed on, handing over the reins to Boyle who, with 15 for 34, bowled the tourists to victory by an innings and 134 runs.

The Australians spent their last day in San Francisco watching a game of baseball – they were much impressed by the high standard of fielding – and driving out to the fashionable suburb of Oakland in "Lucky" Baldwin's drag and four. Finally, at noon on Monday, 28 October, four weeks since arriving in America, they set sail for Sydney on the SS *City of New York.* With the best wishes of the local cricketers sounding in their ears, they glided past the lighthouse on Alcatraz Island, out through the Golden Gate Strait and into the shimmering waters of the Pacific, heading west. "In a few hours," Horan wrote, "the bold coast of California had disappeared entirely from view." Eight days out from San Francisco they anchored briefly in Honolulu, where they went ashore, and on the evening of Tuesday, 19 November, after another 14 days at sea, they sighted the coast of New Zealand. The last stop before their journey's end.

Seventeen

19 November 1878–10 February 1879

"We were made perfect heroes of"

No sooner had the *City of New York* passed the North Heads and breached the smooth waters of Auckland Harbour than two steamships came into view, their decks festooned in bunting and crammed with passengers. The sound of the ships' bells and horns, intermingled with a smattering of voices and loud cheering, rang out across the water. To the Australians, watching from the upper deck, it meant little at first, their minds blunted perhaps after 22 days at sea. It was only when the steamships drew alongside and the cheers rose to a crescendo that the cricketers realised the welcoming committee was for them.

They were genuinely dazzled by what they saw, and, as Horan recorded, the acclamation appeared to hit them like a delightful thunderbolt to the senses: "We were taken completely by surprise at the brilliant and enthusiastic reception accorded us by the good people of Auckland ... Cheer after cheer of generous welcome was sent up [and] in such a hearty way as to thrill us through and through." The full extent of it, though, did not make itself known until the *City of New York* approached the packed Queen Street wharf:

> Then ... we saw the grand display of bunting, and noted the dipping of flags on all the vessels in the harbour, as well as on the housetops. As we came alongside we heard a mighty cheering from the thousands on the pier, and the strains of See the Conquering Hero Comes from the assembled military band, added to the incessant discharge of heavy guns in salutation. We were so astonished at the magnificence of the triumph and the great

excitement of the scene that, to express it in the words of one member of the team, we hardly knew whether we were on our heads or our heels.

After coming ashore and eventually disentangling themselves from the hundreds of well-wishers – everyone wanted to shake them by the hand – the Australians were driven to the Auckland Club on Princes Street for a champagne reception. Flags and banners were hung from every establishment. From there they proceeded to the handsome four-storey Northern Club, a few doors down, for dinner with the prominent citizens and cricketers of the city. During the rounds of speeches and toasts, they were thanked on behalf of the people of New Zealand for the "reputation they had gained for the Australasian Colonies"; they were, after all, part of one family and "the success of one colony was the success of all". Their triumphant tour, another speaker proposed, had established beyond any doubt that Britain's Antipodeans had lost none of their "pluck, vigour and ability"; they were not only able to hold their own against Britons in the mother country, but to beat them on a regular basis. A telegram addressed to David Gregory from Sir George Grey, the Premier of New Zealand, was read out, congratulating them on their great success and assuring them of the keen interest shown by all New Zealanders in their exploits. Indeed, barely a day went by, they learned, when telegrams and newspapers were not eagerly perused for news of their progress or the result of their latest match. The highlight of the evening was undoubtedly Jack Conway's reply. He started by expressing his gratitude for the generosity of the welcome – one that was so warm "each cricketer had blushed profusely"; even he had been startled by the "genuine feeling" of it. They had not always been shown such kindness and consideration on their travels, and on one particularly memorable occasion in England, he recalled, the team had been addressed as Polynesians. He waited for the gales of laughter to subside before concluding with the thought that, were he to take another team to travel to the other side of the world, he would "endeavour to include several New Zealand players". The cheers were still echoing in their ears when they returned to the *City of New York* later that night.

At seven o'clock the next morning they left Auckland on the last leg of their adventure, waved off by a crowd of several hundred who had gathered on the wharf despite the early hour. Once again they would have no luck with the weather across the Tasman Sea. Within hours of rounding the North Heads, the passengers felt the prow of the ship rise and fall with the swell of the oncoming whitecaps and heard the shrill whistle of the wind in the rigging. They were steering straight into a storm. "It was the roughest of the trip," Horan wrote, "heavy seas and head winds prevailing right through." The 1,342-mile passage would last five days in all, causing crowds to wait anxiously outside the telegraph office in Sydney for news of the steamer's location. Eventually, at daybreak on Monday, 25 November, a thin trail of smoke was spotted on the eastern horizon by the lookout on the Sydney Heads telegraph station, and within minutes the news was confirmed: the *City of New York* was on her way.

At least 12 hours behind schedule, but having weathered some of the worst seas the Tasman could throw at her, the *City of New York* steamed proudly towards Sydney Harbour. Just outside the Heads they were met by a flotilla of launches and pleasure cruisers – Spofforth reminisced years later that the "crowded steamers were one of the greatest sights I have ever seen" – and escorted through the harbour entrance in a fanfare of bells and horns. At that moment Sydney seemed to erupt in a riot of colour. "The men-o'-war in Farm Cove were decorated in honour of the occasion," Horan recorded, while all the steamers and ships were "trimmed from stem to stern with flags". Blue ribbon, in recognition of the team's colours, and flags, streamers and banners, "conspicuous amongst which was *Welcome Home*", were strung from every available space in the harbour. Even the private residences on the shores paid their compliments, they observed, and "bunting was hoisted in every direction". Conway later wrote that on "no previous occasion had Sydney been so moved". The Eleven, who had sailed from the city, to the strains of "Cheer, Boys, Cheer!", at the start of their journey eight months earlier, would not have believed their eyes.

Not even the country's first inter-colonial strike – sailors and maritime workers were in dispute with the Australian Steam Navigation Company over its plans to replace them with cheap Chinese labour – could impede the progress of the celebrations. The walkout, supported by the dock hands, was already into its eighth day and many of the strikers no doubt decided to swell the vast crowds that lined the waterfront and surrounding streets. The *Sydney Morning Herald* estimated that more than 20,000 people came to cheer the Eleven home – almost 10% of the city's population. The weather also did its best to put people off: a stiff north-westerly wind sent dust clouds swirling around the streets and whipped up the waves in the harbour. But it failed to dampen the enthusiasm and good humour of the crowds, or to prevent the crews of the Sydney and Mercantile Rowing clubs from joining a procession of boats which accompanied the cricketers' launch to Circular Quay.

On landing, the Eleven "were rushed" and had to push and shove their way as best they could through the throng to reach their four-in-hand – a task that was "managed with some difficulty", according to Horan. Once on board they drove to the town hall for the official welcoming ceremony. The progress was slow, particularly through Pitt Street and George Street where the route was so packed it was "hardly possible for the vehicle to get along", the *Sydney Morning Herald* reported. Strings of flags and banners extended from one side of the street to the other, and the demand for blue ribbon was such that even "the whips of the cabmen, omnibus men and draymen, as well as the harnesses of their horses, were decorated with the favourite colour". "We were made perfect heroes of," Spofforth recalled.

The Eleven were formally welcomed on the steps of the town hall by the mayor, in the presence of such dignitaries as the Premier of New South Wales, James Farnell, and the president of the New South Wales Cricket Association, Richard Driver, and congratulated on their safe return. "Upon your departure from this city a few months ago, few could have hoped that your bold undertaking would be so successful," the mayor announced, having to raise his voice above the huge cheers, "but, however gratifying it may be to your fellow colonists to find that your ability in the field had been proved beyond all expectation, it must be still more pleasing to hear from all quarters that your conduct has been such as to add more lasting laurels to your name as Australians." Richard Driver, conveniently forgetting his association's earlier opposition to the tour, praised the Eleven for their "individual and collective triumphs" and rejoiced that "your success has made the game more popular than ever … Even those who did not know the difference between a ball and no-ball must feel indebted to you for the benefits which the colonies will derive from your efforts." However, he ventured that only a brother cricketer could understand the supreme sacrifice made by the Eleven, or truly estimate the scale of their glorious achievements: "Nothing short of a rare combination of skill, judgment, discipline, endurance, industry, good conduct and inimitable pluck could enable you to have succeeded as you have done." Gregory replied by thanking the people of Sydney for a "princely reception", the magnificence of which had not been surpassed anywhere on their travels. He was proud to lead such a team, he said, and he only hoped that when the next Eleven "goes home" the captain was as little troubled as he had been.

Later, in the evening, the cricketers were introduced on stage at the Theatre Royal by James Farnell to rapturous applause, and presented with gold medals, struck in the shape of a set of stumps with a bat and ball. In a short speech the Premier of New South Wales thanked the Eleven for proving, once and for all, that colonials were not degenerating in the hot Australian sun, as had so often been claimed, but were in fact flourishing. He added that he did not wish to think his own country better than any other in the world, but it must be "admitted on all hands that the gentlemen who had represented us in the mother country had done so both honourably and successfully". It was a theme that would be much repeated in the coming weeks, particularly by the newspapers as they dealt at length with the significance of the tour, and addressed Australia's place both in the old and the new world. Many contemplated just what the country might be capable of achieving were it to demonstrate the same unity of purpose and fortitude as its cricketers. The Federation of the Australian Colonies was still another 23 years in the future, but although the majority of the Eleven saw themselves as Anglo-Australian, considered Great Britain as home and remained fiercely loyal to imperial values, they had, nevertheless, struck the first blow for nationhood. As Chris Hart so succinctly put it in *A History of Australian Cricket*, if nothing else "the independence of the mind had possibly just occurred".

The Eleven returned to their hotel – the Oxford on King Street – through the ribbon-strewn streets of Sydney, a contented and much praised band of cricketers. "We are home," Horan wrote in his diary, "and feel very pleased to find ourselves safe and sound back in Australia once more after our long wanderings over land and sea." But there was to be no time for rest. Four days after their arrival, and more than a month since they last picked up a bat, they were back on the road. Although, in this case, they did not have very far to travel, no more than three miles across the city to Sydney's new ground at Moore Park, where they would take on a fifteen of New South Wales.

———

The Eleven's progress through Australia was meant to be nothing more than a victory parade: an opportunity for them to bask in their glory and for the public to show their appreciation and catch a glimpse of their heroes in the flesh. Celebrations had been planned in every town and city they would visit, with the people of Melbourne in particular eager to match, if not better, the Sydney spectacular. After so long away, they would inevitably notice several changes on their return, while some things had stayed resolutely the same. They were shocked and saddened to learn that Tom Wills, the former captain of Victoria and inventor of Australian Rules Football (he originally devised the game to prevent cricketers from becoming idle during the winter), was in a Melbourne asylum, "being kept under restraint" for alcoholism. An old friend and erstwhile team-mate of Conway's, Wills had been a staunch supporter of the plans to take a representative team to England and, it has been claimed, provided financial assistance for it in its early stages. Meanwhile, the bushranger Ned Kelly remained on the loose, successfully evading all attempts at capture, dividing public opinion and still waging his one-man war against the authorities. Although there was now a reward of £500 on his head – dead or alive – following the cold-blooded killing of three policemen in a gun battle with the gang a month earlier. What the Eleven had not expected to find, however, was that the same critics who had disparaged their tour to England before they left Australia were still making trouble.

A plot to set up a rival Australian XI – the self-styled United Australians – to play Gregory's team on their return had been hatched as early as September, while the tourists were still at sea and sailing to America. "Imagine therefore our surprise, when upon our arrival home ... we discovered that the ambitions of some reception committees in Australia were not to honour our achievements at the banquet table, but to organise teams to play against and beat us!" Horan wrote. "This they did, we presume, so that they could prove that the men who stayed at home were just as good as the eleven which toured."

The driving force behind the scheme was a Melbourne Cricket Club member, H. M. Mackinnon, who described himself "as an old English cricketer". In a letter to Edwin Evans, the highly regarded New South Wales all-rounder who had declined an offer to tour with Gregory's Eleven, Mackinnon attempted to sound out his availability for selection: "We are of the opinion that if we secure your co-operation and that of, say five, of your leading players, we could get together a team that would not go far from licking the now 'Almighties'." The names of the Victorian Tom Kendall – ruthlessly chopped before the Eleven set off for England – and the New South Wales batsmen Ned Sheridan and Nat Thomson, were also among the players Mackinnon was keen to enlist. The proposal was that, once formed, the United Australians would play warm-up games in Sydney, Ballarat, Bendigo and Melbourne before the return of the "Great Uns". Mackinnon told Evans that he was confident he could acquire the Melbourne Cricket Ground "on reasonable terms" for the all-important match with the tourists, and concluded provocatively, "It would be a great crow if we licked 'The Invincibles'."

The Age and the *Herald* immediately lined up behind Gregory's team, and other newspapers swiftly followed suit. In an editorial on 28 September, *The Age* rebuked Mackinnon for not only insulting the Eleven, but the Australian public, "who are anxiously awaiting the advent of our champions to give them a generous welcome". However, it did not reserve its disapproval solely for Mackinnon and his fellow conspirators: "It would seem that Mr Evans, who was unwilling to risk his reputation in the Australian Eleven's hazardous enterprise at its inception, is not unwilling now to obtain crowns and glory when apparently they are to be had merely by holding out the hand." A correspondent for the *Herald*, while strenuously pointing out that his newspaper had been the only one in the colony to consistently support the Eleven, was equally dismissive: "Mr Mackinnon and his friends are the people who were continually croaking about the licking our boys were going to get in the Old Country. I would advise Mr Mackinnon to get up a team of Britishers in the colonies who have learned their cricket at home and let them have a shot at the Australians."

Mackinnon argued that, "while being a second-rate English cricketer", the motives behind the United Australian XI had nothing to do with envy or petty jealousy on his part, but were concerned purely with showing the "actual amount of cricketing ability that was in existence here". Nor could he be accused of attempting to denigrate the colonies, he insisted, as his United Australian players were native-born, with only Kendall belonging to the "evidently despised Britisher category". His protestations cut no ice with either the newspapers or the public, and when the *Herald* challenged him to explain why neither he nor any of his cronies had attended the Eleven's valedictory dinner in Melbourne before their departure for England, he was effectively scuppered. He backed down and apologised; the idea of a United Australia XI was hastily dropped, and Evans, Sheridan and Thomson all lined up for New South Wales against the tourists.

If Mackinnon was still smarting from his public drubbing, the outcome of the match at Moore Park would have no doubt afforded him a wry smile. After winning the toss on the morning of 29 November, Gregory decided to put the fifteen in to bat first despite the excellent condition of the pitch. It was a decision in which he had little choice, Horan reasoned, as "having become accustomed to the subdued English light, our sight of the ball was very much affected by the strong Australian glare". Deprived also of any opportunity to practise before the game, and pitted against opponents "fresh and fit from steady and continuous exercise", the Eleven were under no illusions about the size of their task. However, what followed was worse than they might have feared. They were still struggling to shake the rust from their joints after lunch when Bailey, in attempting to hurl the ball back to Blackham from cover point, sustained a broken arm. The bone was said to have snapped with a "noise like a pistol shot". Bailey had reported feeling pain in his throwing arm before the start of the game, and had mentioned it several times on tour in England; on this occasion he had tied a handkerchief around it as a precaution. Incredibly, it was the first serious injury suffered by a member of the Eleven in almost 13 months of non-stop cricket. It was also the cruellest of blows, for the Tasmanian was not only the most reliable of fieldsmen – he excelled in the deep – but had more than warranted his selection as a run-getter. Not surprisingly, it "took all the spirit and life out of our play," Horan wrote.

Sheridan struck a brisk 41 and Evans an impressive half-century as New South Wales scored 338 – the first time the

Eleven had conceded 300 runs in an innings – with ten of the fifteen reaching double figures in front of a vast crowd of 15,000 on the second day. The bowlers complained that they ached all over: Spofforth "lost his wind after half a dozen overs [and] Allan sent down half-volleys and full-tosses so often as to highly delight the batsmen". Only Boyle, with three for 50 from 37 overs, bowled with his customary accuracy. Reduced to ten men, the tourists folded for 71, and although they managed 251 following on, with Horan hitting a vigorous 57 and Murdoch and Boyle contributing 40 and 38 respectively (Spofforth was too ill to bat in the second innings), it was not enough to stave off defeat by an innings and 16 runs. "It was the Nottinghamshire match all over again," Horan noted, "save in respect of the weather and the ground." The performance, of course, was not a true barometer of the Eleven's strength, and they left no one in any doubt that with the benefit of several days' rest and practice behind them they would prove a very different proposition for their next opponents, a fifteen of Victoria.

But first there was another tumultuous welcome. A special train, consisting of one carriage and a guard's van, was laid on for the Eleven so that they could travel to Melbourne in style. "The engine was decorated with evergreens," the *Herald* reported, "and the carriage tastefully festooned with flowers." Cheering crowds turned out in every town and station they passed through, prompting Conway to liken the journey to "the return of a victorious army". On arrival in the city at Spencer Street Station, they could not move for people. "A good natured rush was made upon the carriage as soon as the doors were opened, and the team received an excited welcome from everybody within reach of them," one reporter wrote. Outside, mounted police kept the crowds in check as the Eleven boarded their carriage for the drive to the town hall on the corner of Swanston and Collins streets for more speech-making. There were the usual displays of bunting and banners along the route and thousands of spectators, some of whom scaled lamp-posts in their eagerness to get a look at the Eleven. Omnibuses, carts and wagons were also crammed full, and "there was hardly a window which was not thronged". Melbourne had pulled out all the stops, and the following evening, Wednesday, 11 December, the team were honoured with a torchlight procession through the city and an open-air concert at the East Melbourne Club's Jolimont ground.

However, not everyone was working together quite so harmoniously. The decision by the Eleven to play their match against Victoria at Jolimont on 12–16 December, as opposed to its more distinguished neighbour, the Melbourne Cricket Ground, was rooted in the squabble between the Eleven and the Melbourne Cricket Club back in March, when Conway had baulked at what he considered the unfavourable terms offered by the MCC for the use of its ground. The East Melbourne Club had, of course, come to the team's rescue, offering to stage their final match on Australian soil before their departure for England, on more liberal terms. It was in receipt of this that Conway pledged to play at Jolimont on the Eleven's return. But, within days of their homecoming, the Victorian Cricket Association informed Conway that it would not sanction the game unless it was switched to Melbourne's premier cricket venue. According to Horan, the terms of the deal were such that the Eleven would have to pick up the tab for the reception, as well as the players' costs and expenses, before accruing the balance of the match profits. "We think that this is a rather new style of welcome-making!" he commented. "The team pays for its own reception!" Conway, though, had no intention of breaking faith with the East Melbourne Club – or being pushed around by anyone – and to the echoes of a turf war rumbling away in the background, the fixture went ahead at Jolimont.

As for the match, the Eleven did what they had done on many occasions in England after a setback and rebounded with a convincing victory. The conditions could not have been more testing, either. By the start of the second day, Horan recorded, "a searing and stiff north-easterly wind was blowing, bringing the heat of the Outback to the shores of Bass Strait" and with it some of the hottest weather of the year. For the next two days the sun was unremitting: "Playing cricket was a torture and just watching was an ordeal." For all that, an estimated 40,000 people attended the first three days of the game, "amongst whom was an astonishing number of ladies, whose colourful costumes enlivened the scene".

Spofforth and Allan were back among the wickets, too, while Murdoch and Alec Bannerman batted exceptionally well; in the case of Murdoch, it was unlikely that he had played a better innings at this point in his career. Needing 263 to win, the New South Welshman hit 153 (surpassing Charles Bannerman's highest score of 133 against Leicestershire) to sweep the tourists home by six wickets after putting on 167 with Alec Bannerman (52 not out). Many who had witnessed Charles Bannerman's unbeaten 165 in Melbourne in 1877 considered it to be the equal of that innings. Certainly, with his timing and flowing strokeplay, Murdoch provided the first tantalising evidence of the great stylist he was to become. He was eventually dismissed by Kendall, who, despite taking seven wickets in the match and wheeling away for 75 overs in the furnace-like heat, failed to persuade the Eleven that they had erred in leaving the left-armer behind.

The Eleven followed that with a draw against a twenty-two of Ballarat, and a five-wicket victory over Geelong, before heading to Adelaide to play an eighteen of South Australia. They were now reinforced by the Victorian batsman Tom Kelly, who had replaced the luckless Bailey; Conway had tried, but failed, to recruit the New South Wales cricketers Edwin Evans and Hugh Massie, while in Sydney. However, in engaging Kelly, who was regarded as one of the finest points in the game, the team would lose nothing in the fielding stakes. Also a highly accomplished attacking batsman, Kelly had played in the second Melbourne "Test" of 1877, when he hit 32 of his 35 runs during Australia's second innings in boundaries. Born in County Waterford in Ireland but brought up in Gloucestershire, where he learned to play his cricket on Durdham Downs alongside the Graces, he had migrated to Australia in 1863, aged 19. According to Spofforth, the flamboyant Thomas Joseph Dart Kelly created quite a spectacle when he became the first man in Australian cricket to wear a blazer: red, white and blue, and with a sash to match.

With Kelly on board, the Eleven arrived in Port Adelaide two days before Christmas to another rousing welcome. On the journey to the town hall, bouquets and festive wreaths were thrown from the balconies into their coach below, and the streets formed "a triumphant archway of flags". Despite there being no South Australian representative in the Eleven (some had lobbied strongly before the start of the tour for the inclusion of the 19-year-old all-rounder George Giffen), the team's progress had been followed with the keenest of interest throughout the colony, enriched no doubt by Conway's sparkling reports in the local press.

There was, however, nothing particularly sparkling about the Eleven's performance when the game against the eighteen got under way at the Adelaide Oval on Boxing Day. Coached by a 21-year-old Englishman Jessie Hide – a Sussex professional and protégé of James Lillywhite, who had arrived in Australia only a month earlier to take up his post – the eighteen triumphed by 20 runs, dismissing the Eleven for just 66 in their second innings.[1] The tourists were in no doubt where the blame lay for their defeat, though, and soon found themselves embroiled in another umpiring controversy. They accused the South Australian official of bias and complained that the pitch cut up so badly after the first hour "that the batsmen had a very rough time of it". They had exhausted much goodwill by the time of their departure, and, as the *South Australian Register* pointed out, if anyone had genuine cause for complaint it was the eighteen: "Mr Kennedy, the Australians' umpire, made three mistakes in one day – all in favour of his 'own side' – and two of them so palpable as to be condemned by nine-tenths of the spectators."

On Sunday, 29 December, the Eleven left Port Adelaide for the return journey to Melbourne. As the most momentous year of their lives ticked over into 1879, they had one last important duty to perform.

Gregory's Eleven were not the only touring team doing the rounds in Australia at that time. Lord Harris's Gentlemen of England (plus Ulyett and Emmett) had arrived in Glenelg aboard the P&O steamship *Assam*, a couple of weeks after the triumphant return of the Australians, and played their first match against an eighteen of South Australia. They had left behind one of the harshest and longest British winters on record when the Thames froze over and snow remained on the ground in some parts of the country for fully three months. While the merry cricketers of England took advantage by staging matches on the ice[2] – one such contest took place at Grantchester Meadows in Cambridge, played over three days between the town and University – Harris's team had stayed fit during their two-month voyage by practising on deck, when the sun was not too hot. This, though, often proved more trouble than it was worth, as a special correspondent for *Sporting Life* reported, "The great drawback to cricket on board is the fact of losing so many balls overboard". The Australians, of course, had experienced the same problem on their voyage to San Francisco. Despite stretching a canvas awning either side of the wicket in an attempt to eradicate the problem, the ball rebounded so quickly off the deck that "five times out of ten, it goes over the side", the correspondent added. "We have lost a dozen since leaving Malta, which makes it rather expensive work – at 7s. 6d. each."

Expensive work or not, the Englishmen had opened their tour with a four-wicket victory at the Adelaide Oval before drawing their second match, with a fifteen of Victoria. They then returned to the Melbourne Cricket Ground on Thursday, 2 January to take on Gregory's Eleven in an eagerly anticipated game billed as "The Gentlemen of England versus The Australian XI", and which is now recognised as the third Test played between the two adversaries. "Long scoring and a close finish were expected," Horan wrote. "However, few were sanguine enough to predict a win for the Englishmen, considering the decided advantage in bowling which we possessed."

Not even a heavy shower, which had softened the wicket an hour before play, could dissuade Lord Harris from electing to bat first after winning the toss. He would quickly come to regret his decision, though, after the Englishmen crumpled to 26 for seven. Once again Spofforth was the scourge. After bowling the aggressive George Ulyett with the second ball of the match, "the Demon" dismissed Vernon Royle and Francis MacKinnon, both clean-bowled, and Tom Emmett – nervelessly caught by Horan off a skier – from successive balls to record Test cricket's first hat-trick. Only a stand of 63 between Harris and the hard-hitting Charles Absolom saved their country from complete humiliation before Harris, who scored his runs crisply and elegantly – his straight-driving was particularly effective – was castled by Garrett for 33. Spofforth returned to the attack to remove the Irishman Leland Hone with the aid of a leg-side catch by Blackham, which *Lillywhite's Companion* described as "little short of marvellous". But the leonine Absolom continued to hit out, riding his luck and "treating all the bowlers in a very unceremonious fashion". He had rattled up 52 runs in no time when, in attempting to hammer his fifth boundary, he was the last man out – splendidly caught by Alec Bannerman off Boyle – with the total on 113.

The ground had started to fill by the afternoon and an estimated 8,000 spectators were present – including George Bailey watching from the grandstand, his broken arm in a sling – when the Australians replied shortly after three o'clock. Their innings was built around a typically resolute 73 from Alec Bannerman, after Charles Bannerman, Murdoch and Horan had all given away their wickets cheaply. Horan accused Charles Bannerman of succumbing to "his insatiable desire to play to the ring ... in stupidly attempting to turn and drive a straight ball from Emmett in the direction of longstop!" Alec Bannerman, however, found a more than capable ally in Spofforth (39). Both batsmen were missed early on, but they put together 64 for the fourth wicket – the highest partnership of the match – to guide the Australians to a respectable 256 on the second day, and a lead of 143. Emmett (seven for 68) and Ulyett contributed a back-breaking 121 of the 160 overs bowled. Indeed, so threadbare was the English attack that Harris was forced to call on Hornby to fill in with seven overs of fast underarm grubbers.

That first-innings advantage of 143 looked even more formidable after the Englishmen were reduced to 34 for four by Spofforth and Allan in rapidly deteriorating light. For the second time in the match Ulyett and Hornby both had their stumps detonated by Spofforth. Harris was the only batsman to resist, scoring a "masterly" 36, but he, too, fell to "the Demon", caught by Horan at long-stop off the last ball of the day, to leave his side teetering on the brink at 103 for six – still 40 runs to the bad. In a fit of pique after his dismissal, Harris was seen to fling his bat the length of the pavilion in a most unsportsmanlike manner. Some lusty blows from Emmett on the third day at least spared the Englishmen the indignity of an innings' defeat before the tireless Spofforth captured the last four wickets, bowling them out for 160 to return match figures of 13 for 110 from 60 overs. Needing just 18, Charles Bannerman and Murdoch knocked off the runs in three overs before lunch to complete a ten-wicket victory. As ever, the glory went to Spofforth. His performance, Horan wrote, was as much a paean to his skill as it was a decisive riposte to those who remained unconvinced of his powers: "It had been thought by many excellent judges that Fred Spofforth would not prove *the Demon* in Australia that he was in England, and that, on the fast true turf of the Melbourne Ground, the Englishmen would score off him with facility. He has, however, amply sustained his English reputation and shown that his bowling does not by any means ... rely for its effectiveness on wet or slow wickets."

Lord Harris would certainly need no persuading on that score. He rated Spofforth the best bowler he had faced, asserting that he "put his natural gift and experience into execution more often and more regularly than any bowler I have known". Privately, though, he was seething about the poor light on the second evening of the match – he would later describe it as "simply execrable" – and believed that it had as much to do with his team's defeat as Spofforth's conjuring tricks with the ball. During the speeches and toasts, he kept his powder dry and contented himself by remarking that "the next best thing to taking a victory well, was to receive a defeat in the becoming manner", which he hoped his team had done. Some might have interpreted this as a veiled comment on the Australians' often graceless and ill-tempered response to defeat – the most recent example of which, against South Australia, was still fresh in the memory. However, Lord Harris would soon have his hands full with far weightier concerns after he and his team found themselves caught in a cricketing storm of quite epic proportions.

———

After their defeat in Melbourne the Englishmen travelled to Sydney, playing a New South Wales XI twice at the Association Ground in Moore Park. They lost the first game at the end of January by five wickets despite New South Wales dropping an exhausted David Gregory on disciplinary grounds; the captain had missed a pre-match practice session and then failed to provide an adequate explanation for his absence. However, Harris's decision to bring a Victorian umpire, George Coulthard, with him to Sydney was hardly a diplomatic masterstroke. A 22-year-old professional, employed as a net bowler by the Melbourne Cricket Club, Coulthard had stood in the Test at Melbourne and so impressed his lordship that he promptly engaged him as the team's umpire for the rest of the tour. Any qualms that the Sydney crowds might have had about Coulthard's competency or impartiality were masked by the ease of New South Wales's victory. But matters took an abrupt turn for the worse in the second fixture, played over 7–10 February.[3]

Coulthard incensed the spectators on the first day by turning down a blatant caught behind against Harris early in his innings; the snick was said to have been heard all around the ground and the captain went on to make 41. "The decision was admittedly a mistake," the *Sydney Morning Herald* reported. When the same umpire gave Billy Murdoch run out the next day, with New South Wales following on (the decision was later said to have been "very close but accurate"), events quickly spiralled out of control. The in-form Murdoch had carried his bat for 82 in the first innings, and a boisterous Saturday crowd of 10,000 hooted and howled their disapproval of Coulthard. Gregory's refusal to send the next batsman to the wicket only inflamed the situation. In a brief exchange between the captains at the pavilion gate, Gregory informed Lord Harris that he objected to Coulthard and wanted him replaced. Harris declined and recalled that the next thing he knew "the ground had been rushed by the mob and our team had been surrounded".

In returning to the field to defend Coulthard, Harris was "struck by some larrikin with a stick" – a blow intended for Coulthard. Hornby collared the assailant and, despite being punched and having his shirt almost ripped from his back, "conveyed his prisoner to the pavilion in triumph". The bluff Yorkshiremen Ulyett and Emmett armed themselves with a stump and, in standing shoulder to shoulder with their captain, were alleged to have addressed the rioters as "nothing but sons of convicts", an accusation that was always strenuously denied. Harris recorded that he and his team remained in the middle for an hour and a half, defying the 2,000-strong mob until the ground was cleared. It was later claimed that "his lordship elbowed his way out through the crowd in a manner so violent as to invite assault". Two attempts were made to restart the game, but, because of Harris's refusal to withdraw Coulthard, the spectators swarmed back on to the pitch and play had to be abandoned for the day.

With most of Saturday's crowd back at work, the game finished swiftly on the Monday. Ulyett took four wickets in four balls, and Lord Harris's team won conclusively by an innings and 41 runs. The damage had been done, though. The newspapers, naturally, were full of it and united in their abhorrence of the riot. The *Sydney Morning Herald* called it a "national humiliation" and "a blot upon the colony", while *The Australasian* appeared more concerned about what tales the

Englishmen might take home with them, asking, almost piti-fully, "What will they say in England?" England, in fact, was consumed by news of the massacre of some 800 British troops by Zulus at Isandlwana and the heroic defence of Rorke's Drift, and did not pay the riot the attention it might otherwise have done. Richard Driver, the president of the New South Wales Cricket Association, issued a statement of regret and the apologies to the Englishmen followed thick and fast. Lord Harris was in his element, dispensing righteous indignation on the one hand and apparent understanding and tolerance on the other. He did not attach any blame to the New South Wales Cricket Association or to the cricketers of Sydney, but admitted that the riot was "an occurrence it was impossible he could forget". Unfortunately, Harris was prepared to say one thing to the association and quite another to the English newspapers. In a letter to the *Daily Telegraph* in London, he was scathing in his assessment of the association, whose behaviour he considered "uncricket-like", and blamed professional gambling men and bookmakers in the pavilion, "aided and abetted" by members of the association, for inciting the riot. That view was later contradicted by Spofforth, who put the blame fairly and squarely on the volatility of inter-colonial rivalry: "There was not the slightest animosity against Lord Harris or any of his team; the whole disturbance was based on the fact that the offender was a Victorian."

Harris did not dilute his words when it came to Gregory either, and clearly believed that, through his obstinacy, he had accelerated the riot: "I implored Gregory, as a friend, and for the sake of the NSW Cricket Association, which I warned him would be the sufferer by it, not to raise the objection [against Coulthard], but he refused to take my view of the case." Some Australian pressmen were not above criticising Gregory for his role and one even claimed that he had been "coerced by certain persons in the pavilion not to send another man in when Murdoch was given out", thereby implying he had some link with the gamblers. However, Gregory's unenviable track record with umpires, whether it was in England, America or Australia, and his unquenchable determination at all times to stand up for his team – usually with little regard for the consequences – strongly suggests otherwise. The riot would rankle bitterly with Harris for some time to come and have serious ramifications for the next Australian XI to tour England. "We never expect to see such scenes of disorder again – we can never forget this one," he concluded his letter in the *Daily Telegraph*.

As for the immediate future, Lord Harris declined to stay in Sydney a day longer than was necessary and returned at once with his team to Melbourne – but not before pulling out of the scheduled game with Gregory's Australians at the Association Ground. Many considered it a petty and quite needless gesture on his part. The encounter, had it gone ahead, would have undoubtedly received Test match status, making it the fourth in the history of the game. By taking this decision, Harris not only prevented the 1878 Australians from playing together one last time, but denied Gregory the signal honour of captaining his country in his home town of Sydney.

———

The Eleven played their last two matches, against Bendigo and Inglewood, and on 10 January their long tour of duty – all of 72 matches – was finally over. Flush from their triumph over Lord Harris's Gentlemen of England at the Melbourne Cricket Ground, they defeated a twenty-two of Bendigo by 23 runs on 8–9 January before travelling to Inglewood for a one-day encounter, where they ended their adventure as they had begun it in Brisbane 14 months earlier with another victory, this time by 121 runs. Charles Bannerman missed out on his fourth century of the tour by eight runs, while Spofforth summoned one final cannonade to take ten for 38, finishing just short of a staggering 800 wickets for the entire trip from almost 3,000 overs. Three days later the Eleven attended a farewell dinner at Trump's Hotel on Collins Street, Melbourne. It was a joyous occasion, spent with family and friends, though the evening was tinged with an obvious sadness when glasses were raised for the last time and the Eleven was declared disbanded. "There is no doubt in the world that we shall carry the pleasant recollections of this tour to the grave," Horan recorded, "in spite of it being downright hard work at cricket."

During the following days the players went their separate ways, back to their colonial teams and to their everyday jobs: Gregory, Alec Bannerman, Garrett, Allan, Horan and Boyle returned to their duties with the civil service, Blackham and Bailey to their banks (Spofforth would not resume work as a clerk at the Bank of New South Wales for another five months), and Murdoch to his solicitor's office in Sydney.[4] Not that any of their lives would ever be ordinary again.

Each man was said to have received a scarcely believable return of between £750 and £800 (worth as much as £63,000 today) from their £50 investment.[5] For Spofforth, who earned £175 per annum and had been granted 12 months' leave without pay, the windfall amounted to the equivalent of four years' wages. It was later disclosed that the dividend was in fact closer to £1,000 per man, and that Conway, the elemental force behind the tour, had been paid an additional 7.5% by the Eleven for his troubles, pocketing £1,200. However, no balance sheet of the tour was ever published or made available. Either way, it was a tidy sum of money for a team that had barely expected to break even, and one that with a little prudent management would set them up for the rest of their days. There was talk of naming a trophy after the Eleven, so that their extraordinary deeds would not be forgotten by future generations, and even tips in the newspapers, "as cricket is now all the rage", on how best to cope with the pitfalls of fame and celebrity.

More significant by far were the legacies of their expedition. On what was little more than a whim and a prayer (or "our somewhat experimental tour" as Spofforth quaintly described it), they introduced "a new brand of Australian cricket to the English market" and changed the game for ever. Their victory over MCC in a single afternoon on 27 May 1878 at Lord's saw to that. It whetted the appetite for international competition, propelled the game into the modern era and shook English cricket, which thought it had nothing to learn from anyone – least of all a band of colonials – out of its fog of complacency. The Eleven were singularly unafraid to ruffle feathers, too, and put a few noses out of joint along the way; it would not have been an Australian team had they done otherwise. After Lord's, English cricketers discerned a formidable adversary in the Australian – one who was "worthy of our steel", in the words of W. G. Grace. The defeat of Lord Harris's team in Melbourne provided further compelling evidence of that fact.

For all their glorious trailblazing, though, it has often been pointed out that Gregory's XI never played a Test match in England. It is true they did not, but in 1878 the term had yet to become part of the sporting vernacular; international competition was still only a gleam in the eye, and the designation of what was or wasn't a "Test" would not be conferred for another 16 years.[6] It fell to Clarence Moody, the esteemed cricket journalist of the *South Australian Register*, to compile a list of which of those early representative matches were deserving of the status Test match. The compendium, published in *Australian Cricket and Cricketers* in 1894, received the seal of approval in both England and Australia and was quickly adopted as the authoritative guide. However, not everyone agreed. Fred Spofforth, writing in *The Cricketer* magazine in May 1921, argued persuasively that Moody's failure to include the match at Lord's was a glaring omission: "This has not been counted as a Test match, but it really was; for in those days cricket was almost solely managed by the Marylebone Club, and they had the call of any cricketer they wanted. It was a fine eleven…" Indeed, eight of that XI played Test cricket; Grace, Hornby and Shaw each captained their country at the highest level, and Vernon led the first team to tour India. It is worth noting also, in support of Spofforth's argument, that several English newspapers of the day were only too eager to award the match international billing despite the resounding nature of MCC's defeat.

If the 1878 Australians did not play the first Test in England, they did, however, set in motion the traditional cycle of international tours, thereby hastening the advent of the Test match age and the birth of the game's most intense and enduring rivalry, the Ashes, four years later. As one writer put it, "Nothing has so profoundly affected English cricket as the tours of the Australians in this country." And, arguably, none more than that of the Eleven. Through their spirit, resilience, perseverance, resourcefulness, cussedness and unyielding competitiveness – seasoned, of course, with a liberal dash of cricketing brilliance – they set the benchmark and created the template for every Australian team that followed in their questing footsteps.

For Spofforth, Blackham, Murdoch, Boyle, Horan, Garrett and Alec Bannerman, the call would come again: the running battles with W. G.; the great trials of strength; Lord's, The Oval, Old Trafford; sleepless nights on the rail; the scream of a midnight whistle. But for now they had earned their rest.

Epilogue

"I made my reputation in May"

The Australians returned to England in the summer of 1880. This time there was no Jack Conway or David Gregory. Conway had been in the process of negotiating another "second joint-stock enterprise" among the 1878 Eleven, but was effectively frozen out by the cricket associations who threw their not inconsiderable weight behind the formation of a combined New South Wales–Victoria touring team. Harry Boyle succeeded Gregory as captain, and with Conway for once outmanoeuvred, George Alexander, a fellow Victorian, was appointed manager in his stead in what amounted to a significant changing of the guard. It was once again a private venture, but, unlike their 1878 predecessors, the Australians left for England with the blessing of the associations billowing their sails.

However, all was far from shipshape. Boyle was clearly unsuited to the complexities of captaincy, and while the SS *Garonne* steamed through the Suez Canal, the players took matters into their hands, replacing him with the more genial and tactically astute Billy Murdoch. It seems, though, that the coup fell some way short of outright mutiny. In all likelihood Boyle had been spared from a chastening experience, and was none too disconsolate at his abrupt return to the ranks. "I did not mind much, but would have been better pleased if they had done it before we left Australia," was his inimitable reaction. Not surprisingly, perhaps, the venture proved ill-starred from start to finish.

Relations between the two countries had plummeted in the wake of the Sydney riot. Lord Harris, still recoiling from its horrors, declared that the Australians were undeserving of their amateur status and should be regarded purely as professionals, adding that he had little desire to meet them on the field of play. Once again James Lillywhite was the agent, but in light of Harris's comments and the prevailing disaffection towards the Australians, he had been unable to provide them with an adequate fixture list. In a desperate state of affairs, the Australians even advertised for matches in the newspapers. Eventually, Harris relented and agreed to lead an England XI in a representative match against the tourists at The Oval (they did not play a single game at Lord's). W. G. Grace – who had already struck up a warm friendship with Murdoch – played no small part in the reintegration of the Australians, and the subsequent healing of the Sydney wounds, bringing much persuasion to bear on the grandiloquent Harris. Hornby, Ulyett and Emmett, however, were not so easily convinced and declined to play. The match, which also owed much to the ingenuity and foresight of the Surrey secretary Charles Alcock, was later recognised as the fourth Test to be played between the two countries, and the first to be staged in England.

The Australians, though, had to take the field without Spofforth, who had incurred a broken finger while batting at Scarborough on the eve of the match. With no "Demon" to plague him as he had done to almost malign effect in 1878, Grace proceeded to record the first Test century by an Englishman – a rollicking 152. Throughout the match Murdoch and Grace had indulged in their own personal duel, and the Australian bet Grace a sovereign that he could outscore him. Remarkably, having recorded a duck in the first innings, he exceeded Grace's 152 by one run, although it was not enough to stave off defeat, and England emerged victorious by five wickets. Murdoch wore the golden sovereign on his watch chain for the rest of his days.

Spofforth's injury weighed heavily on the colonials at The Oval, and *The Australasian* even went as far as to suggest that, had he been fit, "the champion would not have made his large score". They were also profoundly weakened by the absence of Charles Bannerman, who would have travelled but for illness, as they were by the unavailability of Gregory, Horan, Allan, Garrett and Bailey, of the 1878 Eleven. However, of all the Australians who did battle with England during the period between 1877 and the early 1890s, it is the name of one man that still thunders down the years: "the Demon" Spofforth, who mixed ferocity with subtlety, and put the devil into Australian cricket.

———

After the 1878 and 1880 ventures, Spofforth made a further three tours of England, in 1882, 1884 and 1886. At The Oval in 1882 – the match which spawned the Ashes – he bowled Australia to a momentous victory, claiming 14 wickets for 90 runs. England required only 84 to win in their second innings, but such was "the Demon's" giant-killing nerve and skill that he bowled them out for 77. He captured 94 Test wickets in 18 matches – including the first hat-trick – at an average of under 20 apiece, and 853 in all first-class games. In 1888 he moved his family to England, where he became a director of the Star Tea Company.[1] He continued to play cricket, first for Derbyshire, once taking 15 for 81 against Yorkshire at Derby in 1889, and then for Hampstead, regularly topping the bowling averages despite being over 50. Spofforth suffered food poisoning in the summer of 1925 and never recovered full health. He died of chronic colitis, aged 72, at his home in Long Ditton, Surrey, leaving a fortune of £164,000. It seems that the 1878 tour, and the Eleven's devastating defeat of MCC, had been much on his mind during the last few days of his life. Lord Harris, who went to visit him, recalled that among the last things Spofforth said to him were, "The doctors say I shall see the First Test Match [June 12–15]; but I made my reputation in May ..." Monday, 27 May, to be exact. He passed away on 4 June 1926, missing the start of the 26th Ashes series – the trophy forged in the fires of his genius – by a matter of days.

Spofforth's great accomplice, Jack Blackham, revolutionised wicketkeeping in much the same way as "the Demon" did with bowling. Together, they symbolised the menace and majesty of Australian cricket. Blackham kept wicket in 32 of the first 39 Test matches, solidifying his position as his country's premier stumper for a period of almost 20 years; on another three occasions he played purely as a batsman. He toured England with the first eight Australian teams, and captained the 1893 side, although it was not a role he actively sought. He compiled his highest Test score, 74, in his final Test, against England at Sydney, in the 1894–5 series. During the match, a ball forced back the top joint of his thumb, ripping open an old injury and precipitating his retirement. The legacy of standing up to fast bowling also left him with a cavity in his chest and "scarcely a sound finger on either hand". In total, he amassed 853 first-class dismissals, including 60 in Test cricket, 36 of which were caught and 24 stumped. When Grace was once asked to name the best wicketkeeper he had seen, he answered emphatically, "Don't be silly, there has only been one – Jack Blackham." Blackham died in Melbourne at the age of 78 on 28 December 1932.

Blackham's fellow gloveman, Billy Murdoch, served his batting apprenticeship on tour with the Eleven in 1878. He returned two years later to the old country a vastly superior player, scoring the first Test century by an Australian in England. His friendship with W. G. Grace did much to smooth the often troubled waters between 'the Champion' and the Australians. He led his country in a further four campaigns: 1882, 1882–3, 1884 – when he recorded Test cricket's first double hundred – and 1890. He later settled in Sussex, captaining the county with much aplomb between 1893 and 1899. During that time he represented England, keeping wicket against South Africa for W. W. Read's team at Cape Town. He died in Melbourne after collapsing while watching a Test between Australia and South Africa in 1911, aged 56. He was buried in London's Kensal Green Cemetery. Described as the first great Australian batsman – *Wisden* said that his style left "no loophole for criticism" – he scored 896 runs in 18 Tests at an average of 32, and completed 243 first-class dismissals as a wicketkeeper.

Harry Boyle went on another four tours to England in 1882, 1884, 1888 and finally 1890, when he travelled as player/manager. "No one," *Wisden* wrote, "was quicker to discover a batsman's weakness, or more persevering in turning his knowledge to account." The tour of 1882 was the pinnacle of his career: he took the last wicket when Australia gained their historic victory at The Oval, bowling Ted Peate, and finished top of the averages with 144 first-class wickets. He played in 12 Tests and collected 32 wickets. He also claimed 125 first-class catches, the majority of them taken in the position he made his own, "Boyley's silly mid-on". He died in Bendigo on 21 November 1907, three weeks short of his 60th birthday.

Tom Horan returned to England in 1882 when he finished second in the averages behind Murdoch with 1,197 runs, which included his highest score of 141 not out against Gloucestershire. A sturdy backfoot player, he scored his only Test century against England in Melbourne in 1881–2 and also captained Australia twice during the 1884–5 series. In 15 Tests, he scored 471 runs. It is as a journalist, though, that Horan is most fondly remembered, and for 37 years he wrote under the pseudonym "Felix" for *The Australasian*, until his death, at the age of 62, in 1916. His columns "Cricket Chatter" and "Round the Ground", often composed beneath his favourite elms at the MCG, were considered required reading, and paved the way for leading Test cricketers such as Jack Fingleton to follow in his footsteps.

The Sydney-born Alec Bannerman made five more visits to England after 1878, playing in 28 Tests and scoring 1,108 runs. He was as different from his buccaneering brother, Charles, as mercury is to iron, and once took seven and a half hours to score 91 against England at Sydney in 1892. His catch at mid-off to dismiss W. G. Grace at The Oval in 1882 during England's second innings has often been identified as the turning point in that epic battle. Charles Bannerman, a relentless aggressor with a bat in his hands, is immortalised as the scorer of the first Test century; his international career, though, was all too transient. He played only twice more for Australia, making his last appearance in 1879 against Lord Harris's team in Melbourne. Although he continued in first-class cricket until 1888, he was much troubled by ill health and never touched the glorious heights again. It has been suggested, however, that he could not cope with his celebrity status, and that drinking and gambling "played a significant role in his rapid loss of form after 1878". He outlived his younger brother by six years, dying in 1930 aged 79.[2]

Like Charles Bannerman, Frank Allan made just the one visit to England. In his sole Test appearance for Australia, in 1879, he took four wickets for 80 runs. Lord Harris recalled him as a bowler who could swing a ball "like a boomerang", but added, "He was an unhappy, ungainly cricketer, and I shall never forget the contemptuous 'You crab!' hurled at him by one of his indignant comrades for some bungle in the field." He was perhaps, at 28, past his best when he came to England. Nevertheless, he took more than a hundred wickets on tour and scored close to 500 runs despite a batting method that would never be forgotten by all who saw it.

George Bailey missed out on a Test appearance against Lord Harris's XI in 1879 after breaking his arm playing for the Eleven against New South Wales on their return from England. The Tasmanian was held in high regard as a middle-order batsman and was invited to tour again in 1880, but, having been refused the necessary leave by his bank where he gained swift promotion, he declined the offer. His great-great grandson, George Bailey, also a middle-order batsman, made his Test debut against England in the opening Ashes encounter of 2013–14.

David Gregory played in three Tests and made just the one tour to England, although, like Bailey, he turned down the offer to return in 1880. Not long after he was appointed inspector of public accounts and later became paymaster of the Treasury. It was said that his captaincy was "universally admired by Englishmen and Australians alike", but that he lacked the requisite skill at the very highest level as a batsman. Part of a great Australian cricketing dynasty – his four brothers all played for New South Wales, while his nephew, Syd, appeared in 58 Tests – David Gregory died of heart disease in 1919, aged 74. The success of the 1878 tour owed much to his hawkish leadership and "invincible self-confidence", but he rarely passed up an opportunity to give Jack Conway the credit for orchestrating Australian cricket's first great adventure.

"Those prone to sporting nostalgia habitually remember great players more than great coaches, entrepreneurs or organisers," Ronald Conway, Jack's grandson, once wrote. "Yet almost every great cricketer for the last forty years of nineteenth-century Australia owed something to John Conway, from Dave Gregory ... to Victor Trumper, the great turn-of-the-century batsman whose youthful talent Conway recognised and fostered." Conway's eye for a cricketer – he discovered Blackham and championed Horan – never deserted him. He acted as agent for the English teams that visited Australia in 1881–2 and 1884–5, and continued to wield influence as a journalist. He was a member of *The Australasian* staff before, fittingly, handing over the newspaper's cricket duties to Horan, and also wrote for the *Argus*, the Melbourne *Leader* and the *Sydney Mail* under the *nom de plume* "Censor". Jack Conway died on 22 August 1909, aged 69. In an age of overworked sobriquets, he could not have been more deserving of his: "the Father of Australian Cricket".

It is perhaps no surprise that William Evans Midwinter is the only cricketer to have played both for and against Australia. Between 1877 and 1887, he played in 12 Test matches – eight for Australia and four for England. In keeping with the twists and turns of his mind, the *Bulletin* could not resist commenting, "In Australia he plays as an Englishman; in England, as an Australian and he is always a credit to himself and his country, whichever that may be." He became the first cricketer to commute between the two hemispheres, dividing his time, and his loyalties, between Victoria and Gloucestershire. In first-class cricket between 1874 and 1887, he scored 4,493 runs, including three centuries, and took 418 wickets. He died in December 1890 in Kew Asylum, Melbourne, aged 39, after the earlier deaths of his wife and two children, prompting the most solemn of epitaphs from Haygarth's

Scores and Biographies: "May the death of no other cricketer who has taken part in great matches be like his."[3]

Tom Kendall appeared in just two Tests and ended his playing days with Tasmania. He played against Lord Sheffield's English tourists in 1892 and took seven for 79, including the wicket of W. G. Grace whom he clean-bowled for 27, having placed a wager that he would do so. A slow left-armer who bowled off two paces, he was described by *Wisden* once as "perhaps the best Australian bowler who never came to England".

Tom Garrett was 18 years and 232 days old when he played against James Lillywhite's professionals in the Grand Combination Match in 1877. He remained Australia's youngest Test cricketer for another 76 years until eclipsed by the 17-year-old Ian Craig in 1953. Garrett toured England again in 1882 and 1886, taking more than a hundred wickets on both occasions. He also represented Australia in seven series at home, when it was often claimed that he was a more effective and penetrative bowler on hard grounds than Spofforth, a cricketer he placed above all others. His best Test return was six for 71 against England at Sydney in 1882. He became an excellent captain of New South Wales for four years and a mentor to the young Victor Trumper. In a first-class career that spanned 21 years, Garrett captured 445 wickets and scored 3,673 runs. After the death of Jack Blackham in 1932 he became the sole survivor of the 1878 Eleven and of the first two Test matches played in 1877. James Lillywhite, the last of the English survivors, had died in 1929, aged 87. Garrett was greatly revered and his opinions were much in demand. He abhorred bodyline and marvelled at the number of players in a modern touring team. "We took only eleven to England," he would remind people. Supremely fit, he was the only member of the 1878 Eleven to play in every match in Britain, and missed just three of the 72 games in all. He died in Sydney at the age of 85 on 6 August 1943, having seen the world change beyond all recognition since those dim and distant days. He was, in the words of one newspaper, "the youngest of 'old men'". He was also the last of the pioneers.

Notes

One

1   A notable literary figure in Australia, the London-born Clarke was best known for his novel *For the Term of his Natural Life*, a harrowing depiction of life in a penal colony. According to Ronald Conway, Clarke and Jack Conway made a curious pair – "Conway bluff, powerful and jovially extrovert, Clarke a slight man with razor-sharp perceptions, darting about mentally and physically like quicksilver".

2   Lawrence's Aboriginals played 47 matches in England, winning 14, losing 14 and drawing 19. They possessed an exceptional all-rounder in Johnny Mullagh, who scored 1,698 runs and captured 250 wickets during the five-month tour.

3   Caffyn stayed on as a coach for another seven years before returning, reluctantly, to England in 1871 because of his wife's ill-health. A perfectionist, he was described as having a "profound effect on the development of Australian cricket".

Two

1   Sir Home Gordon was a cricket journalist, author and publisher. His earliest recollection of the game was being taken as a boy to Prince's Ground to see the 1878 Australians play the Gentlemen of England, when "spectators were within sixty yards of the wicket and stood in serried ranks in front of the pressmen".

2   The Parsees undertook their first expedition to England in 1886; Charles Alcock, the influential secretary of Surrey Cricket Club, acted as agent for the tourists, who won only one of their 28 matches.

3   Horan records that the players paid a £100 stake; most accounts, however, agree that the figure was £50. The Eleven also withdrew from the inter-colonial matches between Victoria and New South Wales, to foster, in their own words, "togetherness and to get rid of any jealousies" – a decision that further impaired their relations with the two cricketing associations.

4   The match, which started on Boxing Day and was played over four days, resulted in a 31-run victory for a Victoria fifteen, who included Horan, Midwinter, Allan, Blackham and Kendall.

5   Born John Stanley James in Walsall, Staffordshire in 1843, Thomas's early forays into journalism included being imprisoned as a spy in Paris and covering the Franco-Prussian War. However, John Barnes, writing in the *Australian Dictionary of Biography*, suggests that, "his uncorroborated account of success as a London journalist must be treated with reserve". He changed his name to Julian Thomas around 1872 and, after a none too successful spell in America, arrived in Australia in 1875, where his fortunes were swiftly, and all too briefly, transformed. In April 1876 the Melbourne *Argus* published "A Night in the Model Lodging House" written anonymously by James and signed by "A Vagabond", "the first of a series on the social life and public institutions of Melbourne from a point of view unattainable to the majority." So successful were these articles that they were soon published in book form, *The Vagabond Papers*. "James wrote with an experienced and authoritative air," Barnes adds, "casually mentioning associations with prominent men and implying his involvement in public affairs in England and America. But he could not measure up to the image that he had so successfully fixed in the minds of his readers, and the revelation that Julian Thomas was 'The Vagabond' produced an inevitable sense of anti-climax from which he never really recovered." At the time that Thomas rubbed shoulders with Lillywhite and Conway at the White Hart in Melbourne, and mingled with the Eleven on board the *Balclutha*, he was at the height of his popularity. He died "in squalor" at Fitzroy, Melbourne, on 4 September, 1896.

6   The song was composed by the balladeer G. W. Hunt and made famous by the "Great Macdermott" (Gilbert Hastings Macdermott), a former Royal Navy rating who went on to become one of the biggest stars of the English music hall. It was claimed that he bought the song off Hunt for a guinea.

7   The *Chimborazo* struck rocks at the foot of Point Perpendicular, the north head of Jervis Bay. No lives were lost. In fact, the *Sydney Morning Herald* reported that, "The passengers behaved admirably … The ladies and children were placed in the boats first, then the remaining passengers, with some provisions, and away all started as comfortably as if proceeding to a picnic."

Three

1   Grace would not bring another England team to Australia until 1891-2, by which time he was 43.

2   Patrick Gilmore was an Irish-born bandmaster who is credited with writing the song "When Johnny Comes Marching Home", under the pen name Louis Lambert, in 1863. He has been described as one of the principal figures of 19th century American music, and from 1872 until his death in 1892 he led the New York 22nd Regiment Band, or Gilmore's Band as it was more commonly known. The musicians played more than 150 concerts – including 65 in Great Britain and Ireland – during a highly successful European tour in 1878.

Four

1   Gale wrote under the *nom de plume* "The Old Buffer" and was, in the words of *Wisden*, a "prolific" observer of the game, "several books and numberless magazine and newspaper articles coming from his pen". In addition, he championed and discovered several Surrey professionals, including the England batsman Harry Jupp. Among his best known books are *Echoes from Old Cricket Fields* (1871), *The Game of Cricket* (1887) and *Sports and Recreations* (1888). Furthermore, Gale had "a high ideal of the way in which cricket should be played, and in his various writings always insisted on the necessity of good fielding".

2   The perceptions of Australia and its cricketers changed markedly during the 1878 tour. In his paper, *Inventing Australians and Constructing Englishness: Cricket and the Creation of a National Consciousness*, James Bradley writes that, "This transformation broadly represented a shift from one kind of ignorance (that all Australian cricketers were black) to another (that all Australian cricketers were drawn from a similar, but not the same, class background as English professional cricketers). In reality, most of the Australian tourists were professional men or 'white collar' workers and were thus from a very different background to the English professionals." The division between amateurs and professionals in England was, of course, one defined purely by class. The Australians, Bradley adds, "consciously stood aside from this system … claiming amateur status irrespective of their class background".

3   In the opinion of *Lillywhite's Companion*, MCC should have acted "four or five seasons ago", but it added, "cricketers must be thankful that the leading club has, however late in the day, recognised an evil which has been injuring the best interests of the game for some years past."

4   Boyle, who spent the match in the haven of the pavilion, was not quite so accommodating in his assessment of events. In one of his

many letters home to his brother, he wrote that Gregory had been "very foolish to play in such weather ...The wicket was in a very bad state, and it rained nearly all the time our fellows were in the field."

Five

1   A dark style of beer, porter originated in London during the 18th century.

2   Thomas Lord relocated to Lisson Grove, Regent's Park, in 1811 but stayed there for only three years after the land was requisitioned for canal cutting. He moved his ground to St John's Wood three years later.

3   Built in 1876, it could seat as many as 2,000 spectators.

4   C.L.R. James, in *Beyond a Boundary*, writes that Grace was once cheered to the echo for keeping out four shooters in a row at Lord's.

5   MCC paid £30 for a gravestone, inscribing it with the words: "This tablet is erected to the memory of George Summers by the Marylebone Cricket Club, to mark their sense of his qualities as a cricketer, and to testify their regret at the untimely accident on Lord's ground, which cut short a career so full of promise ..."

6   An amateur cricketer who played for Middlesex, Beldam pioneered the art of sports action photography. The potential to freeze fast moving images by the early 1900s transformed photography and enabled Beldam to complete his most famous works, *Great Batsmen: Their Methods at a Glance* (1905), and *Great Bowlers and Fielders* (1906). These "showed for the first time 'action photographs and actual experience'... breaking the tradition of a more staid form of posed photography". Among a cornucopia of action shots, Beldam captured the iconic image of Victor Trumper jumping out to drive at The Oval.

7   This was not the first time Grace and Spofforth had met on the pitch. An unknown 20-year-old, Spofforth played for an eighteen of New South Wales against the English tourists in January 1874, taking two wickets for 16 from 13 overs, after which Grace described him as "a very fair bowler". Spofforth, in fact, claims that their first encounter was made a month earlier in Melbourne: "I had a lark with the Old Man at the nets [it was not unusual for all-comers to bowl at practice sessions]. In those days, though I stood six feet three inches, I only weighed ten stone six. But I could bowl faster than any man in the world." After lolling up, in his own words, a couple of balls in "a funny slow way", he suddenly surprised Grace by unleashing a ball of express pace and "down went his off stump". Spofforth records that

Grace "called out in his quick fashion when not liking anything: 'Where did that come from? Who bowled that?' But I slipped away having done my job." Amusing as the story is, however, it did not take place. Spofforth's biographer, Richard Cashman, revealed that research undertaken by the historian Ric Finlay proved that the young fast bowler and his brother were on a family holiday in Tasmania "for the whole period from 18 December 1873 to 12 January 1874", and could not have been in Melbourne at that time.

Six

1   Although Ned Trickett relinquished his title to the Canadian Ned Hanlon in 1880 – again on the Thames – he inspired a golden age of rowing for his country, in which seven Australians variously held the title of world sculling champion between 1876 and 1907.

2   The gate receipts amounted to £4,742, of which £119 7s. went into the Australian coffers.

Seven

1   Cricket's popularity at that time was undeniable. Nine weeks earlier The Oval had hosted the FA Cup final (the Wanderers beat the Royal Engineers 3-1) in front of a crowd of barely 3,000. The Surrey secretary Charles Alcock, who was also secretary to the Football Association and the guiding force behind the creation of the FA Cup, had pretensions of turning The Oval into the first great all-purpose sporting stadium, staging football and rugby union during the winter (England had beaten Scotland there in February), and cricket and athletics in the summer.

2   It is claimed that the people of Christchurch held a public subscription for Pooley and bought him a pocket watch.

3   The 1878 Epsom Derby was won by Sefton, a three-year-old dark bay stallion ridden by Henry Constable, who started at odds of 100/12 (just over 8/1 today), and romped home by a length and a half in a field of 22. Sefton's damsire was a Melbourne stallion called Western Australian.

Eight

1   The *Argus* reported that "the fame of the Eleven had become so great that every town had made its arrangements, and did not want to be disappointed".

2   A six was awarded only if a ball was hit clean out of the ground; five if it cleared the boundary.

3   The Australian press, which reported the story, did not include E. M. Grace among the Gloucestershire amateurs who were "invariably paid for their services" – an omission, which Derek Birley, writing in *A Social History Of English Cricket*, suggests was "an oversight".

Nine

1   In *W. G. Grace: A Life*, the author Simon Rae confirms that Grace got into a fight in Northampton while playing for the United South XI against a local eighteen in 1873. The first day's play had been much curtailed by rain, and Grace took himself off to a nearby shooting gallery "to while away the idle hours". There, he was confronted by a bystander, who "enquired officiously, 'Why don't you go and play cricket, keeping the crowd waiting like you are doing?' In the heated exchange that ensued he struck W. G. in the face, cutting it with his ring." Grace did not retaliate, "but when Fred [Grace] saw the blood and asked who had hit him, he indicated 'that cad over there against the entrance'. Fred said, 'If you don't go and give him a good hiding, I shall', so Grace strode across and laid into him … blackening both his eyes." The incident, Rae adds, was kept quiet at the time.

Ten

1   Motley made his first-class debut for Yorkshire against I Zingari in September 1879, taking six wickets in the match, including that of the England all-rounder A. G. Steel. Between 1886–8, he played in five first-class games for Wellington in New Zealand, where he recorded his highest first-class score, an unbeaten 58, against Nelson.

2   Hall was named one of *Wisden's* Nine Great Batsmen of the Year for 1890, despite failing to register a century during the 1889 season.

3   The Victorian eighteen included Conway, Murdoch, Allan, Horan, Midwinter and Boyle who, during the match, became the first Australian to clean bowl Grace. Simon Rae asserts that, "There was a widely believed rumour that Grace had backed himself to get through the tour without being bowled."

4   One newspaper reported that "once within the rays", the women in the crowd "shot up their umbrellas as they would parasols to shield them from the sun at mid-day".

Eleven

1   The property was derelict by the early 20th century and by 1926 it was mostly demolished. However, parts of the building, including a baroque octagonal room, designed by the architect James Gibbs, have since been preserved and now form the Orleans House Gallery, attracting some 56,000 visitors a year. In 1973, 16 acres of the grounds were used as the site of Orleans Park School.

2   Jack Pollard, in *The Formative Years of Australian Cricket 1803-93*, states that Tennant was a Melbourne medical student.

3   Hector Henry Hyslop committed suicide at the age of 79 in September 1920, shooting himself "whilst temporarily of unsound mind through illness and suffering". "His jaunty name," writes David Frith, in *Silence of the Heart: Cricket Suicides*, "was matched by his odd career in big cricket." Hyslop also filled in for the 1886 Australians at Harrogate against an Eleven of England, when they found themselves a man short, despite being in his 46th year. His name, Frith adds, will thus be "linked forever with *two* Australian touring teams".

Twelve

1   Tobin, in fact, was born in Kensington, London, in 1859. Between 1880–5 he played in three first-class matches for Victoria, but never fulfilled his early promise, scoring 31 runs with a highest score of 15. He died in South Melbourne, aged 44, in 1904.

2   Hyslop occasionally stepped in for Conway when the Australian manager was prevented from meeting his obligations as a newspaper reporter.

3   Although the County Championship was considered to have started in 1873, it was not until 1890 that it was formally organised; before then the winning county was voted for by the press. In 1878 the title was awarded to Middlesex.

4   During his lifetime Thompson was both an opium addict and a street vagrant. He was "discovered" after sending his poetry to the magazine *Merrie England* and winning the acclaim of Robert Browning. His most famous poem "The Hound of Heaven" describes the pursuit of the human soul by God. Born in Preston in 1859, Thompson died of tuberculosis in 1907 aged 47. The manuscript for his lament "At Lord's" was not found until after his death.

Thirteen

1   The Oval had been made available to the Australians by Charles Alcock.

2   The second combination match played at Melbourne over 31 March–4 April.

3   Home Gordon, in *Background Of Cricket*, recounts that Lillywhite, on his return from Australia, "met the group that had provided the guarantee for the trip, handed them a bag containing eight hundred sovereigns and a dirty piece of paper on which were scribbled in pencil some of the bigger expenses, though not his own wine bill, saying: 'That's the lot for you to carve up between you …'"

4   It was intended that the Australians and the Players of England should play a match at The Oval, with the proceeds to be equally divided between the Thames Calamity Fund, and the two teams. However, *Wisden* records that, "it was not adopted; why was never clearly understood, because, although it was stated The Australians could not find vacant days for the match, such a match – i.e., The Australians v The Players – was actually played at Prince's on the 11th and 12th of September, six days subsequent to the above proposition being made; but although that match was not played on behalf of The Fund, it is but fair to repeat here that the Australians subscribed £100 in aid of that sorely needed help to the bereaved."

Fourteen

1   In *Cricketing Reminiscences and Personal Recollections*, W. G. Grace concludes that, "the removal of Middlesex proved to be the beginning of the decline of cricket at Prince's … First one corner, and then another piece of the picturesque ground at Hans Place, Sloane Square, was cut off by the builders, and … Prince's Cricket Ground soon ceased to exist."

2   The first recorded total of more than 600 in a first-class match.

Fifteen

1   I. D. Walker withdrew from the tour following the sudden death of one of his brothers.

Sixteen

1   According to the *Evening News* in Sydney, Allan's watch was returned from America a few months later, but without an explanatory letter.

Seventeen

1   Hide was engaged at the Adelaide Oval on a salary of £200 a year.

2   One of the most extraordinary of these matches took place at Windsor Park on 9 January 1879, beneath a full moon and in front of several hundred spectators. "The game caused no end of amusement," *Wisden* wrote, "owing to the difficulties encountered by the players while bowling, batting and fielding."

3   Coulthard's fellow umpire was Edmund Barton, who became Australia's first Prime Minister 22 years later.

4   In June 1879, Murdoch was declared bankrupt, and the firm, Murdoch & Murdoch, which he shared with his brother Gilbert, was dissolved with debts of £775; his only assets were clothing valued at £10 and £25 in his bank account.

5   The Eleven agreed to augment Alec Bannerman's fixed sum of £200 by £90 "for good behaviour". Gregory also applied to the New South Wales government for the full payment of his salary, along with those of Garrett, Gibbes and Alec Bannerman, for "the period of our absence". Gregory, who earned £320 per annum, had received half pay during the time he had been away; Gibbes, one-third of his £140 salary; Garrett and Bannerman had received nothing. However, Henry Parkes, the Colonial Secretary, was "no cricket lover" and rejected the petition "out of hand".

6   The term "Test" did not come into regular use until the mid-1880s, when the *Sydney Morning Herald* (3 January, 1883) and the Melbourne *Argus* (16 September, 1884) used it to describe the international matches between England and Australia.

Epilogue

1   In 1886 Spofforth married Phillis Cadman of Derbyshire, the daughter of Joseph Cadman, the owner of the highly lucrative Star Tea Company. Spofforth found life much to his liking in England. "Personally, I see myself as an Englishman," he later remarked, "but other people may take a contrary view." There is no doubt that, in his case, he had truly come home.

2   Jack Pollard, in *The Formative Years of Australian Cricket 1803-93*, writes that Charles Bannerman "like his co-star in the first of all Tests, Tom Kendall, developed a fondness for the bottle. Careless with his cash and his choice of companions, he continued to appear at first-class matches, a striking contrast in stained, crumpled clothes and scruffy shoes to his dapper brother ..." He also stood as an umpire in 12 Tests between 1887 and 1902. His brother, Alec, was a player in two of the matches in which he officiated.

3   Midwinter was driven "hopelessly insane" by the tragic deaths of his baby daughter (pneumonia), his wife (apoplexy) and three-year-old son, all within a year of each other. According to one newspaper report, he "got possession of two revolvers" and "was not secured without a severe struggle". He was confined to Bendigo Hospital before being committed to Kew Asylum. Not only was Midwinter the first man to take five wickets in a Test – a feat he achieved during Australia's victory in the Grand Combination Match – he was also the first "Test" cricketer to die.

List of First-Class Matches Played
by the 1878 Australians in England

Nottinghamshire v Australians at Trent Bridge, Nottingham, 20–22 May (Australians won toss and batted): Australians 63 (A. Shaw 5-20) & 76 (Shaw 6-35); Nottinghamshire 153 (J. Selby 66; T. P. Horan 5-30). Nottinghamshire won by an inning and 14 runs.

MCC v Australians at Lord's, 27 May (MCC won toss and batted): MCC 33 (F. R. Spofforth 6 for 4); & 19 (H. F. Boyle 6 for 3); Australians 41 (Shaw 5 for 10, F. Morley 5-31) & 12-1. The Australians won by nine wickets. *Match was scheduled for three days but completed in only four and a half hours' play. Spofforth claimed a hat-trick in MCC's first innings – the first by an Australian in England.*

Yorkshire v Australians at Huddersfield, 30–31 May – 1 June (Australians won toss and fielded): Yorkshire 72 (Boyle 5-32) & 73 (Spofforth 5-31); Australians 118 (T. Emmett 5-23) & 28-4. The Australians won by six wickets.

Surrey v Australians at The Oval, 3–4 June (Surrey won toss and batted): Surrey 107 (Spofforth 8-52) & 80; Australians 110 (E. D. Barratt 8-58) & 78-5. The Australians won by five wickets. *Match was scheduled for three days but completed in two.*

The Gentlemen of England v Australians at Prince's Ground, Chelsea, 17–18 June (Australians won toss and batted): Australians 75 & 63 (A. G. Steel 7-35); Gentlemen of England 139 (Boyle 7-48). The Gentlemen won by an innings and one run. *Match was scheduled for three days but completed in two.*

Middlesex v Australians at Lord's, 20–22 June (Middlesex won toss and fielded): Australians 165 & 256 (Spofforth 56; R. Henderson 5-96); Middlesex 122 (A. J. Webbe 50; T. W. Garrett 7-38) & 185 (E. Lyttelton 103; F. E. Allan 6-76). The Australians won by 98 runs. *Edward Lyttelton's maiden first-class century included 14 fours and was the only three-figure score conceded by the Australians during 14 months of non-stop cricket. Spofforth's 56 was the maiden first-class half-century by an Australian in England and surpassed his previous best first-class score of 21.*

Yorkshire v Australians at Bramall Lane, Sheffield, 1–2 July (Australians won toss and batted): Australians 88 & 104; Yorkshire 167 & 26-1. Yorkshire won by nine wickets. *Match was scheduled for three days but completed in two.*

Orleans Club v Australians at Orleans Club, Twickenham, 8–9 July (Australians won toss and batted): Australians 171 (A. Bannerman 71; Barratt 5-71) & 172 (Horan 64; Barratt 7-70); Orleans Club 132 (F. E. R. Fryer 61) & 137-2 (I. D. Walker 60no). Match drawn.

Cambridge University v Australians at Lord's, 22–23 July (Cambridge University won toss and batted): Cambridge University 285 (A. Lyttelton 72, A. G. Steel 59); Australians 111 (P. H. Morton 7-45) & 102 (Morton 5-45). Cambridge University won by an innings and 72 runs. *Match was scheduled for three days but completed in two.*

Lancashire v Australians at Old Trafford, Manchester, 16–18 August (Australians won toss and fielded): Lancashire 97 (Spofforth 9-53) & 162; Australians 140 (C. Bannerman 58; R. G. Barlow 5-47) & 47-0. Match drawn. *Spofforth reached 50 first-class wickets for the season when he collected his seventh wicket during Lancashire's first innings.*

Sussex v Australians at Hove, 29–30 August (Sussex won toss and batted): Sussex 80 (Boyle 5-26) & 47 (Spofforth 6-31); Australians 75 (J. Lillywhite 5-25) & 53-3. The Australians won by seven wickets. *Match was scheduled for three days but completed in two.*

The Players v Australians at The Oval, 2–3 September (Players won toss and fielded): Australians 77 (C. Bannerman 51; Barratt 10-43) & 89 (W. McIntyre 6-24); the Players 82 (Spofforth 7-37) & 76 (Spofforth 5-38). The Australians won by eight runs. *The match was scheduled for three days but completed in two. Spofforth recorded his second first-class hat-trick of the tour during the Players' first innings. Boyle captured his 50th first-class wicket of the season in the Players' second inning.*

Gloucestershire v Australians at Clifton, Bristol, 5–6 September (Australians won toss and fielded): Gloucestershire 112 (Spofforth 7-49) & 85 (Spofforth 5-41); Australians 183 (R. F. Miles 5-49) & 17-0. The Australians won by 10 wickets. *Match scheduled for three days but was completed in two.*

The Gentlemen of England v Australia at North Marine Road, Scarborough, 9–10 September (Australians won the toss and batted): Australians 157 (A. G. Steel 6-80) & 249-8 (C. Bannerman 54); The Gentlemen of England 109 (Spofforth 6-44). Match drawn.

The Players v Australians at Prince's Ground, Chelsea, 11–12 September (Australians won toss and batted): Australians 236 (C. Bannerman 61, D. W. Gregory 57); The Players 160 (G. Ulyett 79; Garrett 7-41). Match drawn. *This was the last first-class match to be played at Prince's Ground.*

---

*The Australians won seven, lost four and drew four of their 15 first-class matches in England. The matches against Leicestershire – where Charles Bannerman scored the first century by an Australian in England (133) – and Hull (renamed the United North of England XI), both of which the tourists won, were played against 11 men but did not receive first-class status.

Bibliography

Books and articles:

Altham HS and Swanton EW, *A History of Cricket*, George Allen & Unwin, London, 1938

Argus, *The Australian Cricketers' Tour Through Australia, New Zealand and Great Britain in 1878*, PE Reynolds, Melbourne, Sydney, 1878, compiled from authentic press reports; reprint JW McKenzie, Cambridge, 1980

Barker R, *Ten Great Bowlers*, Chatto & Windus, London, 1967

Barker R & Rosenwater, I *Test Cricket England v Australia*, Batsford, London, 1969

Barrett N, (ed.) *The Daily Telegraph Chronicle Of Cricket*, Guinness Publishing, London, 1994

Batchelor D, *The Book Of Cricket*, Collins, London, 1952

Bedford J (ed.), *The Cricketer's Bedside Book*, Colt Books, Cambridge, 1999

Beldam G and Fry C, *Great Bowlers and Fielders: Their Methods at a Glance*, Macmillan, London, 1906

Bellesiles MA, *1877: America's Year of Living Violently*, The New Press, New York, 2010

Berry S and Peploe R, *Cricket's Burning Passion: Ivo Bligh and the story of the Ashes,* Methuen, London, 2006

Bettesworth WA, *Chats on the Cricket Field*, Merritt & Hatcher, London, 1910

Birley D, *A Social History of English Cricket*, Aurum Press, London, 1999

Blumenfeld R, *R.D.B.'s Diary*, William Heinemann, London, 1930

Bradley J, *Inventing Australians and Constructing Englishness: Cricket and Creation of a National Consciousness 1860-1914*, Sporting Traditions, 1995

Brookes C, *English Cricket: The game and its players through the ages*, Weidenfeld & Nicholson, London, 1978

Cardus N, *Days In The Sun*, Rupert Hart-Davis, London, 1924

Cardus N, *The Summer Game*, Rupert Hart-Davis, London, 1929

Cashman R, *The 'Demon' Spofforth*, New South Wales University Press, Sydney, 1990

Christiansen R, *The Visitors: Culture Shock in Nineteenth Century Britain*, Chatto & Windus, London, 2000

Clarke M, *The Future Australian Race*, Massina, Melbourne, 1877

Clarke T (and others), *The American Railway*, Arno Press, New York, 1976

Conway R, *John Conway and the First Australian Eleven of 1878*, Series 1 & 2, *Margin* Magazine, Mulini Press, Canberra, 1993

Crowley B & Mullins P (ed.), *Cradle Days of Australian Cricket: An Anthology of the writings of 'Felix', TP Horan*, MacMillan, Melbourne, 1989

Cruikshank RJ, *Roaring Century 1846-1946*, Hamish Hamilton, London, 1946

Daft R, *Kings of Cricket*, Arrowsmith, Bristol, 1893

Darwin B, *W.G. Grace*, Duckworth, London, 1948

Davie M & Davie S, (ed.), *The Faber Book of Cricket*, Faber and Faber, London, 1897

Ensor R, *England 1870-1914*, Clarendon Press, Oxford, 1936

Fingleton JH, *Cricket Crisis*, Cassell, London, 1946

Frewin L (ed.), *The Boundary Book: A Lord's Taverners' miscellany of cricket*, Macdonald, London, 1962

Frith D, *England versus Australia: A pictorial history of the Test matches since 1877*, Lutterworth Press and Richard Smart Publishing, London, 1977

Frith D, *Pageant Of Cricket*, Macmillan, London, 1987

Frith D, *Silence of the Heart: Cricket Suicides*, Mainstream, Edinburgh, 2001

Gordon H, *Background Of Cricket*, Arthur Barker, London, 1939

Giffen G, *With Bat and Ball*, Ward, Lock and Co., London, 1899

Grace, W.G. *Cricketing Reminiscences & Personal Recollections*, James Bowden, London, 1899

Green B, *A History Of Cricket*, Barrie & Jenkins, London, 1988

Green B, *Wisden Anthology 1864-1900*, Macdonald and Jane's, London, 1979

Green B, *The Wisden Papers 1888-1946*, Stanley Paul, London, 1989

Green S, *Lord's: The Cathedral Of Cricket*, Tempus, Gloucestershire, 2003

Gregson K, *Australia in Sunderland: The Making of a Test Match*, MX Publishing, London, 2013

Griffiths D, *The Encyclopedia Of The British Press 1422-1992*, Macmillan, London, 1992

Guha R (ed.), *The Picador Book of Cricket*, Picador, London, 2001

Harris L, *A Few Short Runs*, John Murray, London, 1921

Harte C, *A History Of Australian Cricket*, Andre Deutsch, London, 1993

Harwood J, *Holidays and Hard Times 1870s*, Reader's Digest, London, 2009

Hodgson RL, *Cricketing Memories by a Country Vicar*, Methuen, London, 1930

Huggett F, *Victorian England as seen by Punch*, Book Club Associates, London, 1978

James CLR, *Beyond a Boundary*, new edition, Yellow Jersey, London, 2005

Knox M, *Never A Gentlemen's Game*, Hardie Grant, Melbourne, 2012

Kynaston D, *WG's Birthday Party*, Chatto & Windus, London, 1990; reprint Bloomsbury, London, 2011

Lester JA (ed.), *A Century of Philadelphia Cricket*, University of Pennsylvania Press, Philadelphia, 1951

Lewis A, *Double Century: The Story of MCC and Cricket*, Hodder & Stoughton, London, 1987

Levison B (ed.), *All In A Day's Cricket: An anthology of outstanding cricket writing*, Constable, London, 2012

Lillywhite F, *The English Cricketer's Trip to Canada and the United States in 1859*, World's Work Ltd, Surrey, 1980; first published by F Lillywhite in 1860

Low R, *WG Grace: An Intimate Biography*, Metro Books, London, 2004

Major J, *More Than A Game: The Story Of Cricket's Early Years*, Harper Perennial, London, 2008

Mallett A, *Lords' Dreaming: The story of the 1868 Aboriginal tour of England and beyond*, University of Queensland Press, Australia, 2002

Marshall J, *Old Trafford*, Pelham Books, London, 1971

Martin-Jenkins C, *Cricket – A Way Of Life*, Century Publishing, London, 1984

Martin-Jenkins C, *The Complete Who's Who Of Test Cricketers*, Orbis, London, 1980

Martineau GD, *They Made Cricket*, Museum Press, London, 1956

Melville H, *Redburn: His First Voyage*, Richard Bentley, London, 1849

Meredith A, *Summers In Winter: Four England Tours Of Australia*, The Kingswood Press, London, 1990

Midwinter E, *W.G. Grace: His Life and Times*, George Allen & Unwin, London, 1981

Montefiore D, *Cricket in the Doldrums: The Struggle Between Private and Public Control of Australian Cricket in the 1880s*, Australian Society for Sports History, University of Western Sydney, 1992

Morris EE (ed.), *Australia's First Century*, Child and Henry in association with Fine Arts Press, Melbourne, 1980

Moyes AG, *A Century Of Cricketers*, George Harrap, London, 1950)

Moyes AG, *Australian Cricket: A History*, Angus and Robertson, Sydney, 1959

Mullins P & Derriman P, *Bat & Pad: Writings On Australian Cricket 1804-1984*, Oxford University Press, Melbourne, 1984

Parker E, *The History Of Cricket*, Seeley Service, London, 1950

Parker G, *The Midwinter File*, *Wisden Cricketers' Almanack*, Sporting Handbooks, London, 1971

Paterson M, *Life in Victorian Britain: A Social History of Queen Victoria's Reign*, Robinson, London, 2008

Piesee K, *Cricket's Colosseum: 125 years of Test Cricket at the MCG*, Hardie Grant, Melbourne, 2003

Piesee K, *The Ashes: An Illustrated History Of Cricket's Greatest Rivalry*, Penguin Group, Australia, 2007

Pollard J, *The Formative Years Of Australian Cricket 1803-93*, Angus and Robertson, Sydney, 1987

Pollard J, *Australian Cricket: The Game And The Players*, Hodder & Stoughton, Sydney, 1982

Pollard J, *The Complete Illustrated History Of Australian Cricket*, Viking, London, 1995

Pollard J (ed.), *Six and Out: The Legend of Australian and New Zealand Cricket*, reprint: Pollard Publishing, Sydney, 1975

Pullin AW, *Alfred Shaw: His Career and Reminiscences*, Cassell, London, 1902

Pullin AW, *Talks with Old England Cricketers*, Blackwood, London, 1900

Rae S, *W.G. Grace: A Life*, Faber and Faber, London, 1998

Roberts EL, *The Test Cricket Cavalcade 1877-1947*, Arnold, London, 1947

Ryan C (ed.), *Australia: Story of a Cricket Country*, Hardie Grant, Melbourne, 2011

Sentence PD, *Cricket in America, 1710-2000*, McFarland, North Carolina, 2005

Smith ET, *Playing Hard Ball*, Abacus, London, 2002

Smith R, *The ABC Guide To Australian Test Cricketers*, Queen Anne Press, London, 1994

Smith R, *John Arthur and George Bailey – A Tale Of Two Cricketers*, Launceston Historical Society, 1990

Spofforth FR, *In the Days of My Youth: Chapters of Autobiography*, *M.A.P.*, London, 1903

Stevenson RL, *Across the Plains: Other Memories and Essays*, Charles Scribner's, New York, 1905, reprint; first published in Longman's Magazine, London, 1883

Swanton EW, *The World Of Cricket*, Michael Joseph, London, 1966; reprint Collins, London, 1980

Tyson F (ed.), *Horan's Diary: The Australian Touring Team 1877-1879*, ACS Publications, Nottingham, 2001

Ward A, *Cricket's Strangest Matches*, Robson Books, London, 1999

Warner PF, *Lord's 1787-1945*, George Harrap, London, 1946

Warner PF, *The Badminton Library: Cricket*, Longmans, Green, & Co, London, 1920

Webber JR, *The Chronicle of W.G. Grace*, ACS Publications, Nottingham, 1998

Webber R, *The Phoenix History of Cricket*, Phoenix, London, 1960

White J, *London In The 19th Century*, Vintage, London, 2008

Williams M (ed.), *Double Century: 200 Years of Cricket in The Times*, Willow Books, Collins, London, 1985

Wilde S, *Number One: The World's Best Batsmen and Bowlers*, Victor Gollancz, London, 1998

Wilde S, *Wisden Cricketers Of The Year: A Celebration Of Cricket's Greatest Players*, John Wisden and Co, London, 2013

Withington J, *London's Disasters*, The History Press, Gloucestershire, 2003

Woodcock J, *One Hundred Greatest Cricketers*, Macmillan, London, 1998

Wynne-Thomas P, *'Give Me Arthur': A Biography of Arthur Shrewsbury*, Barker, London, 1985

General:
Australian Dictionary of Biography
Conway J, *Australian Cricketers' Annual*
Haygarth A and Lillywhite F, *Cricket Scores and Biographies*
Lillywhite J, *Cricketers' Annual; Cricketer's Companion*
Oxford Dictionary of National Biography
Wisden Cricketers' Almanack

Newspapers, magazines and journals
Advertiser (Adelaide*)*
The Age (Melbourne)
American Cricketer
Argus (Melbourne)
Australasian
Australian Town and County Journal
Bailey's Magazine
Bell's Life (London)
Bell's Life in Victoria
Bendigo Advertiser
Brisbane Courier
Bulletin (Sydney)
Cootamundra Herald
Cricket: A Weekly Record
Cricketer
Daily Alta (California)

Daily Telegraph
Evening News (Sydney)
Examiner (Launceston)
Globe
Guardian
Herald (Melbourne)
Leader (Melbourne)
Home News
Huddersfield Chronicle
Hull Packet
Illustrated London News
Leeds Mercury
Leeds Times
Liverpool Mercury
London Daily News
London Standard
Manchester Evening News
Mercury (Hobart)
Morning Post
Nelson Evening Mail
New York Herald
New York Times
New Zealand Herald
Nottingham Express
Nottingham Daily Guardian
Nottingham Evening Post
Otago Witness
Pall Mall Gazette
Philadelphia Evening Telegraph
Punch
Queenslander
Referee (Sydney)
San Francisco Evening Post
Sheffield Independent
South Australian Advertiser
South Australian Chronicle and Weekly Mail
South Australian Register
Spectator

Sporting Gazette
Sportsman
Sporting Life
Sunderland Echo
Sydney Mail
Sydney Morning Herald
The Times
Vanity Fair
York Herald

Websites

www.19cbaseball.com, www.british-history.@ac.uk,
www.ccmorris.org, www.clydesite.co.uk, www.cricketarchive.co.uk,
www.dreamcricket.com,www.espcricinfo.com,
www.frontiertimes.com, www.germantowncricket.org,
www.hampshirecricket.wordpress.com, www.lccc.co.uk,
cprr.org/Museum/Riding_the_Rails Intro.html, www.npg.org.uk,
www.si.nsw.gov.au, www.victorianlondon.org,
www.victorianweb.org, zythophile.wordpress.com

Collections

C.C. Morris Cricket Library and Collection, Haverford, Philadelphia,
The Roger Mann Collection – Specialist cricket photographs.

Acknowledgments

Many thanks to Bloomsbury Publishing, in particular to Charlotte Atyeo and Jane Lawes for all their hard work, patience and attention to detail, and to Richard Collins for his excellent copy-editing. As ever, I am indebted to Charlie Viney, my agent, for his belief in the project and his enduring friendship. Thanks also to Neil Robinson and the staff at the Lord's library; to Bill Gordon at The Oval; and to David Studham, at the MCG library, for his assistance and knowledge, and for so promptly replying to my many emails. I am particularly grateful to Roger Mann for providing photographs from his collection (not to mention his positive thoughts), and to Kathleen Burns, Joe Lynn and staff at the C. C. Morris Cricket Library in Haverford, Philadelphia, who all gave so generously of their time. Finally, a special thank you to Sharon, who, not for the first time, had her life turned upside down by a cricket book (there must have been many occasions when she wondered whether this particular tour would ever come to an end). However, like the resourceful Kiwi all-rounder she is, she not only provided research and editing skills, along with tireless practical support, encouragement and advice, but also contributed the title (again) to the book. Once more, I could not have done it without you.

Index

Note: In instances where there is more than one note on a page with the same number, these are differentiated by the inclusion of the chapter number before the note number, e.g. 259 n.1:2